DISCARDED

The New Deal and the Unemployed

The New Deal and the Unemployed

The View from New York City

HD
4606
N5
B58
1979

Barbara Blumberg

LAMAR UNIVERSITY LIBRARY

653063

Lewisburg
Bucknell University Press
London: Associated University Presses

© 1979 by Associated University Presses, Inc.

Associated University Presses, Inc.
Cranbury, New Jersey 08512

Associated University Presses
Magdalen House
136–148 Tooley Street
London SE1 2TT, England

Library of Congress Cataloging in Publication Data

Blumberg, Barbara.
　The New Deal and the unemployed.

　　Bibliography: p.
　　Includes index.
　　1. New York (City)—Public works—History.　2. Work relief—New York (City)—History.　I. Title.
HD4606.N5B58 1978　　　331.1'377'097471　　　77-74401
ISBN 0-8387-2129-0

PRINTED IN THE UNITED STATES OF AMERICA

For Mom and Dad, Ira, and Alan

Contents

Preface 9
Acknowledgments 13

1 The Birth of Work Relief in New York City 17
2 Launching the Works Progress Administration: The First Months 45
3 Mr. Ridder Takes the Helm 70
4 Work Relief Reaches Maturity 99
5 The Blue-Collar Projects 124
6 White Collar and White Apron 147
7 The Unemployed in the Classroom and on the Playground 165
8 Unemployed Artists and the WPA 183
9 The WPA Under Attack 121
10 The Last Years 254
11 Some Observations on the New Deal Record 281

Selected Bibliography 307
Index 319

Preface

It has long been observed that each generation rewrites the nation's past, and New Deal historiography certainly conforms to the pattern. In the 1940s and 50s scholarly studies of the depression decade emphasized Franklin Roosevelt's achievements.[1] Arthur Schlesinger, Jr., lauded the president for rejecting the absolutes of both the conservatives and the radicals, the notion that we must choose between unregulated capitalism and socialism. Instead, according to Schlesinger, the New Deal preserved the free enterprise system but managed and modified it in such a way as to make American society more just and humane. Or as Carl Degler put it, a "primary innovation" of the New Deal "was the guaranteeing of a minimum standard of welfare for the people of the nation."[2] There were, of course, some dissenting voices. On the right, historian Edgar Robinson continued to echo Herbert Hoover's charges that Roosevelt had led us down the path to socialism and moral decay, while, from the left, William Appleman Williams dismissed most of the reforms attributed to Roosevelt as a sham.[3]

By the 1960s concerned reformers such as Michael Harrington in his *The Other America* began to remind the country that the poor had far from disappeared, although they were often less visible than they had been thirty years earlier. A younger group of historians, responding to the persistent poverty, racial discrimination, decaying cities, spiraling crime rates, and burgeoning welfare rolls of their own day, took a new look at the Roosevelt era. Rejecting their predecessors' largely favorable assessment of the New Deal, they concentrated on its deficiencies. They pointed to the limited and inadequate coverage of the social security system it enacted, its failure to redistribute wealth, the regressive nature of some of its taxation, and its compromises with bigotry at the expense of blacks.[4] In short, they asked whether the New Deal might not have been "a device . . . of conservatives who used its showy campaigns and appealing rhetoric to put down pressures for real reform . . . and inadvertently perpetuate . . . an intolerable social system."[5]

Perhaps this study of the Roosevelt Administration and the unemployed in New York City can throw some light on the continuing battle between those who stress the humanitarian, innovative, and liberal character of the New Deal and its detractors, who, struck by the incompleteness of 1930s reform, write it off as more shadow than substance. Admittedly, the focus of this inquiry is narrowed to one problem and to the way it was handled in a particular community. Nonetheless, by examining a single program closely we may enhance our understanding of the New Deal as a whole. A discussion of specifics on the municipal level should serve to illustrate generalizations about national developments. For instance, how different was the approach of the Roosevelt Administration toward the jobless in New York from the measures taken earlier? Was the help that was given to the city's destitute adequate? What portion of them benefited and how many were forgotten? Did minority groups receive equal consideration? What was the effect of the New Deal on the quality of urban life? And did the concept of government obligation toward the unemployed undergo a significant and permanent change during these years? These are some of the questions that this study attempts to answer.

Preface

A local history, of course, highlights what is unusual about the subject, as well as illuminates national trends. Mayor Fiorello La Guardia, the militant organizations of the New York unemployed, the radical ferment that permeated metropolitan intellectual and creative circles, and the presence of large numbers of professional, white-collar, and artistic persons on relief all played their parts in giving the New Deal in the city certain unique characteristics. For this reason, any conclusions about the nature of the Roosevelt program that this work reaches need to be corroborated by chronicles of many federal agencies in the 1930s and by how their operations affected various states and localities.

NOTES

1. See as examples Basil Rauch, *History of the New Deal, 1933–1938* (New York, 1944); Arthur M. Schlesinger, Jr., *The Age of Roosevelt,* 3 vols. (Boston, 1957–60); and Carl N. Degler, *Out of Our Past* (New York, 1959).
2. Arthur Schlesinger, Jr., "Sources of the New Deal: Reflections on the Temper of a Time," in *The New Deal: The Critical Issues,* ed. Otis L. Graham, Jr. (Boston, 1971), pp. 118–120; Carl N. Degler, "The Third American Revolution," in *The New Deal: The Critical Issues,* p. 106.
3. For examples of their points of view, see Edgar E. Robinson, *The Roosevelt Leadership: 1933–1945* (New York, 1955) and William Appleman Williams, *The Contours of American History* (New York, 1961).
4. The interpretations of these younger historians may be seen in Paul Conkin, *The New Deal* (New York, 1967); Howard Zinn, ed., *New Deal Thought* (Indianapolis, Ind., 1966); and Barton Bernstein, "The New Deal: The Conservative Achievements of Liberal Reform," in *Towards a New Past,* ed. Barton Bernstein (Westminister, Md., 1968).
5. Graham, *The New Deal,* p. xiv.

Acknowledgments

I wish to thank the Oral History Office of Columbia University for having given me permission to quote from the oral history transcripts of Holger Cahill and Luther Evans. I would also like to thank the New York City Municipal Archives for granting me permission to reproduce from their picture collection the photographs that appear in this volume.

Many people helped to make this book possible. I am greatly indebted to William E. Leuchtenburg of Columbia, who read the manuscript in its entirety. His criticisms, advice, and encouragement proved extremely valuable. David Rothman of Columbia also read the manuscript and suggested changes that improved the work. For the errors, which have inevitably crept in, I take full responsibility. My husband, Alan Krumholz, has assisted me in more ways than I can ever fully acknowledge. He has edited and proofread, made sensible suggestions, and encouraged and cheered me when the going was rough. My parents, Albert and Yvette Schneck, also offered corrections and advice on some of the chapters, for which I want to thank them. Finally, my son, Ira, deserves a lot of credit for patiently accepting the late dinners, divided attention, and other inconveniences of having a mother who was busily writing.

The New Deal and the Unemployed

1
The Birth of Work Relief in New York City

The second winter of the depression approached. August Bauman, a fifty-three-year-old unemployed dishwasher, slumped on a bench in the waiting room of Grand Central Station. When police rushed him to Bellevue Hospital, the doctors diagnosed his malady as starvation. On that same November day William Columbo, seventeen years old, collapsed at Eighty-first Street and Central Park West. Destitute and unable to find work, he had not eaten for five days. No one knew for sure how many other jobless inhabited the metropolitan area. Estimates ranged from three hundred thousand to eight hundred thousand. But whatever the exact numbers, New York abounded with evidence of privation and suffering.

Take the breadlines as an example. On a single day in mid-January 1931, eighty-five thousand people waited for free meals at eighty-one locations in front of churches, the Salvation Army, and other charitable institutions. Many in these lines had formerly been white-collar workers. Often they apologized to the persons serving the food. One man said, "I wouldn't do this, but if I eat here it makes what little there is at home last longer for my wife while I am walking the streets." Still others had no homes to which they could return. More than fifteen hundred unemployed men spent the night of 2 April 1930 in the municipal lodging house, an all-time record since the shelter's opening in 1909. By the end of 1933, the nightly count had grown to seven thousand.

Some of the unemployed provided their own makeshift dwellings. Shanty towns constructed of tar paper, linoleum, driftwood, old automobile bodies, and scrap iron began to spring up around the city. The three largest, inhabited by over five hundred men in the fall and winter of 1932, were situated at the foot of East Tenth Street on the shores of the Hudson River, at Seventy-sixth Street and Riverside Drive, and on the abandoned reservoir site in Central Park. With wry humor the residents named their depression-spawned towns Hardluck-on-the-River or Prosperity Park and tagged their dwellings Grand Hotel and Rain Inn.[1]

Above all, the city's jobless spent the first couple of years of the depression searching for work. By the beginning of 1931, sixty thousand people had registered with the municipal Free Employment Bureau alone. Among the applicants were white-collar personnel, professionals, and skilled and unskilled laborers. An average of five thousand individuals a day lined up at the agency's office, located on Lafayette Street. On a few occasions as many as ten thousand crowded into the headquarters.

Patiently they waited ("shoulders broken by responsibility, faces that look into a black abyss") until the phones rang with calls from potential employers. The positions offered were almost invariably temporary and low paying, and yet men fought for them. A clerk read aloud, "One sandwich man, a dollar and one-half a day. Desk Number 4." A dozen persons flung themselves at the desk, begging for the referral. Later someone wanted to hire two men for one hour apiece to move lumber. Each would earn fifty cents. Nonetheless, the same kind of stampede ensued, while the official

The Birth of Work Relief in New York City

yelled, "For God's sake, men, stand back, this is only one hour's work."

At random, a reporter chose one of the thousands in these employment lines to interview. The man was pale and weary looking, his suit clean but threadbare. At home he had a wife and two children. There was nothing left in the house to eat but half a loaf of bread. The children had not gone to school that morning because their mother did not want to send them with empty stomachs. The man stoutly maintained that they could pull through if only he could get a job, any kind of work, for even as little as one or two days a week.[2]

Private charity, not government, first accepted the challenge of trying to provide jobs for New York's unemployed. Two of the city's oldest philanthropic societies, the Association for Improving the Condition of the Poor and the Charity Organization Society, began to plan a work relief program. In September 1930 these two organizations created the Emergency Employment Committee to raise funds and asked Seward Prosser, chairman of the Bankers Trust Company, to head it. In its money-raising drive the Prosser Committee received assistance from the Catholic Charities Organization and the Jewish Social Services Association.

The Prosser Committee established an Emergency Work Bureau to take charge of selecting employees and assigning them to projects. Immediately the unemployed flocked to its doors. For its first two weeks bureau officials interviewed job seekers from early morning until eleven o'clock at night. Hoping for interviews on the following day, the unemployed sometimes began queuing up at midnight. One applicant said that she had been a secretary for a firm in the financial district and had earned forty-five dollars a week. "I took the president's dictation." Now, "I'm down to what I've got on. Look at my pawn tickets—that's my fur coat and that's my watch," she lamented.

At its peak in January 1931, the Prosser Committee provided work for about twenty-six thousand people and by that spring had raised approximately $8.5 million.[3] Mrs. August Belmont, concerned about jobless single women, instituted a second fund-raising drive in March 1931, which brought in enough money to employ fourteen hundred unmarried women through the summer.[4] But by late July the Prosser Committee had nearly exhausted its resources and had to dismiss many of its workers.

In August a new money-raising committee, under the chairmanship of Harvey Gibson, president of Manufacturers Trust Company, came forward to bolster the efforts of the faltering Emergency Work Bureau. The Gibson Committee's fund-raising campaign enlisted the help of many of the community's leading businessmen and politicians, including the banker Thomas Lamont and former Governor Alfred E. Smith.

In October 1931 the work bureau, now renamed the Emergency Work and Relief Bureau, opened twenty-six new offices where unemployed family heads could register for jobs. Within a week thirty thousand had placed their names with the organization. By December the number had risen to one hundred thousand, including clerks, typists, skilled and unskilled laborers, scholars, writers, musicians, bankers, two ex-diplomats, and one movie director. In their eagerness for work, the unemployed sometimes literally swept all obstacles out of their way. At the Southern Boulevard headquarters of the bureau, fifteen hundred people knocked a police officer aside and tore down the door as they rushed in to the interviewers.[5]

The Gibson Committee never raised enough money to come close to hiring all who applied. At the height of its operations in December 1931, it employed around thirty-two thousand, or less than one-third of those who came to it seeking work. The Committee provided its employees with from twenty-one to twenty-four hours of work a week, for which it paid twelve to fifteen dollars. These people worked for a variety of private and municipal agencies, such as the Park Department, New York University, and neighborhood settlement houses.

Later, state and federal job agencies would follow closely the types of projects developed under the Gibson Committee. Blue-collar personnel, for example, painted, cleaned, and repaired public facilities, resurfaced playgrounds, and planted trees in the parks. Women were put to work in twenty-five sewing rooms where they produced garments and bedding for impoverished families. White-collar and professional people aided the regular staffs at school and public libraries, museums, and botanical gardens.

The Gibson Committee also set a most important precedent in its decision to aid penniless artists and musicians. In December 1932 it hired Audrey McMahon, executive secretary of the College Art Association, to direct projects for painters.[6] She employed one hundred people, approximately one-tenth of the artists then on relief. They completed fifteen murals in churches, schools, and settlements, restored statues and paintings for four churches, and taught arts and crafts to 750 pupils in twelve neighborhood houses. During 1932 and 1933 jobless musicians were also paid to give free concerts in the schools and parks.[7]

All told, the Gibson Committee raised some $31 million, but by 1933 it was running out of money and had to liquidate its projects. Letters from two of its former employees illustrate what the closing of the program meant to the unemployed. "The work I had helped me out of despair. . . . Today I received the notice that work ends next week and under present conditions it seems almost like a death notice." A single girl wrote: "The job with the Work Bureau kept my head above water—I can't fight on if it goes below and losing my job now means just that."

The Gibson Committee's demise demonstrated painfully that private charity alone could not continue to help even a small portion of the jobless. Drives to aid depression victims met with decreasing success. For example, in 1932 nongovernmental sources spent nearly $21 million in New York on relief, but by 1933 this had declined to around $12 million, and in 1934 to less than $5 million. Harvey Gibson acknowledged the inadequacy of private efforts in his final message as chairman when he said: "For some time the problem has been such that sufficient funds could not be raised from private contributions to meet the full need."[8]

Along with trying to create jobs in the early thirties, private charities also publicized the full extent of unemployment and exposed its tragic effects on depression victims. The Welfare Council, which coordinated the efforts of nearly all the groups carrying on relief activities, commissioned social worker Lillian Brandt to make a study of conditions in New York City during the winter of 1930–31. Brandt interviewed nine hundred public health nurses and caseworkers and published some of the following observations:

As the unemployed cut back on their expenditures for food and shelter, their physical health began to deteriorate. The enforced idleness wrought psychological changes, too. Occasionally, the transformations were beneficial, with the individual showing energy, ingenuity, and awakened intellectual interest in the social forces that had created the economic collapse. More often, the prolonged joblessness led to bewilderment, apathy, extreme sensitivity, bitterness, carelessness about personal appearance, and loss of self-respect and the courage to go on looking for work.

A minority of families drew closer together in the face of poverty and idleness, but in the majority of cases the strain weakened conjugal and parental ties. Men sitting at home all day felt that they were "in the way." The children annoyed them. They fought with their wives, who suspected that their husbands could find "something to do if they tried hard enough." At times, the husbands roamed the streets until bedtime "to avoid reproaches and the discomforts of home." Records of local courts and youth shelters confirmed what the caseworkers observed about the destructive effect of unemployment on family life. Between 1928 and 1932 the number of men arraigned in municipal courts for abandoning their wives and children increased by 134 percent. In 1932 the Salvation Army's Nursery and Infant Hospital on Herkimer Street in Brooklyn experienced an unprece-

The Birth of Work Relief in New York City 23

dented demand for its services because of a marked increase in abandonment of babies. Almost all of the health and welfare professionals to whom Brandt talked stated that the unemployed desperately needed more public assistance and that work relief would be far more beneficial than outright grants. Jobs kept up courage and morale and relieved family tensions, while home relief frequently demoralized the taker. Lillian Brandt summarized her findings in these words:

> Most of them [the destitute] really wanted work. When they got it without too long a wait, either from the Emergency Work Bureau or through normal channels, they were happy, they could get along without further assistance and there was no evidence of the development of a dependent attitude.[9]

In the early thirties, then, private philanthropy provided valuable services that influenced the evolution of work relief for years to come. Studies like Lillian Brandt's alerted at least some public officials to the physical and mental deterioration that unemployment caused. The rush of people to apply for the jobs offered by the Prosser and Gibson Committees demonstrated the desire of the idle for work. These agencies initiated many of the white-collar, blue-collar, and arts projects that would later be taken over and expanded by the Federal Emergency Relief Administration, the Civil Works Administration, and eventually the Works Progress Administration. And finally, the social workers who ran these projects were among the first to realize that the crisis was too great for nongovernmental groups to handle.

As the efforts of private charity faltered, municipal authorities met increasing pressure to assume more responsibility for the impoverished. Communists and other radicals led demonstrations demanding work and cash relief from city, state, and federal treasuries. On 6 January 1931 the Welfare Council requested that the city launch a major work relief program of its own. When no response was forthcoming, the executive director of the agency, William Hodson, decided to mobilize public opinion to influence the mayor and council.

Hodson, an intense man, balding and bespectacled, had dedicated himself to social work for many years. Now he organized a meeting at Town Hall for the night of 27 February 1931. He invited more than one thousand representatives of health and relief groups to attend and led them in calling upon New York to appropriate at least $10 million to provide emergency jobs. The city, under the leadership of the high-living Mayor Jimmy Walker, sought permission from the state legislature to issue special revenue bonds and tax notes for such an undertaking. When Albany consented, the mayor entrusted the administration of home and work relief to a commissioner of public welfare, who launched the municipal job program on 24 April 1931.

By November some 17,500 New Yorkers had been hired for the emergency positions, but, unfortunately, politics often played a larger part in getting a man on the payroll than did need. The unemployed themselves believed that this was the case and despaired of obtaining work unless they had "pull" or knew someone with "influence." In 1932 the Joint Legislative (Hofstadter) Committee investigating New York City government confirmed these impressions. Samuel Seabury, counsel for the committee, heard witnesses testify that Democrats received preference over Republicans in ordinary assignments and that "better paid positions were given exclusively to enrolled Democrats."[10]

Aside from this limited and poorly run first venture, extensive governmental work relief (city and state) dated from the Wicks Act. In August 1931 Governor Franklin D. Roosevelt summoned the New York State legislature into special session. Addressing the lawmakers, Roosevelt informed them that neither private charity nor local government could any longer adequately care for the unemployed. Therefore the state must act. Roosevelt pointed out that state government had long recognized some obligation

The Birth of Work Relief in New York City

to help the destitute aged and handicapped. He asserted that the state had the same responsibility toward depression victims. "To these unfortunate citizens aid must be extended by government—not as a matter of charity, but as a matter of social duty," said the governor.

Roosevelt submitted a plan that included the establishment of a Temporary Emergency Relief Administration of three members appointed by the governor. This body would be authorized to apportion a fund of $20 million among the cities and counties to bolster work relief, or, where it was impossible to create jobs, to give home assistance.[11] The money would be raised by a 50 percent increase in the personal income tax. By September the governor's suggestions, incorporated into the Wicks Act, had been signed into law. Thus New York was the first state to assist localities with their relief burden, at a time when the federal government under President Hoover still remained adamant against any direct congressional appropriations for the jobless.

Roosevelt appointed as chairman of the Temporary Emergency Relief Administration Jesse Straus, president of Macy's department store, and an old friend of his.[12] Straus decided to place the day-to-day operations of the TERA in the hands of an executive director trained in welfare work. His first choice, William Hodson, declined the position. Instead, Hodson recommended a fellow social worker, Harry Hopkins, and telephoned him to ask if he wanted the job. Characteristically, Hopkins replied without a moment's hesitation: "I would love it." Within a year Straus resigned, and Hopkins assumed the chairmanship as well as the direction of the agency.

From October 1931, when he became director of the TERA, until December 1938, when Roosevelt appointed him secretary of commerce, Hopkins did more to shape government relief, first in New York and then in Washington, than any other man. To conservatives, he was an irresponsible radical squandering the taxpayers' money and calling those who objected "too damned dumb" to understand. Colleagues and friends saw him as a man totally committed to saving the jobless from destitution and despair.

Hopkins, born and raised in Iowa, arrived in New York City in 1912, soon after graduating from Grinnell College. In the city he began a career in social work, first with a settlement house and, subsequently, with the Association for Improving the Condition of the Poor and the New York Tuberculosis Association. A pale, thin man in frail health most of his life, Hopkins, nonetheless, worked with tremendous energy. He had a talent for cutting through red tape that recommended him to Roosevelt. Despite his dedication, Hopkins was no puritan. Many of the most important decisions concerning relief during the years that he served as head of the WPA he made with his staff on the way to or from the Maryland racetracks. A fellow member of Roosevelt's Administration once said of him: "He had the purity of St. Francis of Assisi combined with the sharp shrewdness of a race track tout."[13]

As director of the TERA, Hopkins issued basic guidelines for New York communities. He urged them to create municipal committees to administer their work and relief activities. These bodies were to propose projects to the TERA that conformed to the following rules: The work had to be done by "force account;" that is, government officials would organize the endeavors and hire labor themselves rather than turning the tasks over to private contractors. The undertakings had to be useful, but must not replace or duplicate operations normally financed by the city's regular budget.[14] The work should be done for a sponsor, who would contribute materials and office space and, in some instances, help supervise the emergency personnel. Municipal and state agencies, such as hospitals and settlement houses, might qualify as sponsors, but private businesses would not. Hopkins later adopted the same guidelines for federal work relief projects.

To qualify for public relief, either work or home, the unemployed had to be New York residents and submit to a "means test" proving their destitution. As an experienced social worker, Hopkins knew that this procedure frequently degraded and humiliated the applicant, but with limited funds and so many jobless needing help, there seemed to be no alternative. The TERA prohibited discrimination in granting aid because of a person's political affiliations, religion, or race.

New York City responded to Hopkins's instructions in the fall of 1931 by establishing an Emergency Work Bureau and a Home Relief Bureau under the direction of the commissioner of public welfare. Within four months, over 90,000 metropolitan families had been accepted for home relief, and the Emergency Work Bureau had placed another 48,000 persons on projects where they worked three days a week for fifteen-dollars pay. The numbers grew steadily, reaching a peak in September 1933 just prior to the start of the Civil Works Administration. In that month, the home relief rolls carried 100,000 families, while 110,000 individuals held emergency jobs.

The people employed by the Emergency Work Bureau, with the help of TERA funds, engaged in a wide variety of tasks. At Fort Washington Park they terraced walks and built stone retaining walls and a replica of the fort that had stood on the grounds one hundred years before. At other parks and playgrounds they installed storm drains, laid cinder paths, constructed wood and concrete benches, and repainted buildings. In Richmond they completely renovated the old court house. The bureau hired forty musicians to give lessons to youngsters at the Greenwich House Music School, the Brooklyn Music School Settlement, and other locations. Additional jobless performers were organized into bands and orchestras that gave free concerts in the parks and at municipal museums. By 1933 the city had also engaged sixty painters to instruct thirty-five hundred pupils in art at thirteen centers in Manhattan, Brooklyn, and The Bronx.[15]

Although the TERA employed more people than had any previous work relief program and completed some worthwhile projects, its expenditures fell far short of needs.[16] By late 1931 an estimated one million people were idle in New York City. In the period prior to the introduction of the Civil Works Administration, less than one-quarter of them received any kind of relief from government. Furthermore, as funds became scarce and had to be divided among the growing ranks of the needy, the Emergency Work Bureau restricted laborers to three days of work every other week. The unemployed families thus had somehow to subsist on fifteen dollars over a two-week period, or about thirty dollars a month. The privation these people suffered can be imagined when one notes that, in September 1933, three-room apartments in The Bronx and Brooklyn rented for between thirty and forty-five dollars a month, and a New York City family of four required close to thirty dollars a month for food alone. It is not surprising under these circumstances that over 20 percent of the city school children examined in 1932 were found to be suffering from malnutrition.[17]

Some of the men closest to the relief situation had suspected even at the time that Roosevelt launched the TERA that state and city resources would not prove sufficient, and, therefore, they continued to advocate federal aid. A steady stream of New York City welfare workers brought this message to Congress. Testifying before the Senate Committee on Manufactures in December 1931, William Hodson stated that the relief needs of the unemployed could not possibly be met without federal money. Paul Kellogg, New York-based editor of *Survey,* the leading social work journal, backed up Hodson's contentions, as did Linton Wells, executive secretary of the Family Welfare Association. Both Governor Roosevelt and Harry Hopkins called upon Congress and the Hoover Administration to act.

Of course, not everyone in the city agreed with them. Many members of the business community, numerous Republicans, and a part of the metropolitan press feared federal action. For instance, in February 1932 the *New York*

The Birth of Work Relief in New York City

Times stated: "It cannot be doubted that the State and the city, together with the splendid response of private contributors, will take care of their own. Federal aid would lessen the sense of local responsibility and check the flow of private charity without relieving the city and State of the ultimate burden."

President Hoover headed the ranks of those who disapproved of federally supported relief, but the desperate circumstances of millions of Americans softened his opposition sufficiently to permit him to sign the Emergency Relief and Construction Act in July 1932. The law authorized the Reconstruction Finance Corporation to lend up to $300 million at 3 percent interest to states and their subdivisions for relief payments. Governor Roosevelt applied for a federal loan and received $6.1 million for his state in January 1933. The TERA in turn granted $1.5 million of the money to New York City.[18] By the closing days of the Hoover Administration, however, both the national fund and New York's share of it had been completely spent.

On 4 March 1933 Franklin D. Roosevelt, who eighteen months before had proclaimed government aid to the unemployed a "matter of social duty," became president of the United States. In the first weeks of his term, the banking and agricultural crises absorbed all of his attention. Harry Hopkins and William Hodson, impatient for action on relief, journeyed to Washington and outlined their plans for a federal program to Roosevelt's secretary of labor, Frances Perkins, an old Albany colleague of Hopkins's. Impressed with their ideas, Perkins arranged an appointment for them with the president. Roosevelt, other members of his official family, and progressives in Congress agreed with the two welfare workers that the time for a national relief system had come.[19] Senators Costigan, La Follette, and Wagner introduced an administration-backed Federal Emergency Relief Bill, which passed Congress on 12 May 1933 with an initial appropriation of $500 million. The law created a Federal Emergency Relief Administration authorized to make grants to the states without expectation of repayment. The distribution of federal funds to the unemployed, however, remained the responsibility of state and local relief administrations. By the end of November 1933 New York had received almost $45 million from the FERA and had in turn funneled the money through the TERA to the local level.[20]

On 1 May 1933 Roosevelt appointed Hopkins, his old TERA chief, to head the new FERA. As federal administrator, the energetic social worker encouraged other states to achieve the relief standards prevalent in New York. In part, this took the form of urging them to use federal funds for more work relief projects instead of solely for welfare handouts. Again citing the experience of private philanthropy and the municipal program in New York, Hopkins and his staff stressed that the projects should be varied in order to extend opportunities to women, professional people, and white-collar jobless. New York City caseworkers, already convinced of the superiority of work over home relief, used FERA money to transfer an additional forty thousand persons from direct assistance to emergency projects.[21]

Hopkins's promotion of job programs, however, met with less success outside of New York. Most states and cities used the bulk of federal money for home relief in the form of groceries, fuel, and now and then a few dollars, since that was the cheapest form of welfare and allowed them to care for the greatest number of people. Hopkins understood this, but he continued to worry about the demoralizing effects of idleness on the unemployed. He felt that the jobless needed work that paid a living wage, and if private industry could not supply it, then the federal government should step into the breach. Many others on the FERA staff in Washington agreed with Hopkins and pressed him to try to persuade Roosevelt to back a nationally operated employment program.

Hopkins hesitated at first, fearing that the president would turn him down. He knew that his proposals would

The Birth of Work Relief in New York City

run into opposition from conservatives and possibly from the unions, which were worried about competition from cheap relief labor. In November 1933, however, armed with the finding that even Samuel Gompers had once advocated a government work program, Hopkins went to see his chief. The relief administrator outlined to Roosevelt a plan to create a new agency called the Civil Works Administration, which would employ four million Americans at least until the following spring. The president not only gave his permission, but agreed to finance the experiment by taking nearly $1 billion from the Public Works Administration, headed by the careful, slow-moving secretary of the interior, Harold Ickes.[22] Overjoyed at his success, Hopkins set as his goal hiring the four million by 15 December 1933.[23]

Meanwhile, important changes had occurred in New York City. The voters there, in November 1933, threw out the corrupt Tammany bosses and elected the Fusion party reformer Fiorello La Guardia as mayor. This combative politician, with his deep capacity for moral indignation, sprang from a background as rich and diverse as the city itself. Born in Greenwich Village to an Italian father and a Jewish mother, La Guardia had spent his childhood on Western military bases, where his father was an army musician. He had been an aviator in World War I and lived in Europe for a time, returning to New York when he was twenty-three. He spent most of the following years in Washington as a congressman.

From his background and travels, La Guardia had picked up a working knowledge of seven languages and the ability to feel at home with and sympathetic to a wide variety of peoples. With boundless energy, humor, and showmanship, La Guardia would soon rival the president in popularity and in grabbing newspaper headlines. The new mayor's activities would encompass racing to fires, guest conducting the New York Philharmonic Orchestra, and reading the comic strips over the radio to New York children.

La Guardia's election marked the beginning of a close collaboration between New York City's government and Washington on depression problems. The mayor, during his campaign, had promised to reorganize the city's relief system and to get more adequate help for the unemployed. In one of his earliest acts after taking office, he appointed the veteran social worker, William Hodson, as his public welfare commissioner. Because Roosevelt admired La Guardia and because of the mayor's obvious interest in the jobless, Hopkins invited La Guardia to assist in planning the Civil Works Administration program.

During November La Guardia conferred with Hopkins, Ickes, and other federal relief officials. The mayor-elect pledged himself to submit a complete works proposal to Washington within twenty-four hours after his inauguration on 1 January 1934. In the meanwhile, he recommended administrative personnel to Hopkins and visited the Architects League to ask its members to help draw blueprints for construction projects.[24]

Hiring in the city began in December 1933. Building on a base of 110,000 persons whom it transferred from the Emergency Work Bureau, the CWA rapidly increased its rolls to better than 169,000 individuals. Counting their dependents, the organization was supporting more than half a million people in the community. The federal government's wage payment for these workers exceeded $12 million a month, while another $2 million monthly, half contributed by the city and half by Washington, went for the materials and equipment their jobs required. During its brief four-month existence, from December through March 1934, the CWA spent over $50 million in New York City.

The jobless responded enthusiastically to the federal work experiment. According to Lillian Brandt, the announcement that the CWA was coming "sounded like the opening of the Gates of Heaven to the unemployed." During November and December, lines of ten thousand to fifteen thousand appeared daily at the Manhattan office of the National Employment Service in hopes of getting on the CWA. Many had to be turned down, however, since the CWA never created enough jobs to cover all who applied.

Several features of the national job program particularly pleased the persons who were hired. The CWA paid prevailing wages; in New York that was $.50 an hour for unskilled and $1.20 for skilled labor. Hours ranged from twenty-four to forty a week, averaging about thirty. Professional and white-collar employees received somewhat less generous compensation, but could in certain categories earn as much as thirty-five dollars a week for thirty-nine hours and never less than fifteen dollars. Aside from those transferred from the Emergency Work Bureau, CWA personnel did not have to submit to a humiliating means test. To qualify for the program the individual only had to be physically fit and desirous of work.[25]

In a four-month period the New York CWA accomplished an amazing amount. It launched over four thousand projects, most of which the FERA, TERA, and city relief program continued after March 1934. Many of those projects eventually formed the nucleus around which the WPA program grew. The undertakings varied from construction to the fine arts. Using unemployed teachers, the CWA opened the first government-sponsored nursery schools in the city. Two hundred fifty other idle educators were assigned to the New York League for the Hard of Hearing, where they were trained to administer hearing tests to elementary school children.

During the CWA period the cultural programs initiated earlier expanded markedly and encompassed new ventures.[26] Emergency jobs for musicians climbed to 950. The individuals holding these positions were organized into orchestras, bands, and chamber ensembles, which played in libraries, hospitals, schools, and over the radio.

The Harlem Community Art Center opened with a faculty of unemployed artists ready to give lessons to interested adults and children. The center, under the direction of a black woman sculptress named Augusta Savage, soon became one of the most respected art schools in New York City, particularly dedicated to encouraging talented young blacks. Also actors, for the first time, began to share in government largess. On 15 January 1934 a drama project that hired 150 thespians started. Some of the actors coached amateur groups. The rest formed several different troupes that performed in the schools and parks.

Despite the CWA's achievements and the approval that millions of New Yorkers gave to the program, the federal experiment came under heavy attack from conservatives. Many businessmen, such as the president of the Chase National Bank in New York City, opposed work relief because of its expense and possible competition with private enterprise. They urged the substitution of home relief. The Republican National Committee charged the CWA with "gross waste" and "downright corruption," while some Southern Democrats denounced the program as unconstitutional and an interference with the supply of cheap agricultural labor in their section of the country. Roosevelt's more conservative advisers also warned him that if he continued the CWA for any length of time, the unemployed might come to feel that the government owed them a living permanently. Then, only force could ever shake them loose from the federal payroll. Lewis Douglas, director of the budget, not only advanced this argument to the president but also continuously urged economy and an end to deficit spending.

Some of the points raised by the opposition carried weight with Roosevelt and joined with his own desire to balance the budget as soon as possible. Therefore, the president ordered Hopkins to liquidate the CWA by the end of March 1934 and return all relief to the FERA. The relief administrator, though deeply disappointed, put loyalty to his chief above all other considerations and began to dismantle the organization he had so recently created.[27]

The White House decision unleashed a storm of protest in New York City. Eight thousand CWA employees attended a rally at Madison Square Garden, demanding the retention of their jobs. Another three thousand adopted a resolution declaring: "We will not accept as final this decision which dooms us to starve." Leaders of relief workers' unions predicted Roosevelt's order would precipitate violence. On 30 March 1934 fifteen hundred persons descended on city hall. There, speaker after speaker addressed the crowd, urging people to join the leagues of the unemployed. When the meeting finally broke up, the demonstrators marched off to the strains of the "Internationale."

A broad cross section of city residents backed up the unemployed in pleading for a reprieve for the CWA. On the evening of 22 January 1934 ten thousand New Yorkers gathered at St. John the Divine Cathedral, among them prominent clergymen, government officials, and educators. La Guardia addressed the throng, begging for continuation of work relief. New York Sen. Robert Wagner sent a telegram disapproving any cutback in the CWA at that time and pledging himself to work for its maintenance. Later both the governor of New York, Herbert Lehman, and Mayor La Guardia conferred with Hopkins and the president to press their views. Lehman warned that the abolition of the CWA would produce "serious social and economic consequences." But Roosevelt remained unswerving in his earlier decision.

On 1 April 1934 the CWA expired, turning its uncompleted projects over to the Emergency Work Bureau. From then until the beginning of the WPA in August 1935, the La Guardia Administration waged a valiant but losing struggle to maintain the work relief program as well as home assistance. With the end of the CWA, the federal government's contribution to metropolitan unemployment relief fell sharply. The CWA had dispensed $12 million on projects in March 1934. By June less than $7 million was being spent on work relief.

The restricted budget forced the Emergency Work Bureau to remove from the projects those hired by the CWA who had not passed a means test—some 20,000 persons. Those who remained suffered both wage and hour cuts.

Finally, during the summer of 1934, in order to make its limited funds help as many destitute individuals as possible, the city relied increasingly on home relief rather than the work program. More than 20,000 people who had been on projects were transferred to direct assistance, and new welfare clients were usually placed on home relief. Thus, eleven months after the CWA's termination the work relief force had fallen from almost 163,000 to approximately 116,000. The home rolls, on the other hand, had grown from under 100,000 to 220,000 families.[28]

Meanwhile, the number of destitute jobless mounted relentlessly, making New York's relief problem just that much more serious. For instance, during May and June 1934 fifteen hundred persons a day applied for aid. Nor could the city hope for any letup since better than one out of every three people who had been gainfully employed in 1930 was out of work by 1935, and only half of the unemployed had applied for relief.

While the city's obligations grew without apparent end, its possible sources of revenue saw no such expansion. Metropolitan residents already paid a variety of special taxes earmarked for relief, including levies on business, public utilities, sales, personal property, and inheritance. Besides, by June 1934 New York City was more than $87 million in debt. Desperate for more revenue, La Guardia frantically rushed to Albany in August 1934 to promote legislation to give the city new taxing power. He also consulted representatives of labor, business, civic, social, and religious groups to get their views on how to raise new monies. While labor and civic groups favored a tax on transportation companies, business opposed it and called for increasing the sales tax. In the long run, New York adopted both proposals, but the revenues still did not equal relief needs.[29]

Relief ran into further complications in the spring of 1935 when it became entangled in municipal politics. The Democratic aldermen, anxious to embarrass La Guardia, embarked on an investigation of the Public Welfare Department. In a series of well-publicized hearings and in its final report the Aldermanic Investigating Committee charged Hodson's department, and especially its work relief efforts, with waste, inefficiency, and lack of adequate planning. The committee particularly ridiculed and criticized the white-collar and research projects.

Others jumped to the defense of Hodson and work relief. The United Neighborhood Houses, a committee representing forty-three settlement houses in the metropolitan area, pointed out that their organizations had close contacts with families on relief and were, therefore, in a position to judge the city's efforts. They adopted a resolution congratulating the Public Welfare Department for handling relief "with intelligence, with humanity and efficiency" and stating that the Works Division "has stimulated a splendid program of educational, cultural, recreational and health activities vitally needed by the community." La Guardia and Hodson both commended the white-collar activities, while Hopkins charged that much of the attack on these projects came from people who basically preferred giving home relief to creating jobs.

The mayor, however, did make one major concession to the aldermen. He transferred control over emergency unemployment relief from Hodson's department to an Emergency Relief Bureau headed by Oswald Knauth. To satisfy the aldermen, who complained that relief had been administered heretofore by fuzzy-headed, do-gooder social workers, La Guardia purposely appointed Knauth, a man with no background in welfare work, but rather a Ph.D. in economics and a member of the board of directors of Macy's department store.[30]

With the end of the CWA, New York advocates of a new and bigger national job program never ceased their activities. Foremost in the campaign were the social workers. The head of the Association for Improving the Condition of the Poor reminded the Roosevelt Administration that work relief was the only honest way to help the ablebodied unemployed, whereas home relief deprived a man of his self-respect. The director of the Charity Organization Society called for a work program for the jobless not on an emergency basis but "organized with a view to dealing as constructively as possible with unemployment as one of the outstanding problems of our modern social order." William Hodson daily watched disappointed people who really wanted jobs and wages accept direct aid reluctantly. For them, he said, there has to be a "new deal."

Progressive municipal politicians agreed. La Guardia, in September 1934, led a delegation from the United States Conference of Mayors (an organization composed of executives of 150 of the largest cities) to Hyde Park to meet with the president. They proposed to Roosevelt a new approach to the unemployment crisis. Washington should assume complete responsibility for the employables on the relief rolls, leaving most of the remaining burden of handicapped and dependent persons to cities, counties, and states.

Creative and intellectual circles in New York also agitated for work relief for struggling talent. As early as 1929, artists and writers had begun to join the militant John Reed Clubs established by the Communist Party. In 1934 painters and sculptors started the Artists' Union and the Artists' Committee of Action specifically to demand more government aid for their penniless members. On 15 December of that year, they participated in a march through Manhattan that culminated at the office of Audrey McMahon, head of the Emergency Relief Bureau's art project. The writers were not far behind. By 1935 they had organized the Writers Union and the Unemployed Writers Association. On 25 February 1935 a group from the Writers Union picketed in front of the Port Authority Building. The line was led by Earl Conrad, who carried a sign reading "Children Need Books. Writers Need a Break. We Demand Projects." Soon after, a delegation of New York poets and fiction writers visited Hopkins in Washington to present a plan they had drawn up for a writers' project.[31]

But what was the mood of the rest of the unemployed?

The Birth of Work Relief in New York City

This question vitally interested local government officials and the federal administration. Determined to find out, Hopkins dispatched FERA personnel to New York and other places to gather information. The account he received from the nation's largest city could hardly have reassured him. It reported that the relief rolls increased daily, but private industry had almost no new openings. Throughout the community, welfare investigators and supervisors talked of "growing unrest" among the unemployed. They feared that "the last year has brought a great many clients to a frame of mind where they will follow a leader." William Hodson confided to Hopkins's FERA observer that "unless the trend began back toward private jobs" the unemployed might insist on "a new social order."

Most of the social workers in closest contact with those on the relief rolls felt that President Roosevelt's popularity was waning. "The next idol is likely to be someone who has a promise and plans for jobs," the welfare workers emphasized. In Queens the unemployed had been relatively quiet in their misery up to that point, but caseworkers noted the growing inroads made by Communists and the Unemployed Councils (unions of the jobless that they suspected were closely allied to the Communist Party). In poorer sections of the city, such as Harlem, the councils exercised even greater influence. Many caseworkers spoke of a "distinct radical trend" among students and recent college graduates on relief as well.

Other welfare officials expressed deep concern for the mental stability of the jobless. Hopkins's observer reported: "The feeling is prevalent among case workers and investigators that a vast majority of people on relief for two years or more are reaching 'the cracking point' and have got to have jobs or go to pieces." One investigator whose district covered the neighborhood surrounding Columbia University reported that "almost everyone of her clients had talked suicide at one time or another." The conclusion appeared inescapable. As the FERA reporter summed it up:

"Jobs is the cry everywhere. . . . All agree that this is the one solution, and with no jobs in private business, they must be created by government."[32]

Fortunately for the unemployed, the situation in Washington had changed considerably between early 1934 and the beginning of 1935. Many of Roosevelt's more conservative advisers, including Lewis Douglas, had broken with their chief and departed from the administration. On the other hand, Hopkins was winning increasing respect from the president. The social worker's advice now appeared sounder to Roosevelt than that of many orthodox economists. Besides, the president appreciated Hopkins's common sense, his efficiency, and the uncomplaining way in which he had liquidated the CWA despite his own feelings.

Furthermore, in the congressional elections of November 1934, the New Deal had won an overwhelming victory. Instead of losing seats as the party in power traditionally did in mid-term contests, the Democrats took twenty-five out of thirty-five Senate races and increased their membership in the House from 312 to 322. Not only were the Republicans weaker than at any other time since the Civil War, but many of the newly elected Democrats were outspokenly progressive. These liberals in Congress called impatiently for further relief and reform measures. Roosevelt could interpret the returns as a vote of confidence and a mandate for bold new action.

Hopkins immediately planned to make the most of the victory. He told Aubrey Williams, a fellow social worker from Alabama, and a group of his other FERA administrators: "Boys—this is our hour. We've got to get everything we want—a works program, social security, wages and hours, everything—now or never." By Thanksgiving, Hopkins and his FERA staff, in consultation with Ickes, had drawn up blueprints for a vast new works program. Hopkins headed south to Warm Springs, Georgia, to sell the plans to the vacationing president.[33]

When the seventy-fourth Congress convened in January 1935, Roosevelt summoned the legislators to join him in a new departure in federal relief. With words that echoed the ideas of Hopkins, Hodson, and other long ignored social workers, the president charged that to dole out direct relief was "to administer a narcotic, a subtle destroyer, to the human spirit." He continued:

> I am not willing that the vitality of our people be further sapped by the giving of cash, of market baskets, of a few hours of weekly work cutting grass, raking leaves, or picking up papers in the public parks. We must preserve not only the bodies of the unemployed from destitution, but also their self-respect, their self-reliance and courage and determination.

Roosevelt proposed that the national government return the care of the handicapped and dependent to the localities and the states, where it had traditionally resided. But, the President went on, the federal government must assume its duty of employing the able-bodied jobless until private industry could once again absorb them. FDR then suggested some guiding principles for a national program. Work projects should be useful, compete as little as possible with business, and spend a high proportion of their funds on labor as compared to materials and equipment. The unemployed should receive security payments, greater than home relief but less than prevailing wages, as an inducement to them to continue to seek outside jobs.[34]

Early in April Congress passed the Emergency Relief Appropriations Bill granting Roosevelt $4.8 billion, the largest single appropriation ever made by a legislative body in the United States up to that time. The administration could now proceed to organize a program that would employ some three million Americans, among them over two hundred thousand New York City residents. Thus the federal government had come finally to commit itself to the principle of work relief. In that decision the past experiences of private and public welfare agencies in New York and the ceaseless pressure of city and state political leaders, as well as the unemployed, had played a significant part.

NOTES

1. *New York Times,* 28 November 1930, p. 2; 24 October 1930, p. 3; 21 January 1931, p. 14; 3 April 1930, p. 15; 16 November 1930, sec. 9, p. 7; 16 December 1933, p. 6; 26 March 1933, sec. 6, p. 12; 3 August 1932, p. 17.

2. Louis Stark, "All I Want Is Work," *New Republic,* 4 February 1931, pp. 317–18; *New York Times,* 16 November 1930, sec. 9, p. 7.

3. Despite the impressive effort, the help covered only a tiny fraction of those who needed it. According to a special census taken by the United States Census Bureau in January 1931, 609,035 New Yorkers were unemployed.

4. John D. Millett, *The Works Progress Administration in New York City* (Chicago, 1938), pp. 2–3; Joanna C. Colcord, *Emergency Work Relief as Carried Out in Twenty-six American Communities* (New York, 1932), p. 138; Gertrude Springer, "The Job Line," *Survey,* 1 February 1931, p. 499; U.S. WPA for N.Y.C. *Final Report of the Work Projects Administration for the City of New York, 1935 to 1943* (New York, 1943), p. 2.

5. *New York Times,* 3 October 1931, p. 1; 1 November 1931, p. 21; 9 December 1931, p. 31; 31 January 1932, sec. 2, p. 1; 28 October 1931, p. 14.

6. McMahon later became the head of the WPA art project in New York City.

7. U.S. WPA for N.Y.C., *The Administration of Work Relief in New York City, August 1936–December 1937,* Report of Brehon B. Somervell to Harry Hopkins (New York, 1938), p. 103; Colcord, *Emergency Work Relief,* pp. 143–44, 147–48; Springer, "The Job Line," pp. 497–99, 523; "Unemployed Help Catalogue Department," *Library Journal,* 1 October 1932, p. 815; William F. McDonald, *Federal Relief Administration and the Arts* (Columbus, Ohio, 1969), pp. 350, 589–90.

8. U.S. WPA for N.Y.C., *Final Report,* p. 2; *New York Times,* 16 March 1933, p. 19; N.Y.C. Mayor's Committee on Unemployment Relief, *Report of Mayor La Guardia's Committee on Unemployment Relief* (New York, 1935), p. 11; "Farewell to the Gibson Alms," *Literary Digest,* 24 June 1933, pp. 17–18.

9. Lillian Brandt, *An Impressionistic View of the Winter of 1930–31 in New York City Based on Statements from Some Nine Hundred Social Workers and Public Health Nurses* (Report to the Welfare Council of N.Y.C., New York, 1 February 1932), pp. 16, 18, 23, 26; *New York Times,* 16 October 1932, p. 24; 13 July 1932, p. 2.

10. *New York Times,* 26 February 1931, p. 11; 28 February 1931, p. 4; Colcord, *Emergency Work Relief,* pp. 152, 156–58; Millett, *The WPA in N.Y.C.,* pp. 4–5; U.S. WPA for N.Y.C., *Administration of Work Relief,* p. 104; Brandt, *An Impressionistic View,* p. 26.

11. The original $20 million appropriation lasted only until March 1932, when the legislature supplemented it with an additional $20 million. New

The Birth of Work Relief in New York City 43

York relief continued to be financed by short-term appropriations thereafter.

12. The other two members of the TERA were Philip Wickser and John Sullivan.

13. New York *Herald Tribune,* 29 August 1931, pp. 1–2; Robert Sherwood, *Roosevelt and Hopkins,* 2 vols. (New York, 1948), 1:18–60.

14. Hopkins included this proviso to discourage cities from saving money by firing regular civil servants and replacing them with cheaper relief workers.

15. *New York Times,* 27 March 1933, p. 17; 17 December 1933, sec. 8, p. 2; "A $20,000,000 Investment in Emergency Jobs," *American City,* 48 (February 1933): 70–71; McDonald, *Federal Relief Administration,* pp. 631, 349.

16. The TERA contributed $46,173,006 to N.Y.C. for unemployment relief between 1 November 1931 and 1 September 1933. Of this money, $21,830,613 went for work relief and the remainder for home relief. *New York Times,* 16 October 1933, p. 11.

17. *New York Times,* 31 December 1931, p. 10; 1–30 September 1933, advertisements; 29 October 1932, p. 17; U.S. WPA, *Intercity Differences in Cost of Living in March 1935, in Fifty-nine Cities,* by Margaret Loomis Stecker (Washington, D.C., 1937), p. 172.

18. *New York Times,* 29 December 1931, p. 1; 30 December 1931, p. 18; 5 January 1933, p. 14; 8 February 1932, p. 16; Millett, *The WPA in N.Y.C.,* p. 8.

19. Frances Perkins, *The Roosevelt I Knew* (New York, 1946), pp. 183–84; Arthur M. Schlesinger, Jr., *The Age of Roosevelt,* vol. 2, *The Coming of the New Deal* (Boston, 1959), p. 264.

20. The last grant to the state from the FERA, before its demise, arrived in October 1935. All told, the FERA between 1933 and 1935 gave New York $374,205,774.

21. The greater expense of employing the destitute rather than just feeding them was offset, partially, by the decision of the TERA in November 1933 to reimburse localities for two-thirds of their relief expenditures instead of the 40 percent paid previously. FERA grants made the increase possible.

22. Roosevelt justified his actions to Ickes with the explanation that Hopkins's CWA would provide immediate but temporary work while the PWA planned and reviewed its projects, cleared up legal matters, and made contracts with private construction companies that would eventually absorb all of the unemployed.

23. Millett, *The WPA in N.Y.C.,* p. 8; Hopkins to All State FERA Administrators, FERA Letter A-5, 22 September 1933, Harry Hopkins Papers, Franklin D. Roosevelt Library, Hyde Park, N.Y.; Jacob Baker to All State FERA Administrators, FERA Letter A-28, 30 October 1933, Harry Hopkins Papers, Franklin D. Roosevelt Library, Hyde Park, N.Y.; Schlesinger,

Coming of the New Deal, pp. 269–70; Sherwood, *Roosevelt and Hopkins,* pp. 62–64.

24. Arthur Mann, *La Guardia Comes to Power, 1933* (Chicago, 1965), pp. 15–33; New York *Herald Tribune,* 24 November 1933, p. 1; *New York Times,* 30 November 1933, p. 7.

25. *New York Times,* 17 December 1933, sec. 8, p. 2; 26 March 1934, p. 14; 28 November 1933, p. 26; Millett, *The WPA in N.Y.C.,* p. 16; Lillian Brandt, *Relief of the Unemployed in NYC, 1929–1937,* (Report to the Welfare Council of N.Y.C. New York, 1938), pp. 174–75.

26. Technically, the funds coming from Ickes's PWA could only be used for construction. Therefore, Hopkins took other money from the FERA to cover these cultural projects and created a sister program to the CWA known as Civil Works Service (CWS).

27. "CWA Nursery Schools for Children," *Literary Digest,* 24 February 1934, p. 21; "Thanks to the CWA," *Survey,* 30 (March 1934): 87; Alain Locke, *The Negro in Art: A Pictorial Record of the Negro Artist and the Negro Theme in Art* (New York, 1940), p. 135; McDonald, *Federal Relief Administration,* pp. 599, 411, 490, 550; *New York Times,* 13 January 1935, sec. 6, p. 8; Sherwood, *Roosevelt and Hopkins,* pp. 68–69; Schlesinger, *Coming of the New Deal,* p. 277.

28. *New York Times,* 26 March 1934, p. 14; 14 March 1934, p. 6; 30 March 1934, p. 1; 31 March 1934, p. 1; 1 April 1934, p. 1; 6 May 1934, p. 8; 10 February 1935, sec. 4, p. 10; New York *Herald Tribune,* 22 January 1934, p. 1; 23 January 1934, p. 1; Isidor Feinstein, "New York's Relief Crisis," *Nation,* 22 August 1934, pp. 213–14.

29. *New York Times,* 24 June 1934, sec. 8, p. 1; N.Y.C. Mayor's Committee, *Report of Mayor La Guardia's Committee,* pp. 8–12; R. Ecker to Hopkins, 31 December 1934, Harry Hopkins Papers, Franklin D. Roosevelt Library, Hyde Park, N.Y.

30. N.Y.C. Aldermanic Committee to Investigate the Administration of Relief, *In the Matter of the Investigation of the Administration of Unemployment Relief in the City of New York* (New York, 8 July 1935), pp. 5, 24, 87, 19, 20, 89, 97, 153; New York *Herald Tribune,* 4 April 1935, pp. 1, 2; 8 April 1935, pp. 1, 6; *New York Times,* 4 April 1935, p. 1; 7 April 1935, sec. 4, p. 11; 7 April 1935, p. 1.

31. *New York Times,* 13 January 1935, sec. 6, p. 8; 23 April 1934, p. 19; 11 June 1934, p. 4; 16 December 1934, p. 17; Fiorello La Guardia Papers, New York City Municipal Archives; McDonald, *Federal Relief Administration,* p. 405; Jerre Mangione, *The Dream and the Deal: The Federal Writers' Project, 1935–1943* (Boston, 1972), pp. 34–38.

32. Narrative Report on New York City from Wayne Parrish, investigator for FERA, to Hopkins, 11 November 1934 and 17 November 1934, Harry Hopkins Papers, Franklin D. Roosevelt Library, Hyde Park, N.Y.

33. Sherwood, *Roosevelt and Hopkins,* pp. 69, 79–80; Schlesinger, *Coming of the New Deal,* p. 277.

34. New York *Herald Tribune,* 5 January 1935, pp. 1, 8.

2

Launching the Works Progress Administration: The First Months

When it voted nearly $5 billion for relief in April 1935, Congress left the organization of the new federal program almost entirely to Franklin Roosevelt. The law stated: "In carrying out the provisions of this joint resolution the President is authorized to establish and prescribe the duties and functions of necessary agencies within the government."[1] Roosevelt exercised this power by distributing some of the money to "pump-priming" and welfare agencies already in existence, such as Harold Ickes's Public Works Administration and the Civilian Conservation Corps. The president also created and handed funds to several new authorities, including the Resettlement Administration and the Rural Electrification Administration, both designed to assist the agricultural poor. By an executive order issued on 6 May 1935, Roosevelt established the Works Progress Administration, of which Hopkins became chief. The presidential directive authorized the WPA to coordinate the efforts of other agencies receiving portions of the 1935 appropriation and to undertake work projects of its own. The WPA was assigned the largest share of the relief dollars, $1.4 billion out of the $4.8 billion voted by Congress. In later years the WPA's coordinating function fell by the wayside, while its role as the primary government agency offering aid and work to the unemployed grew rapidly.[2]

Soon after Roosevelt issued his executive order creating the WPA, he announced who would be eligible for employment under the program. Unlike the earlier CWA, which accepted any able-bodied jobless, the new organization limited positions to those receiving public relief who had registered with the United States Employment Service.[3] In order to give the WPA some leeway in finding workers with necessary but rare skills, the president authorized the agency to seek up to 10 percent of its labor from nonrelief sources. Later the limit was reduced to 5 percent.[4]

The decision to limit participation to those on the relief rolls became inevitable when the president asked Congress for the $4.8 billion appropriation. Although that seemed like an enormous amount, it was far short of what a program to hire all the jobless would cost. Relief officials estimated full coverage would require a minimum of $9 billion. Whether Roosevelt could have wrung such a sum from Congress is doubtful. At any rate, he never suggested it.

Restricting WPA jobs almost entirely to welfare recipients had some unfortunate results. It made the new program appear to many to be merely relief under another name instead of a public works effort paying wages to employees for their legitimate services. Also, it robbed the individual of some of the self-respect that work relief (as opposed to direct assistance) was supposed to foster. For example, in order to obtain welfare certification in New York City the applicant had to answer all personal and financial questions asked by a social worker and sign a form permitting a search of banks to uncover any hidden assets that he might possess. He had to prove that he owned no real estate, other than his family's home, and carried no more than fifteen hundred dollars in life insurance. The social worker, through visits to his residence and other investigations, had to be convinced that the individual lacked any means of supporting himself and his family and that there were no legally responsible relatives who might be called upon for aid. If a destitute person passed all of these tests, he was then accepted on home relief, where, by 1936, he had to remain for at least ten days before he was eligible for WPA placement.

One WPA official, objecting to this and similar procedures in other states, asked how it was possible to preserve a person's pride when "he must submit to the equivalent of a pauper's oath and a most humiliating inquisition." The jobless often raised similar complaints. A letter of protest from a New York group read:

> We have been told many times that we are done with relief—that we have jobs. We exchange work for pay; we do not ask for unearned money. For this reason we believe that reducing us to a relief status constitutes a patent injustice. Moreover, as you must know, submission to a relief questionnaire is universally felt to be degrading and humiliating.[5]

The president and Hopkins explained the nature of the WPA program further through their information circulars to local government officials and directives to WPA administrators. These stated that projects had to be useful and located on public property. All work (with the exception of Federal Project number 1, instituted some months later) had to be sponsored by either a state or municipal agency that was expected to contribute equipment, materials, possibly some cash, and varying degrees of supervision depending on the nature of the endeavor. In fact, the larger the sponsor's proposed contribution, the more likely it was that the WPA would accept its project. Also, Roosevelt cautioned WPA directors in June 1935 to reject any work that could not be completed by 1 July 1936.

The president's directive indicated, along with other evidence, that Roosevelt regarded the unemployment relief program as temporary. Though Congress stipulated that the $4.8 billion might be spent over a two-year period, the president seemed to contemplate exhausting the fund in twelve months and allowed Hopkins to apportion his share of the money accordingly. Roosevelt and his advisers banked heavily on the prospects of a business upturn that would soon reduce the need for federal unemployment relief. Speaking to a meeting of state WPA directors on 18 June 1935, the chief executive voiced the expectation that the coming year would see a pronounced decline in joblessness. "When the hope failed," as one historian of the WPA commented, "the Administration kept on with the program, although it had been launched and was being continued with no considered plan for either its duration or its scale." In June 1936 the president, finding the employment picture not much brighter than the year before, returned to Congress for a supplementary appropriation, thus beginning a pattern of year-by-year or even shorter-term financing of the WPA. Throughout the life of the organization, its directors complained that the uncertainty interfered with adequate long-range planning of projects and therefore caused the work to be carried out less efficiently. It also resulted in feelings of great insecurity among WPA employees.[6]

While the new work relief program was taking shape in Washington, La Guardia moved with alacrity in New York, appointing a Mayor's Committee on Federal Projects. It put together proposals that entailed expenditures of $300 million and promised to create jobs for three hundred thousand people. Although the national administration did not approve all of the plans, New York City found that its fast action paid off. By October over two hundred thousand municipal residents held WPA jobs, while at that date in the rest of the nation the work relief program was either still on the drawing board or, at best, employed only a few thousand people. The first director of the WPA in New York City would later give La Guardia much of the credit for this rapid start.[7]

Besides rushing project proposals to the capital, the tireless mayor also launched a campaign to obtain an independent WPA unit for his city, separate from the rest of the state. Even before the Emergency Relief Bill passed Congress, La Guardia wrote to the executive director of the United States Conference of Mayors, then lobbying for the legislation in Washington, advising him to push for more direct contact between the municipalities and the federal government. The mayor warned that if Washington worked through the governors, "the cities will be frozen out entirely." Apparently, the executives of other cities shared La Guardia's apprehensions, for in April the conference of mayors asked Hopkins to create independent work relief administrations for the nation's twenty-five largest municipalities. Of these twenty-five, only New York got its way when, on 26 June 1935, Hopkins announced that the city would be treated as a "forty-ninth state" unit within the WPA.[8]

It is not entirely clear why Roosevelt and Hopkins granted administrative independence to New York City alone, but one can point to many circumstances that probably aided La Guardia's case. First of all, La Guardia occupied a better position for getting a sympathetic hearing in Washington than did most other mayors. Roosevelt and he had enjoyed a cordial relationship since the presidential election of 1932. Second, the number on welfare in New York topped that in every other city and every state, except Pennsylvania.[9] Nearly 7 percent of all persons receiving relief in the nation between January and August 1935 lived in the metropolis. La Guardia could also stress that his community had spent more on welfare than any other city in the country and had pioneered in work relief. A WPA unit established in New York could immediately take over projects, employing almost one hundred thousand people as well as a functioning staff. With these advantages, a New York City WPA could spring into action almost immediately and thus serve as a pilot program for the rest of the federal unemployment setup.[10]

La Guardia not only obtained a separate WPA unit for his city, but he also had a part in choosing its chief. Hopkins offered the post of New York City WPA administrator to

Gen. Hugh Johnson largely at the mayor's suggestion. La Guardia believed that the municipal work relief program, under attack by the hostile aldermen, badly needed a strong leader to save it. Johnson, a nationally known figure since his direction of the National Recovery Administration, had a reputation for bubbling energy, decisiveness, and drama. Such a man might appeal to the disgruntled aldermen, and, in fact, they did greet the news that he would take the position enthusiastically. Furthermore, La Guardia knew that it was wise to please the predominantly Democratic New York congressional delegation since the appointment of state WPA directors had to be approved by Congress. Johnson, who had worked actively in New York state politics in both Al Smith's campaign for president in 1928 and Roosevelt's in 1932, would have no trouble getting the nod of approval from New York Democrats. The mayor also may have taken into consideration the general's connections and friendships with many of the top officials in the executive branch. Surely he could cut through more red tape and open more doors than a local politician or social worker.

Hugh Johnson, far off in the West in June 1935, had read about the aldermanic investigation and its charge "that there was something very rotten in the State of Denmark," but he considered himself simply an interested spectator until he received a telephone call from Hopkins asking him to head the WPA in New York City. La Guardia, then in Hopkins's office, joined in the conversation and seconded the request. Not willing to commit himself immediately, the general asked some of his friends in the city to look into the situation and advise him. They implored him "to go on further West as promptly as possible." Despite the warnings of his friends, Johnson finally accepted the job on a temporary basis. He agreed to remain only long enough to get the organization on its feet.[11]

Johnson brought to the WPA a wealth of experience in running big government operations. As a young second lieutenant, he had directed distribution of public relief to the victims of the 1906 San Francisco earthquake and fire.

During World War I he had helped write the Selective Service Act and had organized thousands of local draft boards that registered millions of men. He had also served on the War Industries Board under Bernard Baruch. Most recently, the general, who had retired from the army after World War I, but who always retained his title, had headed the NRA, in which capacity he supervised adoption of fair codes of competition for practically every industry and sold the program to the public with great fanfare.

An ebullient man, Johnson possessed many of the traits that make an ideal administrator, such as managerial skill, independence, flexibility, and a tremendous capacity for hard work. However, he also tended toward extremes in his behavior, smoking too much, drinking too much, wrangling with colleagues whom he suspected of nefarious schemes to undermine him, and overreacting to their criticism. These failings had hastened his departure from the NRA. The man's saving graces, however, were his charm and his ability to laugh at himself. For example, with tongue in cheek, he prefaced his autobiography with the defiant answer he first hurled at opponents when he was four years old: "Everybody in the world's a Rink-Stink but Hughie Johnson and he's all right."[12]

On 1 July 1935 Johnson moved into the headquarters of the Emergency Relief Bureau's Works Division, located in the old Port Authority Building in lower Manhattan. He assumed command over the division's administrative staff of approximately three thousand persons. Then he superimposed on this structure a small group of his own advisers, chief among them being his deputy administrator, Alvin Brown, an associate of Johnson's since World War I.

The general also attempted to recruit a staff of engineers who were vital for operating an extensive construction program. But with the limited salaries the WPA paid, obtaining competent personnel was not easy. Johnson attacked the problem in a way that set a precedent increasingly followed by the federal work relief agency all over the nation. He turned to the Army Corps of Engineers. The general chose

Lt. Col. Joseph Mehaffey as his assistant administrator for engineering and named four other officers also to supervise construction activities. Using military careerists served another purpose, too. The officers would be relatively independent of local politics.[13]

On 1 August the New York City ERB transferred its approximately one hundred thousand workers to the WPA, and Johnson pledged himself to double his payroll by 1 October. For the next three weeks, however, Johnson's goal appeared to be unattainable because the new agency ran into some major difficulties. The foremost was a strike against the WPA by AFL unions. The dispute out of which the strike grew had started eight months earlier. In his message to Congress of January 1935, Roosevelt had suggested what he called security payments for the unemployed, a sum greater than they received on welfare but below prevailing pay in private industry. The president considered such remuneration necessary in order to get men to leave direct relief for work, but at the same time to induce them to continue to seek regular nongovernment jobs. The lower wage, of course, also meant that the limited appropriation could be turned into positions for more people.

During the congressional debates on the Emergency Relief Appropriations Bill, no topic aroused greater controversy than the security wage proposal. Organized labor denounced it, claiming that the government rate would give private employers the excuse they needed to attack union scales and replace them with the minimal amounts paid relief workers. For a time Congress considered amending the legislation to provide for payment of prevailing wages, but the lawmakers ultimately accepted the president's wishes and allowed him to establish the pay schedules.

In an executive order issued on 20 May 1935 Roosevelt announced the wage scales for relief employees. He divided the country into four pay regions in which rates ranged from the lowest in the rural South to the highest in the urban Northeast, designated Region 1. Within each area the worker's classification determined the amount of his se-

Launching the WPA: The First Months

curity payment. For New York City, in Region 1, unskilled workers would receive fifty-five dollars a month; intermediate, sixty-five dollars; skilled, eighty-five; and professional and technical, ninety-four. In addition, the president authorized the federal WPA administrator or his representatives to adjust all wages either up or down by as much as 10 percent at their discretion. For these wages, work relief employees would labor between a minimum of 120 hours a month and a maximum of 140.[14]

The president's work relief pay scales aroused immediate protest. The day after Roosevelt announced them, La Guardia telephoned Hopkins to express dismay at how low they were. Later, in a conference with George Meany, president of the New York State Federation of Labor, and Joseph Ryan, head of the City Central Trades and Labor Council, La Guardia promised he would back their efforts to induce Roosevelt to revise the schedules.

To demonstrate union displeasure with Roosevelt's security payments, the New York City Central Trades and Labor Council sponsored a mass meeting at Madison Square Garden on 23 May 1935. There La Guardia, Senator Wagner, William Green, John L. Lewis, Sidney Hillman, and other labor leaders called upon the WPA to pay New York workers the wages prevailing in the area. Political extremists also jumped at the opportunity that the security payments gave them for berating the New Deal. Father Coughlin denounced the meager wages as a "breeder of communism," and Huey Long accused the president of wanting to starve WPA workers.[15]

Johnson, soon after his appointment as local administrator, announced his support of organized labor's position. On 3 July the general said of the security payment, "Labor doesn't like it and I don't like it. It is going to give me a lot of headaches." Meanwhile, Johnson used the authority available to him to assuage labor's feelings as much as possible. He reduced all WPA hours in the city to the minimum 120 and instituted an across-the-board 10 percent wage increase.[16]

Despite the efforts of Johnson, La Guardia, assorted New Deal critics, and the union leaders, neither Roosevelt nor Hopkins changed his earlier stand. On 16 July the federal WPA administrator turned down the demand for the prevailing wage for New York City. Hopkins defended the security payments by pointing out that the majority of the New York residents affected would get more than they had ever realized from home relief or the previous made-work programs, which was true in most cases. The only ones who stood to lose rather than gain under the New York City WPA scales were certain white-collar employees, some of those on the arts and theater projects, and unskilled workers with very large families, since home relief based payments on the number of dependents and the WPA did not.

On the other hand, a study of the cost of living for a family of four in New York City in 1935, conducted by the WPA itself, found that at least $81.84 a month was required to cover just bare essentials such as food, rent, and carfare. Thus an employee in the unskilled or intermediate classification who had a wife and two or more children to support would be earning less than this minimal amount.[17]

The American Federation of Labor, representing for the most part the skilled and therefore better compensated WPA workers, did not object to the security payments on the grounds that they were inadequate as much as they protested the denial of the prevailing-wage principle, which the ERB had long recognized. The bureau had conformed to prevailing hourly rates by deciding how much it could pay a relief worker and then adjusting the number of hours he toiled, accordingly. For instance, common laborers put in 96 hours a month, while the skilled worked fewer than 60. The WPA made a similar accommodation impossible by insisting that all its employees serve 120 hours a month.

One building trades worker expressed the union point of view when he explained why he would not take a WPA position though the agency was offering him more than he had received on either home relief or the municipally run projects.

[Home relief's] worse than . . . prison, take it from me. If there's kids you never quite get enough to eat. It gnaws at you till you can't hardly think of anything but food. So you just set around and set around and the kids holler and your wife tries to be a sport and you're ready to go bugs. Work relief was a whole lot better than that. My union rate was $1.40 and to make our monthly budget of $70.20 I worked six days a month at my trade. Then this WPA comes along. They turned our project over to that. Union men get $93.50 a month and that means $26.30 more a month than we've been seeing lately. But it's this way. If I follow my trade 120 hours for $93.50 it works out to .78¢ an hour. My rate is $1.40. Union rates don't come from sitting down and asking pretty. They was fought for. Now the government is asking us to forget all that and work for under the union rate. I'd rather work any time than sit home and rot. But if I'm going to follow my trade, it's got to be at union rates. I can't scab, can I?[18]

In spite of the arguments of the union men, Hopkins and Roosevelt felt that they had better reasons for not following the precedent of the ERB in adjusting hours of labor so as to approximate prevailing wages. First, the New York City WPA was asking relief recipients to put in fewer than thirty hours a week, which hardly seemed excessive at a time when even the forty-hour week had not yet become standard in private industry. Second, the great majority of people on the relief rolls among whom the WPA would do its hiring belonged to no union. Therefore, the principle that the AFL wanted to uphold had no direct relevance to them. Further, trying to adjust hours for each trade and skill would greatly complicate the paperwork involved in preparing payrolls and in assigning crews to projects.[19]

Regardless of which side had the better case, the unions prepared to do battle. On 12 July after issuing a statement that he had "absolute proof the contractors generally have cut wages to bring them in line with work relief," George Meany declared that the AFL would not permit its members to take WPA jobs at less than prevailing wages. Within a week after the WPA assumed control of all relief projects in the city, the first walkout occurred. One hundred seventy-eight bricklayers, steamfitters, lathers, ironworkers, plumbers, and carpenters on the Astor low-cost housing project quit work, temporarily closing down that operation. Between seven hundred and one thousand other WPA laborers soon followed their example. Then, on 8 August the New York Central Trades and Labor Council officially called a strike despite Hopkins's declaration that "there is no such thing as a strike on a relief job" and Johnson's appeals to that body to reconsider its actions.

The AFL leaders did not seriously expect more than a small portion of the WPA workers to heed their summons, but that would be sufficient if those staying away were skilled building tradespeople. Without them to guide the common laborers, the union strategists reasoned, construction projects would founder and the government's attempt to employ two hundred thousand New Yorkers by the fall would fail. Roosevelt, concerned about restoring employment and wages as quickly as possible, would have to capitulate on the security payments, thus setting a precedent not only for New York but the entire nation.

Quickly the building trades unions gained sympathizers. On 9 August the Bookkeepers, Stenographers, and Accountants Union, an AFL affiliate, authorized a strike or other job action by its members to back up the demand for prevailing wages. The Federation of Architects, Engineers, Chemists, and Technicians praised the strike vote of the skilled unions and announced they would join in a "solidarity action."

Unions of the unemployed not affiliated with the AFL also entered the fray with their own demands. They wanted increased wages, weekly rather than biweekly paychecks, paid vacations, sick leave, government recognition of the newer unions, and collective bargaining. The City Projects Council and the Workers Alliance, which had signed up an assortment of white-collar, skilled, and unskilled work and home relief recipients, directed repeated work stoppages and marches lasting several hours at a time. However, since these groups lacked war chests and since the AFL refused to admit the recently formed unions of the jobless to official membership in the halls of labor, the white-collar, unskilled, and professional workers on the WPA confined their actions to demonstrations, short work stoppages, and pronouncements, as opposed to engaging in all-out strikes.[20]

Roosevelt at first refused to listen to the strikers. However, as the dispute dragged on and seriously hampered Johnson's efforts to recruit skilled laborers (without whom construction projects could not operate and other workers could not function), the president relented. On 17 September he met with La Guardia, Governor Lehman, Hopkins, and Johnson at Hyde Park. There he authorized Hopkins and the general to make peace with the AFL.

After several conferences with Meany and the other leaders of the Central Trades Council, Johnson and Hopkins arrived at a settlement acceptable to both sides. The WPA promised to reduce the work time of skilled labor sufficiently so that each craft earned approximately the hourly pay established by union rates in that trade. In other words, although the laborer received no more in total remuneration, the AFL gained WPA recognition of its prevailing-wage principle. On 19 September Hopkins issued an administrative order eliminating the mandatory 120 hours for relief workers, leaving each state administrator to set the work schedule as he saw fit. Johnson exercised his new power at once, cutting the monthly requirement for some employees to as little as 60 hours, while the less highly skilled and white-collar workers followed schedules that ranged up to 120 hours a month. Shortly afterward, the WPA also agreed to issue weekly paychecks. The other demands of the unions of the unemployed, not affiliated with the AFL, went unheeded since these newer unions had little bargaining power.[21]

The New York City WPA's early difficulties in recruiting workers did not stem entirely from the prevailing-wage dispute. The president's original instructions empowered the

United States Employment Service to help move people from home relief to the WPA. Welfare recipients were to register with the service, which would then compile an accurate file on their skills and qualifications. When the WPA needed laborers, it would place requisitions with the employment agency. This referral procedure soon proved cumbersome. Many reliefers were not aware that they had to register with the service, and it lacked the necessary personnel to compile an occupational classification file. Between 1 and 20 August, although Johnson requested twenty-eight thousand workers from the employment service, it sent only slightly more than five thousand.

After three frustrating weeks, Johnson urged his superiors and colleagues to allow him to simplify the intake procedure. He suggested that home relief caseworkers be held responsible for identifying clients who were employable and for sending them directly to WPA offices for placement. The work relief agency would rely on the employment service only for locating skilled laborers who could not be found on welfare. At a meeting on 23 August the head of the employment service, representatives of the city welfare department, and an administrative assistant to Hopkins, Corrington Gill, agreed to Johnson's proposals. Although the new procedure broke the recruitment bottleneck, it also placed an enormous burden on the WPA staff, which had rapidly to interview thousands of applicants, ascertain their skills and experience, and assign individuals to appropriate projects.

Beginning on Monday, 26 August, the day the change went into effect, relief recipients deluged the intake offices. On some days as many as twenty thousand New Yorkers showed up for interviews. Lines stretched out of the WPA offices and around the block. In the last week of August applicants often began to queue up the night before to assure themselves of being among the first to see the placement officers when headquarters opened the next morning. The WPA staff, at the Port Authority Building and at branch offices established elsewhere in the city, worked feverishly to handle

Launching the WPA: The First Months 59

the rush. At times they hired and assigned to the various projects as many as seven thousand people a day.[22]

Unemployed men and women of every age, occupational background, and race passed by the interviewers' desks telling their stories. There was Clifton Sterling, a forty-three-year-old black man. He had a wife and a child to support. For twenty years he had driven a coal truck in Philadelphia. With the arrival of the depression, he lost his job and came to New York seeking work. He found a position with a charitable organization, running its mess hall, which fed two thousand jobless people a day. In April 1935 the agency, out of funds, closed its doors, and Sterling himself had to go on relief. The WPA employment official assigned Sterling to a construction and maintenance project in Central Park, where he labored 120 hours a month for $60.50.

John Krauss became a fellow employee of Sterling on the maintenance project. A forty-six-year-old white man, Krauss was a veteran of World War I who had served overseas for twenty-one months and had been wounded in combat. After returning to civilian life, he worked as a masseur in a Turkish bath. For three years prior to his WPA placement, however, he had been jobless.

Jacob Kainen, a young graphic artist, was graduated from Pratt Institute in 1930. He found a job drawing greeting cards in pen and ink for the Intaglio Gravure Company. The employment lasted only six months until the firm went bankrupt. "Then I was absolutely indigent," he recalled. "I lived on relief in a condemned house and paid ten dollars a month rent. I had an extension cord so I could get electricity through the transom. I had a heater and I lived on beans." Like many of New York's young artists and intellectuals, he also joined the radical John Reed Club. On 26 August 1935 the WPA hired him to work in the graphics division of the Federal Art Project at $103.40 a month.[23]

Life in the early thirties was not quite as difficult for Allan Angoff. A 1932 graduate of Boston University, he hoped that his journalism major would open the way to

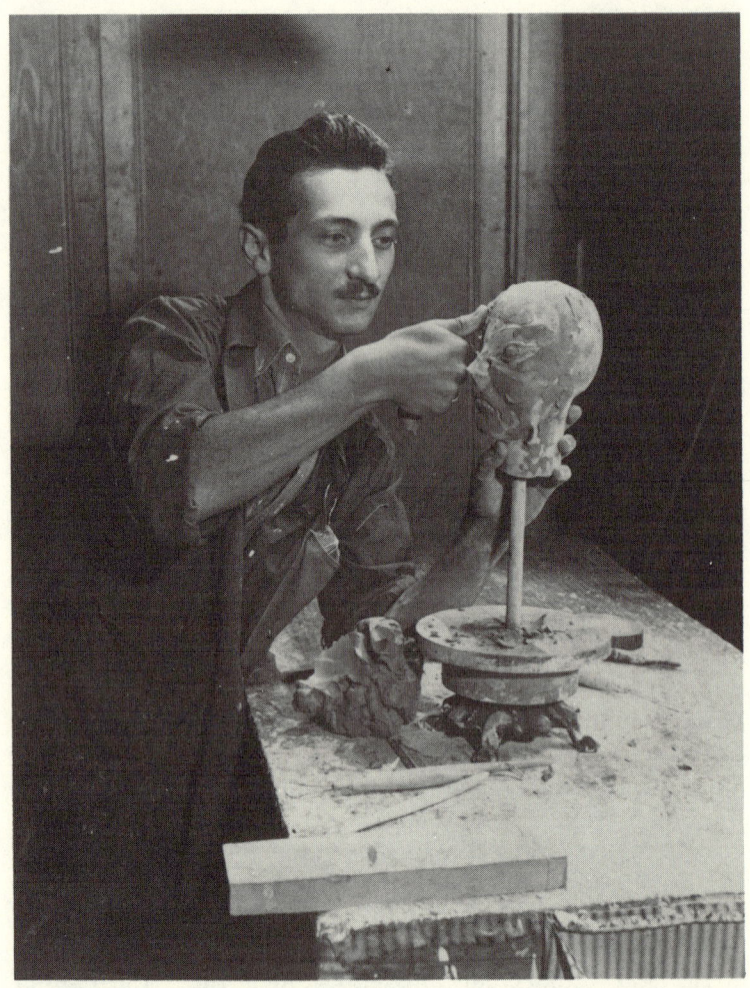

A sculptor employed by the Federal Art Project in New York City modeling a head. *Photo by the Photographic Division, Federal Art Project, WPA.*

employment on a newspaper. He soon discovered that there were no full-time reporters' jobs available and wound up working at the Boston Public Library. He did sell articles now and then to the Boston *Evening Transcript,* the Boston *Herald,* the New York *Post,* and other papers. In 1934 he decided to leave the public library to go to New York. His friends thought he was crazy to give up a steady job in the midst of the depression, but he was young, single, and wanted to try his luck in the exciting metropolis. He rented a room on Seventeenth Street, lived frugally, and managed to get by on what he earned writing articles and book reviews. Often, he did not receive pay for these, but periodicals such as the *American Mercury* allowed him to keep the reviewer's copy of the book, which he then sold at one-quarter of the retail price to local book stores. He joined the Writers Union, becoming friendly with many of his fellow members. When one of them, Earl Conrad, first told Angoff that the government was going to start a project for unemployed writers, he could hardly believe it. If it was true, he knew he wanted to be on it. In August 1935 WPA officials at an old armory on Lexington Avenue began interviewing people for the Writers' Project, and Angoff was one of the lucky applicants hired.

Besides youngsters such as Kainen and Angoff, whose careers had been held back by the depression, older people, some of them the victims of dramatic reversals of fortune, also sought WPA jobs. A fifty-three-year-old former businessman had arrived in this country from Europe twenty-seven years earlier. America had treated him well. He had acquired his own business and invested in the stock market. Then came the crash, and he had lost his life savings, twenty-five thousand dollars. By 1932, his firm was bankrupt, and he was living on relief. On 9 September 1935 the WPA hired him as an unskilled laborer at $60.50 a month. A former assistant manager of one of the city's largest banks became a head clerk for the work relief organization at $93.50 a month. An author of a widely read book on marine salvage operations, with several inventions to his credit, received a position as a timekeeper.

The WPA staff, interviewing thousands of applicants, saw firsthand the toll that poverty and insecurity had taken since 1929. Among thirty thousand unskilled laborers sent to the offices by home relief authorities were nearly six thousand who had to be turned down because of their physical condition. Doctors examining these people for the WPA discovered many of them suffering from extreme nervousness, ulcers, and malnutrition. General Johnson said of these sad cases, "The years of depression and long unemployment have permanently broken so many men in health that they probably will never be employable again."[24]

In those hectic early weeks, the WPA interviewers had no time to check out the applicants' skills or qualifications. People who said they were actors, carpenters, or plumbers were simply taken at their word. Orrick Johns, in charge of the Writers' Project in New York City, recalled the unemployed authors who "filed past and related their sorry tales." "Records of long unemployment, of jobs on vanished publications, and claims of hidden creative talent predominated." He could not stop to verify each story. "In the natural confusion of placing thousands of people on quickly planned work the individual dwindled into a cipher."

Some ridiculously bad assignments resulted from the haste and confusion. Building projects were overloaded with a collection of nondescript employees such as watchmakers, window dressers, garment workers, and waiters. An ex-locomotive engineer became foreman of a construction crew. A man with a wooden leg was sent out to another building site. The supervisor, not having the heart to fire him, transferred him to a different construction project. A year later he was still on the WPA rolls, being shifted from job to job. This confusion took its toll on the efficiency of WPA undertakings as well as on the morale of the work relief personnel. Johnson's successors would have to order extensive reassignments. And these changes could not always be made easily. People entrenched in jobs for which they were ill-suited would fight to retain them rather than take pay cuts or return to home relief.[25]

Whether it placed the majority of the applicants well or not, the WPA, by 15 October 1935, had exceeded Johnson's reemployment goal. Two hundred eight thousand New Yorkers were at work on 340 white-collar and nearly 3,000 engineering projects. The WPA payroll amounted to approximately $740,000 a day in wages for these former welfare recipients. Many of them, who had not been able to earn a penny in several years, regarded their WPA jobs as lifesavers.

There was Anzia Yezierska, for example, who had won recognition with her stories about immigrant life on the lower East Side and had written scripts for Hollywood films in the 1920s. Destitute and unemployed in 1935, she was one of the jobless writers hired by the WPA in New York City. In her autobiography she recalled the exhilaration she and her colleagues on the project experienced when they received their first paychecks:

> We treated one another to beer with the magnanimity of new millionaires. Then we crowded into the smoke-filled banquet hall at the rear of the bar, ordered a feast—a thirty-five cent table-d'hôte dinner—and tossed nickel tips to the waiter. We were as hilarious as slum children around a Christmas tree. Pockets jingled with money. Men who hadn't had a job in years fondled five and ten dollar bills with the tenderness of farmers rejoicing over new crops of grain.

Not all WPA employees rushed out to celebrate, but many of them agreed it felt good to be a wage earner once more. Charles Busch, a forty-four-year-old carpenter, who had run his own shop before the depression ruined him, had been jobless for two years prior to August 1935. He and his family had survived on home relief. Now the WPA was paying him and other skilled laborers to remodel the public baths at Wilson and Willoughby Avenues in Brooklyn, and Busch thanked providence to be off direct assistance and working at his trade again. Even Felix Livotsky, a former tailor, who found himself swinging a pick for the WPA in the city parks, did not complain. Livotsky admitted that he was unaccustomed to the outdoor physical labor, but he had a wife and four children to feed, and he preferred a WPA job to a handout.[26]

All over the city one could see these newly employed laborers at work. In The Bronx, seven hundred WPA employees had begun the development of Orchard Beach, which included enlarging the beach and building restaurants, a bathhouse, and parking lots. Other WPA workers renovated public schools in the borough and constructed buildings and an athletic field on the Bronx campus of Hunter College. In Queens WPA crews were repairing

WPA workers renovating the Duffield Street public bathhouse in Brooklyn, December 1935. These workmen are scraping old plaster from the interior walls preparatory to applying a new finish. *Photo by the Art Service Project, WPA.*

Jamaica Avenue and laying out twenty-six new playgrounds. Staten Islanders watched operations commence on a $2 million project to provide them with a South Shore Boardwalk. The borough president hailed the undertaking as his twenty-year "dream" come true.

With great fanfare, on the afternoon of 28 August Mayor La Guardia, City Park Commissioner Robert Moses, General Johnson, and other city and WPA officials marched from Grand Street to Fourteenth, where ceremonies kicked off the start of WPA construction of Manhattan's East Side Drive.[27] La Guardia had great fun operating steam shovels and jack hammers and then settled down to the less strenuous business of prognosticating that the drive would relieve Manhattan traffic, raise property values, encourage building of new apartments on the East Side, and reclaim the whole section between Grand and Twelfth Streets.

Not all WPA workers swung picks and shovels. Some served the citizens of New York in the fields of recreation, education, and research. For instance, during the summer the WPA hired unemployed musicians to give free band concerts in Brooklyn parks. When schools opened in the fall, teachers on the WPA payroll offered a broad range of adult education classes from Public Speaking to Science in Everyday Life and from Russian Literature to Family Law. Assorted jobless college graduates were placed on research projects of potential use to the community such as studying methods of fuel burning to abate smoke nuisance and surveying the city's airport facilities to determine their capacity and the need for extensions.[28]

By 15 October 1935, then, the WPA had surmounted its troubled start and was operating reasonably well. Hugh Johnson, therefore, felt that he had fulfilled his promise to launch the organization, and he announced his resignation. The city very likely benefited from Johnson's decision not to remain with the work relief agency beyond its formative period. The hectic, dramatic stage of creating a new organization at top speed was just about over. The essential tasks that lay ahead included improvements in organizational structure, tightening up administrative practices, reassigning workers to jobs that best suited their abilities, and reviewing projects to weed out wasteful activities and improve service and efficiency. Johnson was far too fond of the limelight to have been happy supervising these relatively prosaic changes.

The general's early retirement was fortunate in another way as well. Surrounded by so many outside enemies, the WPA required a director who believed in work relief wholeheartedly. But Johnson had grave doubts about the program. He stated publicly as early as June 1935 that turning a $4 billion appropriation into three million jobs was "a practical ban on useful and permanent projects." He called the WPA "a more ambitious kind of leaf raking" and "boondoggling." Upon resigning in October, he had not changed his mind. In his final confidential report to Hopkins he recommended that "the money should be disbursed as direct relief except for worthwhile and necessary work on a basis of cost competitive with contemporary public construction." When the report somehow fell into the hands of the press many months later, it became front-page news and highly embarrassing to the administration and all work relief supporters.[29]

New York City, nonetheless, owed its first WPA administrator a debt of gratitude. In two and one-half months he had carried the new federal agency from the planning stage to a stage at which it ranked as an employer that rivaled any one of the nation's ten largest industrial corporations in the size of its labor force. The administrative experience he brought with him to the assignment helped account for his success. He proved himself able to act quickly, untangle bureaucratic red tape, and anticipate troublesome problems in advance. He demonstrated these abilities when he foresaw the difficulty that the security wage would cause and spoke out against it. Unfortunately, Washington did not listen to him in time to avoid a strike that hampered the reemployment effort for eight weeks. Johnson also eliminated the bottleneck created by the United States Employment Service. The direct contact that he established between home relief and the WPA was eventually copied by most state directors. No doubt, during the hectic first months of the WPA a lot of people wound up in the wrong jobs. But at the same time, 208,000 New Yorkers who would otherwise have been idle and destitute were now gainfully employed.

NOTES

1. Emergency Relief Appropriations Act, 6 April 1935, *49 Stat., L115.*
2. Executive Order no. 7034, 6 May 1935; Grace Adams, *Workers on Relief* (New Haven, Conn., 1939), p. 14; John D. Millett, *The Works Progress Administration in New York City* (Chicago, 1938) p. 28.
3. In addition, only one member of a family could hold a WPA job, and that person would have to be over sixteen years of age. Physically handicapped persons who could be employed without endangering themselves or others were also eligible for positions.
4. Executive Order no. 7060, 5 June 1935; Executive Order no. 7046, 20 May 1935; WPA Bulletin no. 7, 26 July 1935.
5. Arthur Macmahon et al., *The Administration of Work Relief* (Chicago, 1941), pp. 37, 35; Report on the WPA for N.Y.C., Hugh Johnson to Hopkins, 1 July 1935 to 15 October 1935, p. 33, Harry Hopkins Papers, Franklin D. Roosevelt Library, Hyde Park, N.Y.; William F. McDonald, *Federal Relief Administration and the Arts* (Columbus, Ohio, 1969), p. 525; U.S. WPA for N.Y.C., *The Administration of Work Relief in New York City, August 1936–December 1937*, Report of Brehon B. Somervell to Harry Hopkins (New York, 1938), pp. 150–53; U.S. WPA for N.Y.C., *Final Report of the Work Projects Administration for the City of New York, 1935 to 1943* (New York, 1943), p. 91.
6. "Preliminary Statement of Information for Sponsors of WPA Projects," WPA Circular no. 1, 15 July 1935; *New York Herald Tribune,* 18 June 1935, pp. 1, 8; *New York Times,* 18 June 1935, p. 1; 12 June 1935, p. 13; Macmahon, *Administration of Work Relief,* p. 168.
7. *New York Times,* 24 March 1938, p. 16; 4 October 1935, p. 22; Hugh Johnson's Farewell Address to the Administrative Staff of the N.Y.C. WPA, 15 October 1935, Harry Hopkins Papers, Franklin D. Roosevelt Library, Hyde Park, N.Y.
8. La Guardia to Paul V. Betters, 14 February 1935, Fiorello La Guardia Papers, New York City Municipal Archives; Millett, *The WPA in N.Y.C.,* p. 30; *New York Post,* 26 June 1935, pp. 1, 2; *New York Times,* 26 June 1935, p. 1.

68 THE NEW DEAL AND THE UNEMPLOYED

9. By the end of 1934 there were 314,018 families on welfare in N.Y.C., as compared to 100,000 to 160,000 in Chicago, Los Angeles, and Philadelphia, the three cities coming closest in the size of their relief populations.

10. U.S. Congress, House Subcommittee of the Committee on Appropriations, *Hearings on the First Deficiency Appropriations Bill*, 74th Cong., 2d sess. (Washington, D.C., 1936), p. 184; R. Ecker to Hopkins, 31 December 1934, Harry Hopkins Papers, Franklin D. Roosevelt Library, Hyde Park, N.Y.; *New York Times*, 3 July 1935, p. 5; U.S. WPA for N.Y.C., *Brief Review of Developments in New York City during the Past Two Years*, Report of Brehon B. Somervell to Harry Hopkins (New York, 1937), p. 2.

11. *New York Post*, 26 June 1935, p. 2; *New York Times*, 26 June 1935, p. 1; N.Y.C. Aldermanic Committee to Investigate the Administration of Relief, *In the Matter of the Investigation of Administration of Unemployment Relief in the City of New York* (New York, 8 July 1935), p. 187; Johnson's Farewell Address, 15 October 1935, and Memo on Hugh Johnson's Conditions for Accepting Office, Hopkins Papers.

12. Hugh Johnson, *The Blue Eagle from Egg to Earth* (New York, 1935), pp. 24–25, 34–35, 75, 76–77, 87, 89, 100, 102, 116–17, 8; Arthur M. Schlesinger, Jr., *The Age of Roosevelt*, vol. 2, *The Coming of the New Deal* (Boston, 1959), pp. 103–6.

13. Millett, *The WPA in N.Y.C.*, pp. 31–32; Report on WPA, Johnson to Hopkins, pp. 2, 4, Hopkins Papers; *New York Times*, 28 June 1935, p. 1.

14. Report on WPA, Johnson to Hopkins, p. 1, Hopkins Papers; *New York Herald Tribune*, 5 January 1935, p. 8; U.S. *Congressional Record*, 74th Cong., 1st sess., 1935, 79; 924, 928; Executive Order no. 7046, 20 May 1935; WPA Administrative Order no. 13, 8 August 1935.

15. Transcript of a telephone conversation between Hopkins and La Guardia, 21 May 1935, Harry Hopkins Papers, Franklin D. Roosevelt Library, Hyde Park, N.Y.; *New York Post*, 22 May 1935, p. 1; 23 May 1935, pp. 1, 2, 7; *New York Times*, 22 May 1935, p. 1; 23 May 1935, p. 1; 31 August 1935, p. 2.

16. Johnson's increases brought the pay schedules in N.Y.C. to $60.50 a month for unskilled workers, $71.50 for intermediate, $93.50 for skilled, and $103.40 for professional and technical employees.

17. *New York Post*, 3 July 1935, p. 2; 16 July 1935, p. 3; Report on WPA, Johnson to Hopkins, p. 12, Hopkins Papers; *New York Times*, 17 July 1935, p. 28; 23 May 1935, p. 1; 2 June 1935, p. 10; 11 August 1935, p. 10; *Intercity Differences in Cost of Living in March 1935, in Fifty-nine Cities*, by Margaret Loomis Stecker (Washington, D.C., 1937), p. 5.

18. Beulah Amidon, "WPA—Wages and Workers," *Survey Graphic* 24 (October 1935): 493.

19. After Congress wrote the prevailing-wage principle into law in 1936, the N.Y.C. WPA had 125 grades into which workers fit, requiring seventeen different work schedules.

20. *New York Times*, 13 July 1935, p. 1; 8 August 1935, p. 1; 9 August 1935, pp. 1, 2; 10 August 1935, p. 1; 16 August 1935, p. 2; 21 August 1935,

p. 21; New York *Daily News,* 8 August 1935, p. 14; 9 August 1935, pp. 2, 8; New York *Post,* 9 August 1935, p. 12; 10 August 1935, p. 3; Amidon, "WPA—Wages and Workers," p. 497.

21. *New York Times,* 17 September 1935, p. 1; 20 September 1935, p. 1; 18 September 1935, p. 1; 25 September 1935, p. 1; New York *Post,* 14 August 1935, p. 2; 17 September 1935, pp. 1, 20; 19 September 1935, p. 3; 20 September 1935, p. 2; WPA Administrative Order no. 24, 19 September 1935; Report on WPA, Johnson to Hopkins, p. 17, Hopkins Papers.

22. Report on WPA, Johnson to Hopkins, pp. 18, 19, 20–22, 23, 30, Hopkins Papers; Millett, *WPA in N.Y.C.,* pp. 36–37; *New York Times,* 25 August 1935, p. 1; 27 August 1935, p. 1; New York *Post,* 26 August 1935, pp. 1, 6; 27 August 1935, pp. 1, 7; 28 August 1935, pp. 1, 3; U.S. WPA for N.Y.C., *Final Report,* p. 75.

23. New York *World-Telegram,* 11 September 1935, p. 13; Jacob Kainen, "A Dialogue" and "The Graphic Arts Division of the WPA Federal Art Project," in *The New Deal Art Projects: An Anthology of Memoirs,* ed. Francis V. O'Connor (Washington, D.C., 1972), pp. 312–13, 164.

24. Interview of Allan Angoff by the author, 20 November 1976, Teaneck, N.J.; New York *World-Telegram,* 11 September 1935, p. 13; Radio Address of Daniel Ring, assistant administrator in charge of labor, N.Y.C. WPA, 18 June 1936, Papers of the U.S. WPA for N.Y.C., National Archives, Washington, D.C.; *New York Times,* 6 September 1935, p. 1.

25. Orrick Johns, *Time of Our Lives: The Story of My Father and Myself* (New York, 1937), p. 343; U.S. WPA for N.Y.C., *Administration of Work Relief,* pp. 132, 212, 206.

26. *New York Times,* 20 October 1935, p. 11; Anzia Yezierska, *Red Ribbon on a White Horse* (New York, 1950), p. 161; Brooklyn *Eagle,* 10 August 1935, p. 2; New York *World-Telegram,* 11 September 1935, p. 13.

27. The WPA built the East River Drive from Grand to Thirty-fourth Streets, while private contractors under PWA direction completed the rest.

28. Bronx *Home News,* 11 August 1935, p. 1; 16 August 1935, p. 1; New York *World-Telegram,* 11 July 1935, p. 16; 12 August 1935, p. 6; Brooklyn *Eagle,* 7 October 1935, p. 7; 28 August 1935, p. 1; 1 September 1935, p. 6; 11 September 1935, p. 4; *New York Times,* 11 August 1935, sec. 2, p. 3; 1 September 1935, sec. 4, p. 10; 10 July 1935, p. 8.

29. *New York Times,* 26 June 1935, p. 1; 11 April 1936, p. 1; Report on WPA, Johnson to Hopkins, p. 34, Hopkins Papers.

3

Mr. Ridder Takes the Helm

As the German liner, *Bremen,* steamed westward across the Atlantic in September 1935, a radiogram arrived for one of its passengers returning from a holiday in Europe. The message came from Franklin D. Roosevelt and was addressed to Victor Francis Ridder, a forty-nine-year-old German-American publisher. The contents of the wire caught the blond, ruddy-complexioned newspaperman totally by surprise. The Democratic president was asking him, a Republican, to become administrator of the WPA in New York City. Ridder's old friend, Mayor La Guardia, had attached his own appeal to the request, which read simply "Bitte—Fiorello."

The short note from La Guardia hardly indicated what an instrumental part he played in the naming of Victor Ridder to the post. From the time La Guardia learned Johnson was going to resign, the mayor had fretted about who might take over. On 21 September he telephoned Hopkins's assistant, Corrington Gill, to tell him he was "worried sick about Johnson's successor." La Guardia insisted he must talk to Hopkins at once because, as he put it, "I don't want these politicians to put anything over on us." What the mayor feared was the appointment of an administrator with close ties to the Tammany organization or one beholden to the Democratic aldermen or the borough presidents. In a series of conferences with Roosevelt and Hopkins, La Guardia not only forestalled that possibility but managed to convince the others to approve Victor Ridder, one of the mayor's earliest political supporters.

Ridder received the appointment both as a result of La Guardia's persuasiveness and because he appeared to be a well-qualified and popular choice. The new WPA chief came from a prominent New York publishing family with major influence in the German-American community and in local business circles. He and his brothers owned and ran the *Staats-Zeitung*, the city's oldest German-language newspaper, as well as the *Catholic News*, the New York *Journal of Commerce*, and the Long Island *Daily Press*. In addition, Ridder's interest in social work dated back to 1902, when he began teaching classes at the East Side Settlement House. Later he founded the Catholic Committee of Big Brothers and served on the New York Board of Charities (subsequently renamed the State Board of Social Welfare). By the 1930s he also held seats on the TERA, Governor Lehman's Committee on Unemployment Relief, and Mayor La Guardia's committee on the same problem. The *New York Times* commented on the appointment: "Victor Ridder . . . is an excellent choice for successor to General Johnson. . . . He is intimately familiar with the whole relief problem," and "as an old friend of Mayor La Guardia he is assured of the support of the city administration."[1]

On 15 October 1935 Ridder took over the helm of the New York City agency. He inherited from his predecessor an ongoing organization that was employing 208,000 individuals. Most of the hectic period of initiating new projects and assigning thousands of persons to them had passed. Of course, the former publisher also fell heir to many of the problems that had begun to develop under Johnson's leadership. One of these was finding competent foremen to supervise construction activities. As building projects expanded, additional foremen had to be obtained quickly. The New York City WPA had not yet developed tests or standards by which to judge the qualifications of men for these supervisory posts. Besides, the relief rolls yielded few people with past experience in heading construction crews. Consequently, the supervision at WPA work sites sometimes left much to be desired.

A second difficulty that had started during Johnson's tenure persisted as well. WPA hiring ran ahead of its abilities to initiate new projects. Therefore, to provide jobs for as many people as possible, placement officers continued to assign to existing projects more labor than they required. Foremen tended to abet this practice because they wanted to obtain more materials and equipment, and according to WPA rules the cost of supplies had to be kept at a small, fixed percentage of the amount spent for wages. The extra hands, with trifling or nonexistent tasks, leaned on shovels or stood on the curb (which is why the foremen soon nicknamed them the "curbstone payroll"). It was during this first year of the WPA's existence that the public developed the image of the shiftless WPA worker. Most of this overmanning later disappeared, not because the WPA changed its rules or started a sufficient number of new projects but because Washington ordered cutbacks in employment.[2]

Preventing graft represented still another problem for Ridder and his successors. The opportunities and temptation for it were certainly present in an organization that dispensed as much as $5.5 million a week. In tracking down corruption, Ridder and other state administrators had the help of the Division of Investigation created by Hopkins in June 1935. The division was charged with unearthing such offenses as forgeries of work-assignment slips, time sheets, and payrolls; extortion; theft; bribery; and improper political activity, as well as bringing the perpetrators to justice.

In one instance, the division caught a number of foremen who had conspired with truck owners to defraud the government. These dishonest officials were renting twice as much equipment as their projects required and splitting the fees for excess vehicles with the owners. Ridder fired the men involved, and to prevent this abuse from recurring, he discontinued the authority of each project foreman to requisition his own machinery, substituting a more centralized checkup system. In another case, the division uncovered a ring of "fixers" who were selling forged WPA work-assignment cards to persons who were ineligible for placement because they lacked relief certification. Because of the continuing diligence of the Division of Investigation there was remarkably little graft in the New York City WPA, even though it disbursed huge sums of money.[3]

Ridder sometimes found keeping politics out of WPA more difficult than snuffing out dishonesty. Undoubtedly, in New York City as elsewhere, political considerations and friendships influenced the choice of the top directors. Both Johnson and Ridder received their posts in part because of their longtime associations with officials in the Roosevelt Administration or with Mayor La Guardia. They, in turn, staffed the various divisions of the work relief organization with former colleagues and friends in whom they had confidence. In addition, New York City congressmen and members of the La Guardia Administration from time to time asked the heads of the WPA to place certain individuals in project jobs. As early as July 1935 Johnson received recommendations from Congressman William Sirovich on behalf of several of his constituents, and the general promised to give the matter "prompt attention." Ridder generally did the same if the persons recommended were unemployed and needy. He and his successors, however, drew the line at turning the WPA into simply a source of patronage for politicians. Their refusal to do so led to many complaints, such as the one Congressman Samuel Dickstein sent to Ridder in November 1935:

> I do not believe that I received one assignment as a result of any recommendations made by me to the U.S. Works

Progress Administration since its existence. . . . [W]hether you are interested or not you cannot conduct campaigns with not even a laborer's job for deserving Americans.[4]

If the placement of individuals in WPA jobs was not completely free of political considerations, Ridder and his successors were scrupulous in resisting the temptation to influence people working for the agency. For example, the New York administrator asked Washington about the propriety of enclosing within WPA wage envelopes circulars backing a state bond issue to raise money for unemployment relief. Hopkins replied promptly, "I think as a matter of general policy, circulars should not be enclosed with payroll checks no matter how worthy the cause," and such material was never distributed. In letters of instructions to state directors in February and March 1936, moreover, Hopkins stated that the WPA would not employ in an administrative capacity anyone running for elective office. In addition, WPA workers were not required to contribute to any political party or candidate, and persons soliciting such contributions from them were subject to immediate dismissal. Ridder ordered that these regulations be prominently posted at all project locations.[5]

In the first months of Ridder's tenure, while he strove to improve the operation of the WPA, the program reached its peak in the number of destitute New Yorkers it employed, the amount of money it pumped into the city's economy, and the projects it undertook. When the publisher replaced Johnson in mid-October, the payroll listed 208,000 workers. By February 1936 the ranks had grown to over 246,000, the largest the New York agency would ever be. As the numbers carried rose, so, of course, did the WPA's expenditures. Between November 1935 and February 1936, monthly outlay jumped from a little over $20 million to nearly $23 million. Most of the money went directly to the workers in the form of wages—approximately $16 million in November and almost $19.5 million in February. Clearly, the New York City WPA had become one of the biggest enterprises in the country, employing more people than the War Department of its day and more than any private corporation in the city.[6]

These statistics, however, do not adequately illustrate the impact the WPA made on the lives of many New Yorkers. To some a job meant the return to a secure place as family head. One black clerical worker, after three weeks on a white-collar project, put it this way:

> Now I can look my children straight in the eyes. I've regained my self-respect. Relief is all right to keep one from starving, but well—it takes something from you. Sitting around and waiting for your case worker to bring you a check and the kids in the house find you contribute nothing toward their support, very soon they begin to lose respect for you. It's different now. I'm the breadwinner of the house and everybody respects me.

Many young people fresh out of school found in government work relief their only chance for a job. Frank Montano graduated from New York University's School of Architecture *cum laude* in June 1934, but he could find no work of any kind. Then, in January 1936, Montano was taken in with the WPA expansion and assigned to the Park Department. The income provided for his basic needs, and the limited hours required by his WPA employment left him time to continue studying architecture on his own. That spring he entered some of his drawings in the international contest run by the French Society of Beaux-Arts Architects. In June he said good-bye to the WPA and departed for Paris, for he had won first prize, a thirty-six-hundred-dollar scholarship for eighteen months of instruction at the Ecole des Beaux Arts. Although most of the youth hired by the WPA were not as talented as Frank Montano and did not leave the agency for promising outside careers as quickly as he, they did gain work experience from the WPA and a way of supporting themselves until private employment became available.

November 1935, artists of the WPA Poster Project designing posters for New York City's antinoise campaign. Fifty artists were employed on this project. *Photo by the Art Service Project, WPA.*

The WPA in New York touched the lives of many more than those who worked for it. From its expanding projects an ever-greater portion of the city's inhabitants benefited in one way or another. Between 1 August 1935 and July 1936 the WPA laid 48 miles of sewers in New York, removed 33 miles of surface car tracks, began 100 playgrounds and 11 swimming pools, reconditioned 26 armories and 1 million square feet of Coney Island Boardwalk, built 126 miles of roads in Queens, and repaired and painted 50 bridges. But these projects far from exhausted its undertakings. Poor litigants in twenty-eight municipal and four small claims courts received free legal aid from a staff of twenty-four WPA attorneys. By July 1936, 122 limited-income families had moved into the Astor Low Cost Housing Project, now renamed First Houses, where they rented new apartments at an average cost of six dollars a room per month. In May twenty-five thousand New Yorkers crowded on to the Sheep Meadow in Central Park to watch a rollicking four-hour variety show presented by WPA artists, actors, musicians, and writers. Among the acts was an all-black review called "Dixie to Broadway" featuring such old-time favorites of the black theater as Anita Bush, Eddie Frye, and Walter Cumbley.[7]

Unfortunately, not all those who needed the WPA received their fair share of its help. Women claimed that in the first months of the program they were largely bypassed. Despite instructions from Washington that state WPA directors should make jobs available for women on relief, the New York City agency had hired only some nineteen thousand females, representing about 8 percent of its total labor force by December 1935. At that date the Emergency Relief Bureau listed thirty-three thousand women on home relief who were able-bodied and eligible for positions under WPA rules. Victor Ridder announced his intention of placing as many of these women as possible and appealed to the public to suggest new projects offering suitable opportunities for females.

A first step toward eliminating the sexual imbalance came with the creation of a Women's and Professional Division soon after Johnson's departure. National headquarters insisted that this division must be headed by a woman. In compliance, Ridder appointed his executive secretary, Mary Tinney, to the new post. Tinney, a native of Brooklyn who held a master's degree from the University of Chicago, had years of experience as a social worker. Previous to 1936 she had been with the Brooklyn Bureau of Charities, served as a supervisor for home relief, and been a member of the New York City Department of Hospitals.

The New York City WPA also initiated several new undertakings designed specifically to employ women. For instance, early in 1936 the Women's Division opened five schools of beauty culture to teach sixteen hundred jobless women cosmetology skills that might help them obtain work in privately owned beauty parlors. Another project, under the supervision of Ruth Ayres, a former economics teacher at New York University, hired six hundred interviewers, mostly women, to question New York families about their income and expenditures. Eventually, the data gathered would be compiled into a municipal cost-of-living survey thought to be of value to economists, businessmen, and the government.

Despite the attention that Ridder and Mary Tinney gave to female employment, the WPA never wholly solved the problem of finding enough suitable jobs for women. Construction activities were easier to design than service and white-collar projects. Also, swimming pools, roads, and airports were more popular with city officials and the public since they could be readily seen. As a result, building projects predominated, and they offered few opportunities for women. Besides, the WPA could offer a job to only one member of a family, and officials looked upon the man, if one was present in a household, as the natural breadwinner. Thus, throughout the WPA's existence the proportion of females assigned remained small, hovering around 10 percent of the agency's total labor force.[8]

During Johnson's regime, black New Yorkers also charged the WPA with discrimination. In fact, the news of the general's appointment aroused dismay among black leaders. T. Arnold Hill of the National Urban League sent wires to La Guardia and Hopkins in June 1935, protesting the choice. Hill asserted that as NRA director the general had failed completely to recognize blacks and that he had hired none for either administrative or clerical positions. The next month the executive secretary of the Brooklyn Urban League lodged a similar complaint with Hopkins. When Johnson resigned in the fall, the black leaders were no happier about his performance than they had been in June. A committee calling itself the Joint Conference Against Discriminatory Practices announced that it intended to hold a meeting at the Abyssinian Baptist Church on 23

October to denounce the "rampant discrimination in the WPA."

At that time blacks comprised approximately 8 percent of the WPA's labor force. Since, according to the census of 1930, they constituted roughly 5 percent of the city's adult population, they appeared to be overrepresented on work relief. On the other hand, blacks faced a far more desperate unemployment problem than whites. While in the community at large around one out of every three workers was jobless, in Harlem the figure climbed to one out of two. Further, more than four of every ten black families in New York City were living on welfare in 1935–36—roughly double the ratio found among white families.

Soon after Ridder took over the direction of the WPA in the city, he voiced his sympathy for jobless blacks. He agreed that blacks had suffered discrimination and insisted it must stop at once. The injustice arose not from overall WPA policy, which he maintained had always favored fair play, but from "the narrow-mindedness and prejudice of individuals."[9] To illustrate past wrongs and his intention to right them, Ridder stated that he had learned that among sixty dentists hired by the agency not one was black. He immediately sought out and placed an unemployed black dentist on the project.

The former publisher endeavored to integrate other service programs as well. In April, for example, he assigned the first two blacks to the WPA's medical staff—a female surgeon and a registered nurse. He also established a twenty-one-man advisory committee on black problems headed by the Reverend John H. Johnson, pastor of St. Martin's Church and prominent Harlem civil rights leader.[10]

In his attempt to improve relations with the black community, Ridder received the valuable assistance of Mary Tinney, who conceived the idea of staging a week-long festival and exhibit to begin on 8 June 1936, displaying the work of the WPA in Harlem. When the show opened to the public, it featured displays from various fields such as education, recreation, art, music, and theater. The photographs, paintings, pamphlets, and demonstrations told an impressive story. More than ten thousand residents of Harlem attended the WPA's adult education classes, which operated in eighty centers and employed 158 teachers, mostly black. The WPA black drama unit, which staged its plays at the Lafayette Theater—often to a packed house—employed over 140 black actors, writers, and stagehands. Its productions included *The Conjure Man Dies* and Orson Welles's adaptation of *Macbeth*, with its setting moved to Haiti and its witches transformed into practitioners of voodoo. The WPA ran three music centers uptown where thirty-five hundred children and adults took lessons in voice, instruments, and music appreciation. Another fifteen hundred persons attended the free art classes conducted at neighborhood centers, schools, and churches.

These activities proved very important in the lives of two young black people. One was Jacob Lawrence, recognized today as one of America's leading black artists. His mother moved the family from Philadelphia to Harlem in 1929 or 30, when Lawrence was entering his teens. Lawrence was enrolled in the New York public schools and after class worked at odd jobs—in a laundry, a bakery, and a print shop, and delivering newspapers. But his great love was art. From childhood he had displayed considerable talent, although there was never any money for formal instruction. Then, in the mid-1930s, Lawrence found his way to the WPA's Harlem Art Workshop. There he studied under two established black artists, Henry Bannarn and Charles Alston. Alston quickly recognized the unique style and ability of his pupil and actively encouraged him. In 1938 the twenty-one-year-old Lawrence had the first exhibit of his paintings of Harlem street life. That same year, his WPA teachers arranged for Lawrence (now old enough to be eligible) to join the Art Project. For the next eighteen months he earned twenty-five dollars a week, enabling him to devote himself full time to his painting.

A poster announcing free art instruction at one of the many centers throughout the community staffed by WPA art teachers. Photo by the Photographic Division, Federal Art Project, WPA.

Ellen Tarry, in 1936, belonged to a writers' group in Harlem. Like most of its members, she was unemployed. Someone in the group introduced her to the poet and novelist Claude McKay, who was then a supervisor on the New York City WPA Writers' Project. McKay invited Tarry to come by the office for an interview. At the interview, she showed one of the supervisors clippings from her newspaper work in Alabama, and he was sufficiently impressed to offer her a job if she could get relief certification. After some delay, she managed to convince welfare officials that she was indeed without any means of support and became eligible first for home relief and then transfer to the WPA. The Writers' Project put her to work gathering material on the underground railroad and black churches. Though she did not know it at the time, the information she collected and the essays she wrote on it were intended to be incorporated eventually in a history of blacks in New York. Each morning she discussed the progress of her research with her supervisor and then trudged off to the Forty-second Street library or the Schomberg Collection in the library on 135th Street. "I practically lived at those two places. . . ," she recalled. Many years later she wrote:

> I never cease to be grateful for the opportunity I had to retain my skills as a writer because if a writer gets rusty there's a possibility you die from the rust. That is why I'm always glad to acknowledge the debt I owe the Federal Government, the WPA and the Roosevelt Administration. If it hadn't been for them, I might have done nothing more. Now my ninth book is coming out in the spring.[11]

Apparently, then, Ridder and Tinney did make real improvements. The proportion of black workers on the New York City WPA rose from 8 percent in the fall of 1935 to 12 percent by April 1936, which meant an additional five thousand jobs for blacks. The blacks' share continued to climb even after Ridder's departure, and by November 1937 blacks held slightly over 13 percent of the work relief jobs. The complaints from civil rights organizations declined. Perhaps not all black leaders would go as far in their praise, but an editorial in *Opportunity,* the journal of the National Urban League, proclaimed:

> It is to the eternal credit of the administrative officers of the WPA that discrimination on various projects because of race has been kept to a minimum. . . . In the northern communities, particularly in the urban centers, the Negro has been afforded his first real opportunity for employment in white-collar occupations.

Blacks continued, however, to be concentrated in the lowest-paying, unskilled category on the New York City WPA throughout its existence. As late as 1937 nearly three-fourths of the blacks were classified as common laborers, while only 5 percent of black work relief personnel held professional and technical positions and one-half of 1 percent ranked as supervisors. These figures probably indicate both discrimination and lack of education and skills among blacks. Also, WPA placement officers tended to assign people to positions similar to the ones they had held in private employment. Many black women thus wound up on housekeeping projects.[12]

Besides coping with complaints of discrimination from women and blacks, Ridder also had to handle attacks made by certain local government officials. Troubles with Robert Moses, city park commissioner, began almost immediately after the birth of the new organization. He continuously argued with Johnson about who should control WPA projects in the city's parks. Moses demanded the right to hire and fire WPA laborers, establish his own work rules for them, and appoint his own supervisors. The general refused to yield these functions to Moses, pointing out that the WPA was a federalized program, and, therefore, the agency must oversee the spending of its funds. The dispute had not been satisfactorily settled when Ridder succeeded Johnson.

The commissioner first locked horns with Ridder in December after the WPA had set up a labor appeals board to hear the complaints of aggrieved employees. On the 29th, Robert Moses wrote to the administrator: "We cannot permit your appeals board to interfere with promotions, discipline or other administrative matters on Park Department projects." Moses also took the opportunity to reiterate his stand. "All this is simply another way of saying that if you will let the Park Department run the relief projects, confining yourself to furnishing materials and checking results, you will have nothing to regret or be ashamed of." In this instance Ridder allowed the commissioner to have his way. The WPA chief signed an agreement with Moses providing that the Park Department could settle its own labor complaints, but must notify the WPA of the outcome in each case.

The concession did not mollify Moses. Next he refused to display WPA signs on park projects. He protested that these posters were propaganda that advertised "the federal administration to the general public." Only after La Guardia interceded at Hopkins's request did the stubborn commissioner relent, grudgingly permitting one placard per project. And he never tired of reiterating his contention that "detailed control and operation from Washington is beyond the limit of government capacity. If there is to be federal aid, it should be done through the states and municipalities and with the federal government interesting itself only in progress of work and completion on time within the funds available."[13]

Queens Borough President George U. Harvey, a conservative Republican with gubernatorial ambitions, voiced even more severe criticism of the WPA than did Moses. Harvey testified before a Senate subcommittee on 19 May 1936 that the WPA failed to help the poor in his borough because "the money is going to overhead and not going to the men in the street that need it." According to him, the federal agency had built up a vast, unnecessary bureaucracy that ate up at least 25 percent of the relief funds.

The next day Ridder sent the Senate subcommittee a

long letter of rebuttal, totally denying Harvey's figures. The New York director pointed out that the ratio of administrators to laborers in Queens was almost identical to what it had been prior to 1935 under the city-operated work relief program even though the WPA undertook larger and more ambitious construction projects.[14]

Harvey made no public reply to Ridder but precipitated a new battle instead. On 28 May he informed the press that the work relief agency's paving of Jamaica Avenue was so poor that the county could not accept the job. Since the Queens official decided to air his views in the newspapers, Ridder had little alternative but to carry on the fight in the headlines. Accompanied by reporters, he toured the highway in question and pronounced it acceptable. Engineers from the City Department of Finance backed up Ridder's evaluation. Perhaps the most impartial assessment was expressed by a policeman who walked a beat in the area. "Of course, this road isn't so hot. But you should have seen it before the WPA came here. . . . [W]hat do you expect a bunch of shoemakers to work like asphalt men. Most of them never seen asphalt before they got this job."

Convinced that Harvey's charges amounted to a political grandstand play, Ridder determined to call his bluff. He withdrew all WPA laborers from road construction in the borough and assigned them elsewhere. He also threatened that, if the controversy continued, he would terminate all projects in Queens. Still hoping to capitalize on the situation, Harvey directed the placing of signs reading "This job stopped by WPA because I told the truth—George U. Harvey, President, Borough of Queens" on the deserted work sites.

The clash between the two men became the occasion for a great outpouring of support for the WPA in Harvey's home territory. When La Guardia asked Queens residents to let him know if they wanted work relief continued in their community, the mail he received ran "overwhelmingly in favor." Perhaps more surprising, the business organizations of the borough also acclaimed the WPA. The president of the Queensboro Chamber of Commerce wrote directly to Hopkins, urging retention of the program.

La Guardia finally stepped in as peacemaker. He talked Harvey into rescinding his rejection of the Jamaica Avenue paving, and the borough president promised that in the future he would bring his criticisms to Ridder first rather than run to the press. Ridder, in turn, reassigned his labor force to their former activities and allowed the highway department of the borough to do the final surfacing on all roads constructed in Queens.[15] Aside from the acrimonious exchanges with Moses and Harvey, reasonable harmony prevailed between the WPA and local authorities throughout Ridder's tenure and that of his successors as well.

To the former publisher, the problem of handling Moses and Harvey must have seemed like child's play in comparison to the difficulties that beset him when he was forced to reduce the WPA rolls in the spring of 1936. Early in March Ridder received word from Hopkins that some forty thousand employees would have to be dropped by June. This order came at a time when the city found its welfare case load growing by five thousand a month, and it was estimated that one hundred thousand able-bodied New Yorkers who met all requirements for WPA work still subsisted on home relief because jobs had not yet been created for them.

Roosevelt's gamble that an economic upturn would soon eliminate the need for a massive federal work relief effort did not pan out. Although business seemed to enjoy increased profits and activity, the small advances barely touched the gigantic reserve of unemployed Americans. Consequently, the number of men and women dependent on the government rose rather than decreased, and the original $4.8 billion grant from Congress for depression work relief was almost gone. The appropriation that the legislators expected to last for two years was nearly exhausted in less than one. Therefore, Roosevelt would have to return to Congress to request supplemental funds in the late spring. The lawmakers would most likely grant additional money, but the president doubted that Capitol Hill would allow the WPA to spend at the level it had maintained during its first year.

In fact, a growing chorus of voices told Roosevelt that outlays must be trimmed. Within his official family, pressure came from the Treasury Department and the Bureau of the Budget, both desiring to reduce deficit spending. Hopkins did not fully counter this force since he tended to estimate work relief needs on the low side rather than have the president reject his requests. Big business saw disaster ahead if the administration did not reverse its course. J. P. Morgan predicted that, unless the government reduced spending and taxation, every fortune in America would be wiped out within thirty years and with them the spirit of initiative that had made the country great. Herbert Hoover headed the list of conservative politicians who called for a balanced budget, an end to "unnecessary" public works, and the return of relief to local authorities. The *New York Times* represented perhaps the majority view of the nation's press in an April editorial that stated:

> A start must be made somewhere, sometime in the inevitable Federal retreat from this business of trying to provide actual work for all the country's destitute employables until industry absorbs them. It simply cannot be done. However superior in theory, it is too wasteful and expensive a method of relief to be continued indefinitely on anything like the present scale.

The words of Congressman James Buchanan, chairman of the House Appropriations Committee, also sounded ominous concerning the chances for big work relief grants in the future. As early as the fall of 1935 he announced that he opposed any new money for welfare except on a direct relief basis.

Influenced by these cries for economy, the president decided to ask for about $1.5 billion, a much more modest sum than he had requested the previous year. In June 1936 Congress gave Roosevelt what he suggested, making cutbacks in the WPA unavoidable. The desire of Roosevelt and the majority on Capitol Hill to save money and to balance the budget had taken priority over the needs of the jobless. In the months ahead about one million Americans, among them fifty thousand New Yorkers, were released from the program, most to subsist on home relief or private charity.[16]

In New York City the decision to economize at the expense of the unemployed aroused tremendous protest and resistance. La Guardia joined with the executives of fifty other Eastern cities to beg Roosevelt to reconsider. At one point the mayor proclaimed: "For God's sake, stop issuing bulletins on how many you are going to take off WPA before July 1. You don't know what it means in the way of anxiety to all these people. I'll tell the whole world we [the city] can't take care of them." As if to illustrate La Guardia's words, two weeks later Catherine Brunson, a nineteen-year-old black woman, jumped out of the window of her fifth floor apartment. The young mother took her life after her husband, a laborer on the WPA, received his pink slip. Friends said the loss of the job was more than she could bear, for without it she did not know how she and her husband could feed and clothe their infant son.

In April four hundred civic leaders attended a meeting sponsored by the major social work agencies in the city, such as the United Neighborhood Houses and the Welfare Council. Speaker after speaker hailed the WPA's contribution to the well-being of the community and warned against cuts. Private industry would not employ most of those slated for firing, they predicted, with the result that the discarded workers very likely faced prolonged idleness, loss of skills, and perhaps permanent dependency. The gathering adopted a resolution calling on Roosevelt to prevent such tragic developments.

Wires, letters, and statements from the unions of the jobless also poured in to Congress, the president, and the newspapers. A typical one read: "We are determined not to be sacrificed on the axe of Roosevelt economy. We will not be made the victims of the Liberty League to insure the re-election of Mr. Roosevelt. This reduction is the last straw for us."[17]

The unemployed also took direct action to try to prevent their being sacrificed. In March the various organizations of the jobless began almost daily picketing of WPA headquarters in the Port Authority Building. On the 19th and 20th, the demonstrators invaded the offices and occupied them until police emerged from the huge elevators on which they had loaded their patrol wagons, surrounded the crowd, and forcefully dragged the protestors into the vans. After these wild melees, Ridder hired armed guards to patrol the corridors and keep out unauthorized persons. Unable to seize the building, the demonstrators reverted to mass picketing outside. On many days two thousand to three thousand persons congregated on the street below the central offices, shouting and chanting:

> Here's our answer, Mr. Ridder,
> You had better reconsider;
> Stop the layoffs, Mr. Ridder,
> Or we'll get Rid'er you.

At times they blocked the entrances and made it nearly impossible for employees to enter or leave. Rumors circulated that the Port Authority refused to renew the WPA's lease in June 1936 because it was fed up with the disruptions.[18]

In May and June artists, architects, engineers, and technicians staged short-lived strikes against the local WPA, demanding more work and the end of all layoffs. After reading about the sit-down strikes then going on in France, another group of employees decided to apply the technique in their struggle. They occupied the offices of their particular projects around the clock. Ellen Tarry remembered taking candy bars and coffees to her friends who were locked in all night.

The disturbances and strikes became more and more irritating to Ridder, who finally concluded that most of the trouble was inspired by the unemployed unions that were nothing but Communist front groups. He decided he must root out these subversives and warn the public about their insidious activities. In speeches around the community during the spring and summer he labeled the demonstrators "rats" and "vermin" and appealed to the vast majority of peaceful workers on the projects to cooperate with him in a drive against the radicals whose only interest was to destroy the WPA.

The New York administrator also took the position that henceforth he would refuse to see delegations from any group that picketed his headquarters. He justified this decision with the assertion that "the same gang of Communist outsiders" would continue to create disturbances whether the WPA dropped two thousand or forty thousand employees. "The size of the cut has nothing to do with it. These delegations don't come to have interviews, they come to have a riot." Further, he vowed he would fire any employee participating in a demonstration.[19]

As a counteroffensive against the agitators, Ridder encouraged the formation of anti-Communist groups among WPA workers, especially on the arts projects. At his suggestion, Maj. William Ball, an employee of the WPA drama program, organized the Veterans' Theater League. The league soon occupied itself with investigating fellow project members, submitting evidence of their radical activities to the Justice Department, disrupting stage performances of plays they considered un-American, and handing statements to the press charging that the Theatre Project had been taken over by radicals. Another right-wing group of WPA employees, calling itself the American Writers Association, engaged in similar antics, proclaiming that virtually every white-collar project harbored a Communist cell of three to ten members and that these units controlled the unions of the unemployed.[20]

In fact, many of the accusations Ridder and his allies made against the unions of the unemployed were true. The Communists and Socialists had led the way in organizing the jobless. By 1933 in New York City four associations of destitute victims of the depression existed, each tied to a different radical political movement: the Unemployed Councils initiated by the Communist Party, the Workers' Unemployed Leagues founded by the Socialist Party, the Workers' Committee on Unemployment started by the League for Industrial Democracy, and the Association of the Unemployed affiliated with the Lovestonite faction of the Communists. These groups engaged in neighborhood actions against evictions, sit-ins for more aid at welfare stations, hunger marches, and noisy demonstrations for federal public works and relief programs.

After the national government entered the field of work relief, radicals established several other unions to represent those hired on the projects. In July 1935 Willis Morgan, a former insurance salesman, founded the City Projects Council among white-collar employees of the WPA. At about the same time, Joseph Gilbert, who ran as the Communist candidate for the New York Supreme Court in 1935, established a rival organization, the Project Workers Union, and another Communist, Marcel Scherer, began to unite professional workers in his Federation of Architects, Engineers, Chemists, and Technicians.

In the spring of 1936 this hodgepodge of radical associations achieved some unity when the Unemployed Councils, the Unemployed Leagues, the City Projects Council, and a number of others joined together in a single nationwide union, the Workers Alliance of America. David Lasser, a long time Socialist, became national president, but the key position of organizational secretary went to Herbert Benjamin, a Communist who was originally from Ohio.

Before and after they united, the radicals kept up steady agitation for greater aid to the destitute, whether on home or work relief. They fought for the prevailing wage on the WPA, demanded paid sick leave and vacations, and led the outcry against layoffs. Their tactics included strikes, sit-ins, marches on Washington, parades, and occasional riots. Undoubtedly, the left-wingers who established and directed these unions hoped not only to achieve increased benefits for their followers but also to radicalize them and make converts for the Communist or Socialist party. They frequently distributed party publications to their members and attempted to enlist them in causes dear to the left, such as support for the Loyalists in Spain.[21]

While Ridder was right that most of the leaders were Communists, he ignored the important reasons why a minority of the workers on the New York City WPA (the exact membership was always hard to determine) joined these radical associations. In an agency the size of the New York City WPA some injustice toward particular workers inevitably occurred. There might be difficulty in getting an initial assignment, paychecks arrived late, reclassifications and promotions took too long, foremen occasionally abused their powers, and there were arbitrary layoffs and firings. These were the kinds of complaints the unemployed unions took up and often got redressed. The AFL unions, on the other hand, aside from trying to maintain the prevailing-wage principle for their own skilled members, made no attempt to organize work relief personnel or to help them get fair treatment.

Allan Angoff, who worked on the Writers' Project, recalled that the Writers Union assisted its members in getting relief certification so that they qualified for WPA placement, and the union protested vigorously when its people received pink slips. He joined the organization because it offered social contact with other writers. "At the meetings, there was an exciting exchange of ideas," he remembered, and "you could sometimes pick up tips on where to look for jobs." Alan Buxton, a teacher and recreation director on the WPA, did not become a member of the Workers Alliance although his friends and coworkers kept urging him to sign up as a matter of solidarity. Despite the fact that he did not join (the leadership was a bit too radical for his taste), he admitted that the Workers Alliance advised him on how to obtain home relief, and the union was "very protective" of the project workers.

The radical unions also attracted some of the jobless because they spoke out more consistently than anyone else for increased government benefits to the destitute. They initiated mass letter writing to Congress, testified before committees on behalf of bills that provided generous sums for welfare, and sent frequent delegations to the national officers of the WPA to encourage them to interpret the agency's rules in a manner most favorable to the unemployed. They even campaigned actively in local and federal elections on a basis of rewarding the friends of the WPA and punishing insensitive or hostile politicians. Finally, the frantic demonstrations against the layoffs might have occurred even without the radical leadership. People who had held WPA jobs did not look kindly on the loss of income and the humiliation they would suffer even if they were reaccepted on home relief. Naturally, they struggled to stay on the projects against all odds.

Ridder's drive against the Communists won him both friends and enemies. The American Legion expressed its appreciation for his efforts with a testimonial to his "faithful public stewardship" and "nobility of character." The *Nation,* on the other hand, accused him of lack of sympathy toward the workers who suffered bitter insecurity, and concluded: "He is behaving like a typical fascist autocrat. The sooner he is removed the better."

Hopkins and his Washington staff were far from pleased with Ridder's handling of labor matters and his antiradical campaign. They doubted that the Communists intended to wreck the WPA, and their policy from the first favored permitting radicals to organize while employed by the WPA as long as they performed their assigned tasks faithfully. As Ridder's attacks on left-wing demonstrators mounted, the national administrators decided to investigate. Hopkins sent David Niles, one of his aides, to the city to see what was happening. The worried Niles telephoned his chief: "I think you ought to step into the Ridder situation. He has the place [Port Authority offices] like an armed camp with guards with guns. One of Ridder's own assistants came over to me to plead with me to do something about it."[22]

Hopkins hesitated for a while since he disliked interfering with his state directors. In May, however, he decided that Ridder's orders must be countermanded. Rather than single out the New York administrator, Hopkins sent a letter to all local heads forbidding the use of WPA funds to hire armed guards. Where protection of property and personnel seemed necessary, it should be provided by the regular police force in the community. Further, Hopkins reminded his subordinates of their responsibility to "maintain fair and friendly relations with the workers." "This administration," the message warned, "will not permit" discrimination against employees because of their "beliefs, organizational activities, or affiliations." More specifically, Aubrey Williams, deputy administrator, told Ridder that he should recognize the Workers Alliance and its fellow unions as legitimate labor representatives and bargain with them in exactly the same way he did with AFL affiliates. In addition, Williams approved the right of dissatisfied WPA employees to picket local offices as long as they remained peaceful.

The reaction of the national leaders toward his efforts embittered Ridder and hastened his decision to resign. As early as May 1936 the New York director protested the undermining of his antiradical drive. In a letter to Hopkins he complained:

> I found my friend Mr. Willis Morgan, whose whole object in life is to break up the WPA via the City Projects Council, sitting in the Labor Offices in Washington hobnobing with the officials. . . . What is the use of my trying to do everything possible to keep our workers out of the communist organizations if you encourage the heads of these organizations?

Ridder also took issue with Aubrey Williams for approving demonstrations in front of the Manhattan headquarters, saying that the federal official must have in mind a different kind of picketing from that which the radical agitators had carried on in New York.[23]

On 1 August 1936, after guiding the local WPA for ten

and one-half months, Ridder resigned. He left behind a payroll of some two hundred thousand workers and a vast network of ongoing projects. During his tenure he had displayed concern for women and blacks who wanted work relief jobs and had combated corruption and local political interference with the WPA. Ridder, however, was unfortunate to serve at an extremely difficult time. Enforcing the national decision to cut back employment became his responsibility. Very likely any man trying to implement that order would have met heated resistance and vilification. Ridder's mistake was in overreacting. By embarking on his anti-Communist crusade he lost the confidence of the federal administration and jeopardized amicable cooperation between the WPA and those dependent on it.

NOTES

1. John D. Millett, *The Works Progress Administration in New York City* (Chicago, 1938), p. 46; Transcript of a telephone conversation between La Guardia and Corrington Gill, 21 September 1935, Harry Hopkins Papers, Franklin D. Roosevelt Library, Hyde Park, N.Y.; *New York Times*, 27 September 1935, p. 20.

2. U.S. WPA for N.Y.C., *The Administration of Work Relief in New York City, August 1936–December 1937*, Report of Brehon B. Somervell to Harry Hopkins (New York, 1938), pp. 209, 271, 210, 206, 132, 136, 212, 227.

3. WPA Bulletin no. 11, 26 June 1935, Harry Hopkins Papers, Franklin D. Roosevelt Library, Hyde Park, N.Y.; Brooklyn *Eagle*, 20 February 1936, p. 5; 27 February 1936, pp. 1, 2; *New York Times*, 22 November 1935, p. 1.

4. Col. Lawrence Westbrook to Hugh Johnson, 12 July 1935, and Johnson to Westbrook, 17 July 1935, Harry Hopkins Papers, Franklin D. Roosevelt Library, Hyde Park, N.Y.; Dickstein to Ridder, 7 November 1935, Papers of the U.S. WPA for N.Y.C., National Archives, Washington, D.C.

5. Ridder to Jacob Baker, 21 October 1935, and Hopkins to Ridder, 28 October 1935, Papers of the U.S. WPA for N.Y.C., National Archives, Washington, D.C.; WPA General Letter no. 2, 21 February 1936, and WPA General Letter no. 8, 13 March 1936, Harry Hopkins Papers, Franklin D. Roosevelt Library, Hyde Park, N.Y.

6. *New York Times*, 20 October 1935, sec. 4, p. 11; 28 November 1935, p. 19; U.S. Congress, House Subcommittee of the Committee on Appropriations, *Hearings on the Emergency Relief Appropriations Act of 1937*,

75th Cong., 1st sess. (Washington, D.C., 1936), pp. 118–123; U.S. WPA for N.Y.C., *Administration of Work Relief*, pp. 113, 365; New York *Herald Tribune*, 16 April 1936, p. 1; U.S. WPA for N.Y.C., *Reports on Public Assistance to the Administrator of the Works Progress Administration for the City of New York*, by Donald D. Lescohier (New York, 1939), p. 165.

7. WPA for New York State, "The WPA and the Negro," p. 5, Papers of the U.S. WPA for N.Y.C., New York City Public Library, Arthur Schomburg Collection; New York *Herald Tribune*, 9 June 1936, p. 18; *New York Times*, 1 September 1936, p 20; New York *Herald Tribune*, 12 May 1936, p. 1; 9 April 1936, p. 14; 3 May 1936, p. 27; New York *Post*, 2 July 1936, sec. 2, p. 1.

8. WPA Bulletin no. 28, 27 September 1935, and WPA Bulletin no. 37, 30 December 1935, Hopkins Papers; *New York Times*, 18 December 1935, p. 8; 20 December 1935, p. 14; 6 February 1936, p. 17; New York *World-Telegram*, 20 December 1935, p. 15; Millett, *The WPA in N.Y.C.*, pp. 73, 105–6; New York *Herald Tribune*, 6 December 1935, p. 1; 22 April 1936, p. 1; U.S. WPA for N.Y.C., *Reports on Public Assistance*, p. 154; U.S. WPA for N.Y.C., *Administration of Work Relief*, p. 125.

9. Roosevelt's Executive Order no. 7046, 20 May 1935, stated that workers who are "qualified . . . to be assigned to work projects shall not be discriminated against on any grounds whatsoever." Hopkins reiterated the policy in WPA Administrative Orders nos. 41 and 44, 22 June 1936 and 11 July 1936. Workers "shall not be discriminated against on any grounds whatsoever, such as race, religion, or political affiliation."

10. U.S. WPA for N.Y.C., *Final Report of the Work Projects Administration for the City of New York, 1935–1943* (New York, 1943), p. 98; *New York Times*, 27 June 1935, p. 7; Henry Ashcroft, executive secretary, Brooklyn Urban League, to Hopkins, 1 July 1935, Papers of the U.S. WPA for N.Y.C., National Archives, Washington, D.C.; U.S. Department of Labor, *Family Income and Expenditure in New York City, 1935–1936*, 2 vols. (Washington, D.C., 1941), 1:6; *New York Times*, 20 October 1935, sec. 2, p. 1; *Amsterdam News*, 18 July 1936, p. 8; *New York Times*, 31 March 1935, sec. 4, p. 11; New York *World-Telegram*, 6 November 1935, p. 21; WPA for New York State, "The WPA and the Negro," p. 14.

11. Mary Tinney to Jacob Baker, 1 June 1936, and Harlem Festival and Exhibit, 8–13 June 1936, Papers of the U.S. WPA for N.Y.C., National Archives, Washington, D.C.; *Amsterdam News*, 6 June 1936, p. 1; 23 November 1935, p. 1; 18 April 1936, p. 1; Milton W. Brown, *Jacob Lawrence* (New York, 1974), pp. 9–11; Ellen Tarry, "How the History Was Assembled: One Writer's Memories," in *The Negro in New York: An Informal Social History* ed. Roi Ottley and William J. Weatherby (New York, 1967), pp. XI–XII.

12. U.S. WPA for N.Y.C., *Administration of Work Relief*, p. 147; Editorial, *Opportunity* 17, no. 2 (February 1939): 34.

13. Report on the WPA for N.Y.C., Hugh Johnson to Hopkins, 1 July 1935–15 October 1935, pp. 25–27, Harry Hopkins Papers, Franklin D. Roose-

Mr. Ridder Takes the Helm

velt Library, Hyde Park, N.Y.; *New York Times,* 11 September 1935, p. 1; 12 September 1935, p. 1; Report of the Stone Study Group on the Administration of the New York City WPA, November 1935, Papers of the U.S. WPA for N.Y.C., National Archives, Washington, D.C.; New York *Herald Tribune,* 4 January 1936, p. 8; Report of the Operations Division, N.Y.C. WPA, 1 January–30 June 1936, Fiorello La Guardia Papers, New York City Municipal Archives; Hopkins to All State Administrators, 27 February 1936, WPA General Letter no. 185, Harry Hopkins Papers, Franklin D. Roosevelt Library, Hyde Park, N.Y.; New York *World-Telegram,* 13 March 1936, p. 12; 14 March 1936, pp. 1, 4; New York *Post,* 14 March 1936, p. 1; Transcript of a telephone conversation between Hopkins and La Guardia, 12 March 1936, Harry Hopkins Papers, Franklin D. Roosevelt Library, Hyde Park, N.Y.; New York *Post,* 16 March 1936, p. 26; New York *World-Telegram,* 16 March 1936, p. 11; Moses to La Guardia, 5 November 1936, Fiorello La Guardia Papers, New York City Municipal Archives.

14. U.S. Congress, Senate Subcommittee of the Committee on Appropriations, *Hearings on the 1st Deficiency Appropriations Bill for 1936,* 74th Cong., 2d sess., (Washington, D.C., 1936), pp. 466, 467, 469, 470, 480, 493–97, 498, 499.

15. New York *Post,* 29 May 1936, p. 3; *New York Times,* 30 May 1936, p. 1; 5 June 1936, p. 1; 3 June 1936, p. 7; New York *Herald Tribune,* 30 May 1936, p. 1; 31 May 1936, p. 19; 3 June 1936, p. 17; 2 June 1936, p. 13; New York *Post,* 4 June 1936, p. 1.

16. *New York Times,* 5 March 1936, p. 1; 6 March 1936, p. 2; U.S. Congress, House Subcommittee of the Committee on Appropriations, *Hearings on the 1st Deficiency Appropriations Bill,* 74th Cong., 2d sess. (Washington, D.C., 1936), p. 126; New York *Herald Tribune,* 30 November 1935, p. 1; 17 November 1935, p. 1; 28 November 1935, p. 1; *New York Times,* 11 April 1936, p. 14; Arthur Macmahon et al., *The Administration of Work Relief* (Chicago, 1941), pp. 174, 131–32, 185.

17. New York *World-Telegram,* 12 March 1936, pp. 1, 2; *New York Times,* 27 March 1936, p. 1; 5 March 1936, p. 1; 15 March 1936, p. 31; 10 April 1936, p. 7; *Amsterdam News,* 4 April 1936, p. 1.

18. After the Port Authority refused to renew the lease, Ridder found an old warehouse and garage at 70 Columbus Ave. between Sixty-second and Sixty-third Streets that he had converted into an office building. The staff made the entire move over a single weekend in July 1936. On Monday morning the WPA opened for business as if 70 Columbus Ave. had always been its home.

19. New York *Herald Tribune,* 2 April 1936, p. 9; 3 April 1936, p. 18; New York *Post,* 19 March 1936, p. 20; 21 March 1936, p. 3; *New York Times,* 29 March 1936, sec. 2, p. 1; 2 March 1936, p. 2; 24 March 1936, p. 19; 3 April 1936, p. 25; David Ziskind, *One Thousand Strikes of Government Employees* (New York, 1940), pp. 173, 175; Tarry, "How the History Was Assembled," p. XI.

20. Col. Lawrence Westbrook to Hopkins, 20 April 1936, Papers of the

U.S. WPA for N.Y.C., National Archives, Washington, D.C.; New York *Sun,* 13 April 1936, p. 3; 14 April 1936, p. 21.

21. Bernard Karsh, "The Impact of the Political Left," in *Labor and the New Deal,* ed. Milton Derber and E. Young (Madison, Wis., 1957), pp. 91–93; Samuel Applebaum, "History of the Workers Alliance of America," *Work* (national edition), 24 September 1938, pp. 8–9; Allen Raymond, New York *Herald Tribune,* 9 April 1936, p. 1; 10 April 1936, p. 19; 13 April 1936, p. 17; U.S. Congress, "Statement of David Lasser," Senate Subcommittee, *Hearings, 1936,* pp. 309–12.

22. Interview of Allan Angoff by the author, 20 November 1976, Teaneck, N.J.; Interview of Dr. Alan Buxton by the author, 22 November 1976, Paramus, N.J.; Millett, *The WPA in N.Y.C.,* p. 54; *New York Times,* 15 July 1936, p. 17; *Nation,* 8 April 1936, p. 438; Transcript of a telephone conversation between Niles and Hopkins, 24 March 1936, Harry Hopkins Papers, Franklin D. Roosevelt Library, Hyde Park, N.Y.

23. Hopkins to All State Administrators, 11 May 1936, WPA General Letter no. 28, Hopkins Papers; *New York Times,* 14 June 1936, p. 9; 25 July 1936, p. 15; Ridder to Hopkins, 23 May 1936, Papers of the U.S. WPA for N.Y.C., National Archives, Washington, D.C.; *New York Times,* 25 July 1936, p. 15.

4

Work Relief Reaches Maturity

On 1 August 1936, exactly twelve months after the WPA assumed control over all work relief in New York City, Col. Brehon B. Somervell, its third administrator, took command. He was forty-four years old, a trim, lanky man with graying hair and a close-cropped mustache. He spoke with a slight Southern drawl, a reminder of his childhood spent in Little Rock, and he seldom raised his voice. Although Somervell was a man of considerable sophistication who had lived in Europe, the Middle East, and various parts of the United States, he liked to affect a homespun, Will Rogers sort of manner, referring to himself as "just a country boy from Arkansas trying to get along in the big city."

Prior to his assignment with the New York WPA, Somervell had pursued a highly successful army career. Graduated from West Point in 1914, sixth in his class, he went on to serve in the Corps of Engineers, first in Mexico and then in France during World War I. While briefly transferred to an infantry unit at the front, he earned a Distinguished Service Cross. During the 1920s Somervell directed river and harbor improvement activities in the New York area for the Corps of Engineers. On leaves from the army he worked as an engineer for the League of Nations, and in 1933-34, he acted as economic and transportation adviser to the Turkish government. The following year Somervell was one of the officers that the WPA borrowed from the army to supervise construction projects. Initially, the WPA assigned him to its program in the Southern states.

The WPA's hiring of Somervell was part of a growing tendency in the work relief agency to rely on personnel from the Army Corps of Engineers. Hopkins had at first resisted using career military men, fearing that the "brass hats" would be unsympathetic toward the unemployed and might impose rigid, arbitrary discipline upon them. Finding enough competent civilian engineers proved difficult, however, because of the low pay and lack of security offered by the WPA. After a few construction projects were badly botched for want of an adequate engineering staff, Hopkins dropped his earlier opposition to military personnel. He talked the army into lending Col. Francis Harrington to the WPA, where he became chief engineer in the Washington office. Within months, Harrington placed dozens of other army officers throughout the relief organization, among them Brehon Somervell.[1]

Apparently, Hopkins chose Somervell to succeed Ridder as head of the New York City WPA because the local agency was heavily committed to building projects and clearly needed a top-notch engineer to supervise them. Hopkins had heard Ridder say that his greatest handicap in directing the program was his lack of technical background. By bringing in an army officer from outside, moreover, Hopkins avoided the rival claims of municipal politicians. He would favor neither the city Democratic organization nor La Guardia and his Fusion backers. Hopkins's appointee, Somervell, went along with the nonpartisanship quite naturally since he preferred to surround himself with young army careerists (such as the man he made his deputy administrator, Maj. Edmund Levy) rather than local political figures.

Although La Guardia felt relieved at not having a Tammany Democrat imposed on him, he was not completely reconciled to accepting Hopkins's candidate. During the first months of Somervell's tenure, the mayor quarreled with the local WPA chief frequently, especially when the colonel put pressure on La Guardia to increase sponsors' contributions to the projects. By November La Guardia was shouting over the phone at Hopkins's deputy, Aubrey Williams: "This Arkansas 'cracker' isn't going to work here at all. I am not going to let a two by four soldier come in and run New York. Get this 'cracker' out of here." Williams managed to calm the irate mayor on this and other occasions. In time, Somervell and La Guardia resolved their differences and established a close working relationship. Indeed, the mayor eventually fought with the army when it wanted to recall Somervell to active duty.[2]

Somervell's appointment brought with it a temporary truce between the New York WPA and the left-wing unions. Since Ridder had completed the layoff ordered by Washington, the new administrator reassured the remaining two hundred thousand that they were secure for the time being. He also rejected his predecessor's anti-Communist drive. He asserted that no "red" menace existed in the WPA; in any event, he would not weed out radicals because federal policy prohibited discrimination against anyone for his political beliefs.[3] Somervell simply imposed a rule that Communists must not agitate or recruit members while at work.

Unlike Ridder, Somervell declared that he did not object to picketing in front of WPA headquarters. He reaffirmed, in principle, the right of workers to join any group they desired, but, along with President Roosevelt, he denied that there could be a strike against work relief. If the employees walked out, Somervell would discontinue the project. The colonel, moreover, received and talked to many more protest delegations than had either Johnson or Ridder, and he agreed to notify the labor organizations of the outcome of every grievance case they brought.[4]

In the fall of 1936, however, the interlude of stability and peace ended abruptly. The supplemental appropriation that Congress had voted the previous spring, which was supposed to finance the WPA through June 1937, was already running low. To make the remaining funds last, Hopkins would have to introduce rigid economy measures. He decided that the first place fat might be trimmed was on Federal Project number 1, which employed actors, musicians, writers, artists, and historical researchers. Until then, this creative section of the WPA had exercised the special privilege of hiring up to 25 percent of its personnel from non-relief sources, as opposed to the 10 percent restriction on all other projects.[5] Hopkins now rescinded that special treatment and ordered the dismissal of all but 10 percent of those on Federal Project number 1 who could not pass a relief means test. As a result of this change, between fifteen hundred and two thousand persons in New York City stood to lose their jobs. The local WPA would also have to lay off approximately 20 percent of its employees across the board by 1 January 1937. Hopkins hoped that most of those released would be absorbed by private industry, since factory employment, construction, and trade were showing signs of revival, and since the welfare case load in New York had declined slightly.

As the ax began to fall, those under it were less optimistic than Hopkins and responded with frenzied demonstrations. The work relief unions led sit-down strikes and stoppages almost daily. Hour after hour pickets circled the converted warehouse at 70 Columbus Avenue, the location of the WPA central offices since the previous July. On the evening of 1 December, 219 artists seized and occupied the headquarters of their project on Thirty-ninth Street, declaring that they would stay until the dismissals stopped. When the police ordered them to vacate the building, they locked hands and refused to budge. The patrolmen waded into the defiant crowd with clubs swinging. Men and women fought back with fists, teeth, and nails. By the time the battle ended, thirteen injured workers, one with a fractured skull, and four policemen required hospital care. The City Projects Council, Artists' Union, and allied groups charged police brutality.[6]

La Guardia made no secret about where his sympathies lay. Not only did he instruct the police commissioner not to arrest any more sit-down strikers, but he also cabled the president, who was visiting South America: "We find that employment has not kept pace with improved business conditions. Any suggestion of wholesale dismissals or substantial reductions at this time is simply out of the question." He followed his wire with a trip to Washington to plead with Hopkins to reconsider. The mayor pointed out that, of those dropped in the previous curtailment, more than half, unable to find outside jobs, had simply returned to home relief. La Guardia predicted that the same thing was likely to happen to any people Somervell dismissed, imposing an impossible burden on local resources.

Meanwhile, Somervell, on the firing line in New York, responded to the uproar with firmness. He threatened to discharge all who interfered with normal activities, stayed out on strike for more than two days, or seized buildings. Hopkins, who could order layoffs, found it hard to follow up with reprisals against protesting workers. He called Somervell to Washington and advised him to take no punitive action against strikers or sit-downers except for docking their pay for the hours missed.

Whether Somervell liked their tactics or not, the demonstrators, with the help of La Guardia, apparently swayed Hopkins, who not only halted the cutbacks but gave the colonel permission to reinstate persons already laid off if they had relief certification. Hopkins also told Somervell he did not have to enforce strictly the 10 percent nonrelief limit on Federal Project number 1.[7] In short, Hopkins's distaste for going to the president with requests for still more money had been overcome by the organized resistance. This showed that, even with a sympathetic person in charge, the unemployed had to be vociferous in order to keep themselves from being sacrificed on the altar of economy and balanced budgets.

The decision not to go through with the curtailment meant that on his return from South America Roosevelt would have to ask Congress for another supplemental appropriation to carry on the WPA until 1 July 1937. Opinion varied markedly, however, concerning how much the president should request. Roosevelt, optimistic about continued business improvement and declining joblessness, proposed to the lawmakers a sum of $650 million. If private industry absorbed approximately 25 percent of the individuals dependent on the WPA during the winter and spring, the work relief agency could operate on that amount.

The big-city mayors, headed by La Guardia, were less sanguine about economic revival and called for a deficiency grant of $877.5 million. The left-wing unions declared that nothing less than $1.25 billion would meet the needs of the unemployed. To gain support for their demand, the Workers Alliance organized marches in New York and Washington. On Capitol Hill, however, only a handful of progressives headed by Congressman Gerald Boileau of Wisconsin listened sympathetically to the mayors and the unions of the jobless. In January 1937, after the usual protests from conservatives about excessive spending, Congress voted exactly what Roosevelt requested.[8]

Developments in the following months partly vindicated the president's bright expectations—in February 1937, factory employment reached its highest peak since December 1929—but, unfortunately, business did not absorb anywhere near one-quarter of those on the WPA rolls. Hopkins soon realized that he could only make his funds stretch over the remaining half year until July 1937 by renewed belt tightening. First, he ordered a reduction in supervisory personnel on Federal Project number 1. Then he cut back the nonrelief job quota on all other projects from 10 to 5 percent, causing the discharge of some three thousand New Yorkers. Finally, in April 1937 he announced major layoffs, fifty thousand in New York City alone. Each of these moves, of course, produced waves of protest and turmoil.

Members of the Architects, Engineers, Chemists, and Technicians Union staged an eight-day strike in April. Some of them seized the headquarters of the projects where they worked, and when they refused to leave, police arrested eighty-five of them. The City Projects Council called repeated three-hour work stoppages. The cast and stage crew of a WPA dance production occupied the Nora Bayes Theater, where they had been presenting their program. The sympathetic audience joined pickets from the teachers', artists', and writers' unions marching in front of the theater. At the last minute, La Guardia and the municipal Board of Estimate rescued the fifty thousand local WPA workers slated for discharge by pledging a city contribution of seven hundred thousand dollars a month until 30 June to supplement inadequate federal funds for Somervell's agency.[9]

With a major cutback narrowly averted, all concerned turned their attention to the question of appropriations for fiscal year 1937–38. The positions in the almost ceaseless struggle over federal welfare expenditures were by now long familiar. On the one side stood those committed to providing jobs for as many of the unemployed as possible, if not all. These included the U.S. Conference of Mayors, headed by La Guardia; a few liberals and radicals in Congress, such as Jerry Voorhis of California, Maury Maverick of Texas, and Boileau of Wisconsin; and the left-wing unions of relief workers.[10]

On the other hand, most Republicans and many Democrats wished to reduce federal responsibility for the jobless. Some of them feared that continuing major national aid would create a class of parasitic men and women permanently dependent on government. Others, such as Bertrand Snell of New York, leader of the Republicans in the House, claimed: "Reckless Federal spending still is moving the nation inexorably along the path toward a disastrous inflation." Treasury Secretary Henry Morganthau never stopped hoping to balance the budget, and Senate Majority Leader Joseph Robinson suggested curtailment of the relief program as the only way to avoid new taxes.

At the end of April Roosevelt took a position between the warring camps, though one considerably closer to the economizers than to the spenders. Apparently, he did so out of concern over budget deficits and the belief that he lacked the votes in Congress for more than $1.5 billion for 1937–38. The president proposed an appropriation of this amount, thereby displeasing both the cost-conscious and the defenders of the unemployed. The unions of the WPA workers marched on Washington, picketed, struck, and sat down in Times Square, tying up traffic for an evening. La Guardia testified before Congress about the inadequacy of Roosevelt's figure. At the same time the more conservative forces on Capitol Hill briefly backed a move by Sen. James Byrnes of South Carolina and Congressman Clifton Woodrum of Virginia to slice $500 million off the appropriation.

Although the Byrnes-Woodrum maneuver failed, and the president received what he requested, Congress revealed its desire for thrift by writing into the Emergency Relief Appropriations Act of June 1937 a clause saying that this time the money must last the entire year; there would be no supplements. That proviso seemed to indicate that Roosevelt had been correct in his surmise that he could not get a bigger appropriation from Capitol Hill. After the bill passed and the president signed it, a New York *Post* editorial made a most pertinent comment concerning the whole performance:

> Congress has never had the courage to declare its endorsement of the policy of firing destitute men and women from WPA. It has done it by indirection, by passing an inadequate appropriation bill and letting nature and economy take their course. We think it is high time Congress did declare itself on WPA policy. Does it want to give jobs to employables? Does it believe in firing jobless, hopeless, moneyless Americans? Which?[11]

The editorial writer, with some justification, might have addressed the questions to the president as well as Congress.

Soon enough, New Yorkers felt the consequences of the inadequate appropriation. Following instructions from Washington, Somervell announced that he would have to drop thirty-five thousand workers before the fall. The colonel explained that he intended to fire the least competent and those longest with the WPA first. The new work relief law also contained a provision requiring that he dismiss all aliens who had not filed for citizenship, of whom there were about eighteen hundred on his payroll.

The new round of cutbacks set in motion desperate individual responses and hysterical demonstrations. Two young secretaries, discharged by the WPA, attempted to jump out of windows. One hundred dismissed teachers forced their way into the offices of the Adult Education Project and wildly resisted police trying to remove them. In the course of the scuffle the determined instructors broke windows, smashed furniture, punched, scratched, and bit. One young lady battled so furiously that during the struggle most of her clothes were ripped off. As the officers arrested the almost nude girl, she screamed: "My job is my life! I'll fight with my life for my job!" Still other protestors attempted to seize and destroy personnel records so that the WPA could not tell how long anyone had been on work relief. In July 1937 two hundred employees, who had been laid off, participated in a mass job hunt, organized by the Workers Alliance. Wearing white tags that read "WPA dismissed worker looking for a job," they visited firms in the Empire State Building, the offices of the Metropolitan Life Insurance Company, and the National Association of Manufacturers. At all the establishments they heard the same thing—no jobs available.

Relief officials released statistics in mid-August that indicated that most of those laid off had not fared well. Almost twenty-four thousand of the thirty-five thousand employees dropped by the WPA had reapplied for home relief. Welfare authorities guessed that few of the other eleven thousand held jobs. The majority of them probably were living on savings or credit for the time being. Labor leaders confirmed the conjecture. One City Projects Council organizer said that among two thousand members of his union whom Somervell had fired, he did not know of a single one who had found a position. A spokesman for the Teachers' Union claimed that only six of the fourteen hundred dismissed WPA instructors were working. Further, the welfare officials pointed out that the dwindling federal program hurt business. The loss of trade of former WPA employees cost shopkeepers approximately $2 million a month.

In September Somervell pronounced the WPA bloodletting virtually over. The mighty 200,000-man organization that the colonel had inherited from Ridder now stood at 130,000. Between 11,000 and 12,000 had left the rolls voluntarily to take outside employment opportunities. The rest were the victims of forced cutback.[12] But almost no one anticipated how soon Somervell would reverse the whole process and begin augmenting the agency's personnel once more.

As early as the fall of 1937, stark evidence of the so-called Roosevelt recession abounded. After a year and one-quarter of decline, New York City's welfare rolls began climbing again at the rate of 5,000 new cases a month. By November, Somervell estimated unemployment among able-bodied municipal residents at 615,000. As conditions worsened with the coming of winter, the United States experienced the fastest drop in private industry and employment in its history. Could a president who had refused to see idle men wait on breadlines in 1935 turn his back on the mounting army of jobless now?

Roosevelt answered this question in the negative for at least two reasons: his humanitarian concern for the underprivileged and his desire to boost the economy. Earlier, he had listened to the budget balancers, and the result appeared to be recession. His pump-priming advisers, such as Marriner Eccles and Hopkins, now preached stepped-up federal spending as the way to prosperity. Backing up their counsel came the pleas of La Guardia. Speaking for the United States Conference of Mayors, he begged the president to expand WPA quotas for the hard winter months ahead.

Despite Congress's previous assertion that it would authorize no more welfare spending during the fiscal year, Roosevelt determined to ask the lawmakers to reconsider in light of the unforeseen downturn. Early in February the president went before the legislators seeking a deficiency appropriation of $250 million to expand the WPA until 1 July. This request ran into little opposition in Congress, for even the budget-minded found it hard to ignore the mass suffering that the sharp recession had spawned. Before the month was out the Senate approved the emergency fund, sixty-seven to one; the House favored it with almost as lopsided a majority. Fueled by the supplementary money, the WPA, between February and June 1938, added to its rolls nearly one million people, approximately twenty-two thousand of whom lived in New York City.[13]

No sooner had Congress passed the deficiency bill than the president realized that he must advise the lawmakers as to the needs of the WPA for the next fiscal year. Roosevelt, surrounded by conflicting advice and uncertain what course the economy might take, decided to ask Capitol Hill to provide money for six months instead of twelve. That way in January, with the situation perhaps clarified, Washington could review work relief needs again. For 30 June to the start of 1939, Roosevelt succeeded in obtaining from the legislators a sum of $1.425 billion, enough to guarantee expanded WPA employment through the remainder of 1938. In New York City the agency's rolls climbed steadily, reaching over 175,000 by the fall.[14] Now, as Somervell hired rather than fired people, his labor problems diminished to minor complaints and skirmishes.

Although so much of his energy during 1936 and 1937 went into coping with labor disputes and adjusting to ever-changing employment quotas, Somervell still managed to concentrate on what interested him most—turning the New York City WPA into a smooth-running organization that would rival the efficiency of business corporations or the best-run federal departments. To be sure, the colonel understood there were certain limitations within which the WPA had to function since it was both a relief and a public works institution. For instance, it generally had to tailor its program to the skills of persons on welfare rather than hiring personnel to fit the undertakings. The law required it not to compete with private industry or displace municipal civil servants through its work. It had to spend less than the optimum amount on machinery and equipment so that more of its limited funds might go directly to its laborers. But within these boundaries, Somervell intended to give the taxpayer the greatest value per dollar possible in services and construction.

To achieve his objective, Somervell turned first to upgrading his administrative staff. He was not satisfied with the men and women he encountered when he first took command. He accused many of them of buck-passing, lacking training and ability, getting bogged down in details, reluctance to demote bungling subordinates, and failure to require an honest day's labor from those under them. Ruthlessly, Somervell proceeded to clean house. He instructed the Employment Division of the WPA to comb the records of all supervisory personnel. If it found anyone who had lied about his education and previous experience, it was to demote him. He also directed the division to prepare comprehensive oral and written examinations. All future management appointees had to pass these competitive tests.

Somervell activated a field inspection unit designed to visit all projects regularly and review their progress. On the basis of a field inspection report and the evaluation of his immediate superior, each foreman and administrator would be rated once every six months. An individual marked unsatisfactory received a warning. If he did not improve, he was suspended and/or finally dropped. Under these new rules, by the end of 1937 Somervell had demoted or fired nearly five thousand foremen and administrators, including forty-two who held top positions in the central office.[15]

This shake-up did not make the colonel popular with many of his employees. They complained that from his ninth-floor office at 70 Columbus Avenue, with its huge maps of the five boroughs, he issued orders as if he were a commander directing his troops. In fact, some of his critics insisted "that he periodically inspect[ed] his office staff for dirty fingernails and baggy trousers." Apparently, there were those in the Washington headquarters who saw him in the same light. Florence Kerr, the national director of Women's and Professional Projects, considered Somervell "bright" but "a martinet of the first order."

Dismissing incompetent directors proved easier than replacing them with good men. Throughout its existence the WPA experienced trouble in attracting enough top-notch engineers, technicians, and executives. The relief rolls almost never contained enough people of this type, and the rule that all but 5 percent of the WPA's employees should come from welfare severely limited outside hiring. Furthermore, the low salaries and uncertainty about the life span of the organization tended to cause the best administrators to shy away from federal work relief jobs.

Operating within the framework of WPA restrictions, Somervell did what he could to draw and hold able executives. He recruited army engineers whenever possible, and he made the most of the Public Works Administration's curtailment, which took place in 1937. When the PWA closed out several of its construction jobs in the metropolitan area, the colonel grabbed the discharged supervisors. By October he had hired twenty-eight PWA engineers, including the man who had been regional director of that agency. Somervell also experimented with in-service training programs as a way of improving the effectiveness of his staff.[16]

Opinions varied concerning Somervell's success in forging an efficient management team. The colonel himself never felt his staff quite measured up to the standards maintained in the world of business or other governmental departments. He advocated bringing WPA directors under civil service. When they were selected by the same competitive exams and enjoyed the same salaries and benefits as other federal workers, they would perform equally well. The House Committee on Appropriations, in 1939, heard contradictory testimony: Ralph Hale, chief investigator for the General Accounting Office in New York City, characterized the supervisory and administrative practices of the local WPA as so "loose" that they caused undue waste of federal money, while La Guardia stated that Somervell's agency operated with "the highest degree of efficiency of any undertaking of that magnitude . . . . I visited from cellar to garret and I invite comparison with any administration of any railroad, or any insurance company, or any large contracting company."

The army officer's drive to improve the effectiveness of his organization encompassed the rank-and-file employee as well as the supervisor. When the colonel replaced Ridder in August 1936, the latter had corrected some of the poor initial assignment of personnel, but there was still much left to do. Somervell was convinced that some workers held jobs for which they were not qualified and that the productivity of most could be increased. Within the limits imposed by WPA regulations, he proposed to change the situation.

Somervell could not control the process by which people were referred to his organization. This rested in the hands of relief officials who initially certified persons as eligible for welfare. To qualify for public assistance in New York, one had to meet the following tests: one had to be a resident of the state for at least two years and of the city for one; one must possess next to no assets in the form of insurance policies, bank accounts, real estate, or other property; one had to demonstrate one's willingness to work by being registered with the United States Employment Service; and one must have so little income from all sources that one could not support oneself and one's family. A man with a wife and two children, for example, would have to show that his resources to cover the cost of food, gas, light, rent, and other household expenses amounted to less than $61.10 a month.

Once relief officials accepted an applicant for welfare, they classified him as employable or unemployable and kept records of his past occupational experience. When the WPA had jobs to fill, it forwarded a requisition to the Welfare Department, specifying types and numbers of personnel needed. The relief authorities then chose from their files individuals who seemed to fit the openings, giving preference to those longest on the rolls. Social workers instructed these clients to report to the WPA Intake Office at 70 Columbus Avenue. There, bearing a card signed by Welfare Commissioner William Hodson, the lucky person sat on a green wooden bench waiting for an interview. In the early days of the federal program the intake officer who received him usually accepted the person's word as to his skills. The intake officer gave him an assignment slip stating his name, address, rate of pay, classification, and place of work, as well as a WPA identification card, and sent the new employee to the project that had requested the additional labor. Somervell complained that the occupational inventories kept by the Welfare Department were almost worthless; since the WPA was not doing its own screening, many unsuitable placements were made.[17]

To remedy the situation, the colonel ordered the Qualifications Section of the WPA to develop a series of tests that could be administered to all personnel in classifications above unskilled. In drawing up the exams, the WPA officials received the assistance of Columbia University educators, business and union representatives, and members of engineering and professional societies. For skilled craftsmen, the WPA created practical trials directed by journeymen in the field; that is, bricklayers put up a wall, painters mixed and applied their paints. By September 1937 all WPA skilled mechanics had undergone examination. Seventeen percent, or about four thousand, failed and were demoted. Thereafter, anyone wishing initial placement or promotion to a skilled blue-collar job would have to give a demonstration of his abilities. The WPA also began to require qualifying procedures for white-collar people. Lawyers, teachers, typists, architects, and others took oral and written exams and performance tests where applicable.[18]

In January 1938 Somervell took a further step to increase the conscientiousness of his employees. He instituted a system of ratings for diligence and skill to be applied to each individual on the payroll once every six months. The colonel announced that in case of renewed cutbacks, he intended to drop workers with the poorest ratings first. Somervell, moreover, instructed foremen to issue a warning to any crew member who seemed indifferent to his responsibilities. If the warning failed to produce a change in attitude, the supervisor could suspend and ultimately dismiss the offending subordinate. On the other hand, to try to prevent abuses of authority, the WPA allowed a suspended or discharged employee to appeal his foreman's decision to independent review officers.[19]

In his drive for efficiency, Somervell even experimented with a pay incentive plan not altogether unlike the Russian Stakhonovite system. Workers in the WPA sewing shops were producing only about one-quarter as many garments a day as private clothing manufacturers required of their help. Early in 1937 the colonel replaced the antiquated equipment with one thousand of the latest high-speed sewing machines and hired a new supervisory staff for the project. Then the WPA divided the operators into three categories. The most skillful and fastest received a 20 percent wage boost. Those in the second best group earned 10 percent more than formerly. Employees in the lowest classification could qualify for the intermediate or top grade by improving their standards of quality and quantity.

Apparently the plan succeeded, for production more than doubled. With basically the same size labor force, the sewing project completed nearly 6 million garments in 1939 as compared to about 2 million in 1936. The improvement allowed the WPA to meet the clothing needs of every man, woman, and child on welfare in the community, giving the destitute decent wardrobes and adequate household linen that they otherwise could not afford.[20]

Along with ratings and pay incentives went job training designed to make the employee more useful on the WPA and more attractive to private companies. All timekeepers, or for that matter any WPA worker who wanted to qualify for such a position, took an eleven-week course in preparing payroll sheets, computing hourly rates, and other technical procedures. Women hired by the WPA as domestic help underwent one week of training in housework, menu planning, child care, and home nursing. Everyone on the recreation and education projects received training in teaching techniques and group leadership, followed by several months of practice under the guidance of people with experience in these areas. In addition, thousands of unskilled laborers learned at least the rudiments of carpentry, bricklaying, sheet-metal work, or plastering from the WPA.

Many observers, nonetheless, believed that the WPA could have provided much more vocational training. A group of businessmen and academicians, led by Wisconsin economics professor Donald Lescohier, who studied the New York WPA, recommended that the agency push ahead boldly in this field. But even the WPA's modest training efforts aroused the ire of organized labor. The executive council of the AFL, fearful of competition for its members, denounced the use of public funds to upgrade unskilled or semiskilled workers.[21]

Somervell claimed that his reforms (testing, rating, tougher labor discipline, pay incentives, and training) had greatly improved the WPA's performance and its usefulness both to the unemployed and to the city. In construction, the colonel estimated, the monthly output per man over the period August 1936 to December 1937 rose 152 percent above that of the previous year. The *New York Times,* generally not enthusiastic about the WPA, agreed with the administrator's assessment. In a 1940 editorial the paper stated that, since taking office, Somervell had increased the efficiency of relief construction to a point where it approached the standards maintained by private contractors, and that charges of boondoggling had become rare.

Other outside observers also noted the gains in productivity and efficiency. Charles Keutgen, a deputy commissioner in the municipal water supply, gas and electric department, resented the jests about WPA shovel leaners that still circulated in 1937. After watching these much-maligned laborers replace twenty-six hundred feet of sewer in West Brighton, the commissioner wrote the Staten Island *Advance* to set the record straight:

> I want to call attention to the way WPA men worked on this job. Anyone who saw them must have seen that whatever may have occurred on other jobs, there was no basis for jokes on this one. It was hard heavy work done under difficulties. Yet the entire job was completed in twenty-two days and this meant every man on the job was earning his pay every day and doing a full day's work.

The left-wing unions saw the colonel's regime in a different light. One cartoon in the Workers Alliance newspaper depicted Somervell as Simon Legree waving a huge blacksnake whip over a cowering WPA worker. The leaders of the alliance complained: "The worst offenders against the rights of labor are the various army officers who have been foisted upon the program. . . . WPA workers are forced to suffer under the regime of swivel-chair colonels, majors, and captains who regard and treat workers with insufferable contempt." They frequently identified Somervell as a prime example.[22]

Besides driving himself and his employees hard, Somervell believed that the WPA could give the taxpayers better results for their money if his organization planned its projects more carefully. When he first took over the New York administration, he found many of the construction jobs operating in a slipshod manner, without adequate blueprints, progress schedules, and estimates of needed labor and materials. To remedy the situation, the colonel forbade any project to begin until it had a complete set of architectural blueprints or engineering specifications, either drawn up by the sponsor or the WPA itself. In 1937 the WPA began to use standardized progress sheets on all building activities; these sheets set completion dates for each phase of the work, listed the materials and equipment required, specified the number of laborers to be employed, and estimated total cost. Seemingly, this systematic planning resulted in greater efficiency. Between April and November 1937, for example, the pace of highway construction in Queens increased 77 percent.

These innovations put the individual project on a businesslike basis, but they did nothing toward integrating the separate undertakings into a comprehensive program. Before Somervell could achieve this, certain difficulties beyond his control had to be overcome. First, there was the resistance to long-term planning displayed by both city and federal authorities because they could only guess what the life span of the WPA might be. Why lay out a master plan of municipal improvements covering a year or two if within six months Roosevelt might decide to abandon the federal work relief experiment? Second, the local office found it hard to plan a program because Washington doled out funds to the New York City WPA for thirty days at a time. Since Somervell never knew from one month to the next how much he would receive, committing himself to a year or even a six-months schedule of activities became impossible. The WPA was even more uncertain about city contributions than national ones. Although Hopkins continually encouraged his officials to try to get large donations of materials, equipment, and money from sponsors, Somervell initially had little luck in pinning La Guardia down to a fixed payment over a stated time period.[23]

In 1937, however, two important developments enabled the colonel and his staff to begin adopting master plans covering a period of six months to one year. In the spring Hopkins announced that he intended to inform his state directors of the minimum cash allotments they might expect from 1 July through 31 December 1937. This introduced a new stability that the New York WPA had never enjoyed before. Meanwhile, the colonel worked out agreements with La Guardia and the Board of Estimate covering the amount of sponsors' contributions that the WPA could anticipate over specified periods. For the first half of 1937, this amounted to $700,000 a month; for the second half, $750,000 a month; and for 1938, about $39 million or 22 percent of the total cost of the WPA program in New York that year.[24] With these pledges guiding him, Somervell and his staff drafted a rough outline of activities for the WPA during the latter part of 1937 and a much more comprehensive package for 1938.[25]

By 1939 the planning of the WPA program had become quite sophisticated. That year's master plan was developed in the following manner: starting in June 1938, the various municipal departments, as well as federal and state sponsors, began sending Somervell complete lists of undertakings they wanted the WPA to perform for them in 1939; these suggestion sheets contained a description of the items, the order of their priority, the wages and nonpayroll costs of each, the dates on which the sponsor would have blueprints and specifications ready, and the approximate time for initiating and finishing every job. The WPA checked and analyzed the enumerated requests, eliminating proposals that appeared to violate any of its regulations, required more skilled labor than was likely to be available on the welfare rolls, or seemed too expensive for the organization to manage. Somervell's staff compiled the remaining items into a tentative program based on expected federal, state, and local revenues. The city budget director then made corrections and revisions according to his estimates of New York's financial capability. Finally, the colonel and La Guardia endorsed the entire package, sending it to Washington with their blessings.

The projects that received endorsement in the capital were subsequently listed in a master plan that Somervell had printed and distributed to every official connected with relief and public works in the community. In that way, each could see clearly what the WPA intended to achieve in the year ahead and how his individual effort fitted into the overall scheme. Fortunately, the plan was flexible as well as specific. The schedule adopted in January assumed a work force of 175,000 throughout 1939 and a total budget of over $200 million.[26] When, in the spring, national headquarters cut both the labor quota and fund allocations and Congress introduced a host of new restrictions, the master plan held disorganization to a minimum and permitted relatively smooth contraction.[27]

Because of the careful planning and many other changes that Somervell introduced, the New York City WPA operated at its peak effectiveness between 1936 and 1939. To be sure, the strife and insecurity produced by constantly fluctuating and inadequate employment quotas continued. And conservatives and liberals come no closer to agreeing on what the federal government ought to spend to assist the jobless. The WPA, nonetheless, proceeded under the colonel's guidance not only to employ between one hundred thousand and two hundred thousand New Yorkers, but also to use their abilities more efficiently than in its early days. Somervell's imposition of strict discipline and emphasis on productivity did not endear him to his workers, but his introduction of better engineering practices and more careful planning enabled the New York WPA to tackle the biggest projects in the nation. Let us now turn our attention to these undertakings and their effect upon the well-being of metropolitan residents.

NOTES

1. The army's willingness to lend these men probably stemmed from the fact that enrollment in the armed forces was very low in the middle thirties, leaving many officers with few regular duties to perform or soldiers to command. Furthermore, the WPA was working on a number of projects beneficial to national defense, such as the construction of airports, the reconditioning of forts and army barracks, and the resurfacing of military roads.

2. *New Yorker*, 10 February 1940, pp. 24, 22–27; Robert Sherwood, *Roosevelt and Hopkins*, 2 vols. (New York, 1948), 1:92–93; *New York Times*, 27 June 1936, p. 19; New York *Herald Tribune*, 4 July 1936, p. 1; U.S. Congress, House Subcommittee of the Committee on Appropriations, *Hearings on the Emergency Relief Appropriations Act of 1941*, 76th Cong., 3d sess. (Washington, D.C., 1940), p. 665; Transcript of a telephone conversation between La Guardia and Williams, 27 November 1936, Aubrey Williams Papers, Franklin D. Roosevelt Library, Hyde Park, N.Y.

3. By 1938, Somervell had changed his mind about the Communist threat. He wrote in a report to Hopkins that the Workers Alliance and other Communist-dominated unions had gained a foothold in the WPA and were guilty of all manner of obstructionist tactics. However, the colonel still did not propose firing anyone simply for belonging to the Communist party or one of the left-wing unions.

4. New York *Herald Tribune*, 4 July 1936, p. 1; *New York Times*, 12 August 1936, p. 6; 5 August 1936, p. 6; 23 October 1936, p. 7; 25 August 1936, p. 21; John D. Millett, *The Works Progress Administration in New York City* (Chicago, 1938), p. 139.

5. The larger nonrelief quota for the arts projects was permitted originally because their directors argued that the success of the program depended on attracting highly talented people to organize and lead the work (more than the relief rolls could supply) and because artists as a group were frequently too proud to apply for welfare even when they qualified.

6. New York *Herald Tribune*, 11 August 1936, p. 17; 12 September 1936, p. 8; 25 November 1936, p. 10; 26 November 1936, p. 12; 5 December 1936, p. 8; 22 November 1936, p. 22; *New York Times*, 1 December 1936, p. 6; 2 December 1936, p. 8; 25 November 1936, p. 2; U.S. WPA for N.Y.C., *The Administration of Work Relief in New York City, August 1936–December 1937*, Report of Brehon B. Somervell to Harry Hopkins (New York, 1938), p. 183; New York *Post*, 2 December 1936, p. 15.

7. New York *Post*, 5 December 1936, p. 5; 9 December 1936, pp. 1, 19; 10 December 1936, p. 3; New York *Herald Tribune*, 5 December 1936, p. 8; 4 December 1936, pp. 1, 9; 8 December 1936, p. 12; 10 December 1936, p. 17; New York *World-Telegram*, 4 December 1936, p. 20; *New York Times*, 5 December 1936, p. 1; 6 December 1936, p. 2; 12 December 1936, p. 10; Somervell to Hopkins, 10 December 1936, Papers of the U.S. WPA for N.Y.C., National Archives, Washington, D.C.

8. New York *Post*, 8 January 1937, p. 1; New York *World-Telegram*, 8 January 1937, p. 23; New York *Herald Tribune*, 3 January 1937, p. 28; 16 January 1937, p. 34; *New York Times*, 10 January 1937, sec. 2, p. 1.

9. New York *Herald Tribune*, 24 March 1937, p. 8; 1 April 1937, p. 1; U.S. WPA for N.Y.C., *Administration of Work Relief*, p. 183; New York *Post*, 24 February 1937, p. 11; 2 March 1937, pp. 1, 6; *New York Times*, 25 February 1937, p. 1; 28 February 1937, p. 1; 1 April 1937, p. 14; 8 April 1937, p. 15; 1 March 1937, p. 3; 10 March 1937, p. 20; 11 March 1937, p. 25; 1 April 1937, p. 17; 16 May 1937, p. 16; New York *Herald Tribune*, 1 April 1937, p. 1; 8 April 1937, p. 15.

10. Even within this camp, conceptions of how much the WPA would need between 1 July 1937 and 30 June 1938 varied. The U.S. Conference of Mayors called for $2.2 billion. The Workers Alliance and other radical unions backed a bill introduced by Congressman Boileau which would earmark $3 billion for work relief.

11. New York *Post*, 20 May 1937, p. 12; 20 April 1937, p. 1; U.S. Congress, Senate Subcommittee of the Committee on Appropriations, *Hearings on the Emergency Relief Appropriations Act of 1937*, 75th Cong., 1st sess. (Washington, D.C., 1936), p. 257; U.S. Congress, House Subcommittee of the Committee on Appropriations, *Hearings on the Emergency Relief Appropriations Act of 1937*, 75th Cong., 1st sess. (Washington, D.C., 1936), pp. 326, 346–50; New York *Herald Tribune*, 1 March 1937, p. 1; 1 April 1937, p. 11; 10 April 1937, p. 1; 12 April 1937, p. 7; 13 April 1937, p. 15; 22 April 1937, p. 1; *New York Times*, 14 May 1937, p. 1; 16 May 1937, p. 16; 20 May 1937, p. 1; 23 May 1937, p. 1; 28 May 1937, p. 1; 20 June 1937, p. 13; 4 May 1937, p. 1; Arthur Macmahon et al., *The Administration of Work Relief* (Chicago, 1941), p. 133; New York *Post*, 5 August 1937, p. 6.

12. New York *Post*, 22 June 1937, p. 1; *New York Times*, 23 June 1937, p. 1; 2 July 1937, p. 1; 12 October 1937, p. 29; Hopkins to All State Administrators, 17 July 1937, WPA General Letter no. 147, Harry Hopkins Papers, Franklin D. Roosevelt Library, Hyde Park, N.Y.; New York *Journal*, 23 June 1937, p. 3; New York *Daily News*, 3 July 1937, p. 3; New York *Herald Tribune*, 1 July 1937, p. 1; 2 July 1937, p. 1; 16 July 1937, p. 16; New York *World-Telegram*, 14 August 1937, p. 4; U.S. WPA for N.Y.C., "The Number of Employees Working for the WPA in New York City, 1937 and 1938," *General Statistical Bulletin*, 30 April 1938–31 December 1938 (New York, 1939).

13. New York *Herald Tribune*, 12 December 1937, p. 34; 4 January 1938, p. 5; 16 February 1938, p. 7; 16 November 1937, p. 1; 3 February 1938, p. 16; 11 February 1938, p. 1; 24 February 1938, p. 1; *New York Times*, 29 January 1938, p. 17; 29 April 1938, p. 42.

14. New York *Herald Tribune*, 15 June 1938, p. 1; U.S. WPA for N.Y.C., "Number of Employees Working for WPA," *General Statistical Bulletin*, 30 April 1938–31 December 1938.

15. U.S. WPA for N.Y.C., *Reports on Public Assistance to the Administrator of the Works Progress Administration for the City of New York*, by Donald D. Lescohier (New York, 1939), p. 169; U.S. WPA for N.Y.C., *Administration of Work Relief*, pp. 209, 271, 210, 206, 207, 286, 48.

16. *New Yorker*, 17 February 1940, p. 28; Jane D. Mathews, *The Federal Theatre, 1935–1939* (Princeton, N.J., 1967), p. 104; U.S. WPA for N.Y.C., *Reports on Public Assistance*, pp. 168, 169, 170; U.S. WPA for N.Y.C., *Administration of Work Relief*, pp. 208, 210, 366; *New York Times*, 21 November 1937, p. 8; U.S. WPA for N.Y.C., *The Employment Program* (New York, 1939), p. 21.

17. U.S. WPA for N.Y.C., *Administration of Work Relief*, pp. 366, 48–49, 150–53; U.S. Congress, House Subcommittee of the Committee on Appropriations, *Investigation and Study of the WPA*, 76th Cong., 1st sess., (Washington, D.C., 1939), pt. 1, pp. 932, 365; Donald Howard, *The WPA and Federal Relief Policy* (New York, 1943), pp. 380–86; U.S. WPA for N.Y.C., *The Employment Program*, pp. 7–9.

18. In 1939 a committee chaired by Dr. D. B. Steinman, a member of the New York State Board of Examiners for Professional Engineers, evaluated all of the WPA's technical exams and unanimously approved them as practical and just.

19. Somervell to Francis Harrington, 24 February 1938, Papers of the U.S. WPA for N.Y.C., National Archives, Washington, D.C.; U.S. WPA for N.Y.C., *The Employment Program,* pp. 13–14; U.S. WPA for N.Y.C., *Administration of Work Relief,* pp. 164–66, 175; *New York Times,* 19 October 1937, p. 12; 11 December 1937, p. 11; 29 November 1938, p. 4.

20. U.S. WPA for N.Y.C., *Administration of Work Relief,* pp. 176, 284; Final Report of the Sewing Project in New York City: A Record of Program Operation and Accomplishments, Papers of the U.S. WPA for N.Y.C., National Archives, Washington, D.C.; U.S. Congress, House Subcommittee, *Hearings, 1941,* p. 539.

21. U.S. WPA for N.Y.C., *The Employment Program,* pp. 19–23; U.S. WPA for N.Y.C, *Final Report of the Work Projects Administration for the City of New York, 1935–1943* (New York, 1943), pp. 25–27; U.S. WPA for N.Y.C., *Reports on Public Assistance,* p. 160; American Federation of Labor, *Report of Proceedings of the Fifty-sixth Annual Convention* (Washington, D.C., 1936), p. 152; Joseph McInerney, *Carpenter,* July 1938, pp. 17–18.

22. U.S. WPA for N.Y.C., *Administration of Work Relief,* pp. 235, 216; *New York Times,* 8 November 1940, p. 23; Staten Island *Advance,* 22 April 1937, p. 22; *New Yorker,* 10 February 1940, p. 22, and 17 February 1940, p. 28; U.S. Congress, House Subcommittee, *Investigation and Study of WPA,* pt. 1, p. 166.

23. U.S. WPA for N.Y.C., *Administration of Work Relief,* pp. 202, 128, 228, 216, 416, 195, 203, 414; U.S. WPA for N.Y.C., *Reports on Public Assistance,* pp. 166, 163; Somervell to Corrington Gill, 16 August 1936, Papers of the U.S. WPA for N.Y.C., National Archives, Washington, D.C.; U.S. Congress, House Subcommittee, *Investigation and Study of WPA,* pt. 2, pp. 1381–90.

24. New York was able to raise the additional money because it had received authorization from Albany to enact a series of new and increased taxes and permission to spend part of the state's welfare contribution to the city to buy supplies for the WPA. Between 1935 and 1938 funds from the state could only be used for home relief.

25. As part of his effort to integrate all WPA work into a single well-planned program, Somervell finally brought the independent Moses to terms. The colonel allowed the park commissioner to complete an extensive schedule of activities under his own direction with the WPA paying the bills through the calendar year 1937. But starting 1 January 1938 city park-sponsored projects came under the full control of WPA personnel and followed federal regulations.

26. The city's share was estimated at $33,232,690.

27. Macmahon, *Administration of Work Relief*, p. 133; U.S. WPA for N.Y.C., *Final Report*, pp. 39, 242; U.S. WPA for N.Y.C., *Administration of Work Relief*, pp. 203, 414, 43; *New York Times*, 24 March 1938, p. 16; 26 June 1937, p 3; 24 January 1938, p 1; U.S. WPA for N.Y.C., *Brief Review of Developments in New York City during the Past Two Years*, Report of Brehon B. Somervell to Harry Hopkins (New York, 1937), p. 27; *New York Times*, 14 August 1938, p. 1; 24 December 1938, p. 2; U.S. Congress, House Subcommittee, "Report of Brehon Somervell, Feb. 14, 1940, to House Committee on Appropriations," *Hearings, 1941*, pp. 524, 526; *Reports on Public Assistance*, pp. 163, 166; *New York Times*, 19 February 1940, p. 1.

5

The Blue-Collar Projects

The depression of the 1930s not only brought unemployment, despair, and family disorganization to millions of Americans, but it often spelled disaster for the cities in which many of them lived. With tax receipts dropping sharply as business and personal income fell, the urban communities found it difficult to provide normal services, meet payrolls, and maintain (not to mention expand) municipal plants and facilities. At a time when they could afford it least, they also struggled to give the victims of the depression minimal aid to prevent outright starvation.

New York City certainly shared the desperate plight of other American metropolises. Caught between rising relief costs and shrinking revenues, local government allowed services to deteriorate and public needs to go unmet. In 1934 large areas in the parks were in a dilapidated, unkempt condition. Residents suffered through a stifling summer with only two public swimming pools in the entire city. Many of the 164 playgrounds that the community provided for its children were poorly equipped. Frequently, in congested, low-income neighborhoods, there were no safe play areas at all. The Long Island *Press* described Jamaica Avenue of the early 1930s (one of the main thoroughfares of the borough of Queens) as "bumpy, rutted, lined with dangerous abandoned trolley tracks," while another principal artery, Queens Boulevard, "was almost impassable in spots." In the late 1920s the city constructed a nine-story building intended to house the Queens General Hospital, but as late as 1935 it stood an unopened, empty shell because the municipal government lacked the funds to finish the interior and equip it.

The coming of Roosevelt's New Deal helped rescue the cities of the United States from the bankruptcy and decay into which they were falling. In 1933 the Federal Emergency Relief Administration assumed a large share of the cost of welfare. Then, in 1935, the WPA replaced the earlier organization. By providing jobs for able-bodied depression victims, the WPA made available to communities a free, gigantic labor force to perform long-deferred services and engage in repairs, renovations, and a vast amount of new construction. In fact, these Roosevelt agencies provided the first massive infusion of federal aid to urban areas in American history.

The extent and impact of this urban subsidy, especially in the form of rebuilding American cities, has gone largely without notice in histories of the 1930s. When the huge construction program undertaken by the New Deal is mentioned, the agency usually given credit is the Public Works Administration. The WPA, on the other hand, tends to be characterized as primarily a relief organization, valuable for putting purchasing power in the hands of the jobless, but generally occupied with light, rather inconsequential projects.

Such a description of the WPA hardly does the agency justice. In New York City, service, artistic, and clerical undertakings were important, but above all the WPA concentrated on construction. During its first two years of existence the local WPA spent nearly 82 percent of its funds on repairing or making additions to city property. Until growing war preparations in the early 1940s curtailed civilian building everywhere in the country, the WPA continued to devote between two-thirds and three-fourths of its efforts to engineering and construction projects. The number of people it employed on these undertakings reached a peak of 200,000 in January 1936. Between 1936 and 1939 the people assigned to construction jobs averaged from 90,000 to 125,000 a month.[1]

Besides providing jobs for the unemployed, these activities involved the purchase of massive quantities of materials and equipment, some paid for by the federal treasury, some by city and state governments. But in either case the need for these supplies created an important market for heavy industry. In developing La Guardia Airport, for example, the New York City WPA used 20,000 tons of construction steel, 102,000 cubic yards of concrete, and enough electric lighting equipment to illuminate 700 miles of streets.

Perhaps one can best appreciate the magnitude of the building program by comparing the WPA's endeavors with those of other government units and business. In the years 1937 and 1938 New York City WPA activities accounted for 60 percent of all construction underway in the metropolis. By the end of 1937 the local WPA had erected 379 new buildings and expanded or remodeled 1,740 others, while the rival PWA put up 58 structures. The fact that in the second half of the 1930s La Guardia budgeted only around 13 percent of municipal revenue for physical improvements and spent the rest on services to residents shows just how greatly New York relied on federal public works, and especially the WPA, to make repairs and additions to city property.[2]

Instead of praising the WPA for making available to New Yorkers numerous facilities that they could not have afforded otherwise, spokesmen for the construction industry frequently charged the WPA with unfair government competition that hurt their business and put union men out of jobs. The evidence does not substantiate their claims since the volume of new building done under private contract rose dramatically between 1935 and 1938, reaching its highest level since World War I. And municipal officials did not slight free enterprise and try to have all community needs filled by the WPA. From 1936 to 1938 city appropriations for work by private contractors increased substantially over those in the preceding two years. Spending climbed from a low of about $16 million in 1935 to over $73 million in the first nine months of 1938. Donald Lescohier, a professor of economics at the University of Wisconsin, after making his study of the New York WPA, declared: "It is impossible to state the extent to which work undertaken by the WPA might have been done by customary methods had there been no WPA. The status of city finances during the past few years, however, supports the belief that little, if any, of the WPA operations would have been undertaken by other means."

Park and playground development in the thirties illustrate well the contrast between what might have happened without the WPA and the benefits that the city actually enjoyed. For the year 1936 New York Park Commissioner Robert Moses estimated that maintaining the existing properties and erecting a minimal amount of new facilities required a municipal appropriation of just under $8 million. The La Guardia Administration found it impossible to grant him more than $5 million. Moses, critical as he was of the WPA, nonetheless turned to it for the help that the city could not provide. Utilizing its labor force, he undertook the largest park- and playground-building program ever carried out in an urban area. The federal organization assigned more than one-third of its blue-collar employees to jobs in the parks during the first months of 1936. Thereafter, other municipal officials competed more successfully with Moses for work relief laborers, but the Park Department continued to use some 18 percent of all WPA construction personnel between 1937 and 1942. Not only did Moses command the lion's share of WPA manpower, but his department also obtained the work relief agency's biggest allocations of funds. For instance, between August 1936 and December 1937 the WPA poured about $130 million into New York recreational facilities.[3]

What did this signify to city dwellers looking for entertainment and relaxation? It meant that on a hot summer day a youngster might plunge into a municipal swimming pool in his neighborhood, since the WPA completed seventeen of them in seven and one-half years; or for Queens residents who preferred the ocean, Jacob Riis Park beckoned. After the New York WPA expanded and remodeled it, the transformed beach opened to the public in June 1937. The new bathhouse could accomodate ten thousand people. WPA workers had broadened the beach by bringing in sand from Rockaway Inlet and had lengthened the boardwalk to more than a mile. Other improvements included a swimming pool, a boat basin, shuffleboard and deck tennis courts, and more greenery. The entire project cost approximately $10,000,000, and although the city expected to spend about $130,000 a year to maintain the property, it would more than pay for itself. Fees collected for admission, lockers, and parking promised to bring in around $134,000 annually.

The following month, ten thousand Staten Islanders participated in the festivities that officially opened the Franklin D. Roosevelt Boardwalk and Beach on the south shore, stretching one and one-half miles from Sea Avenue in Fort Wadsworth to Woodland Beach. The $2 million development took eighteen months to finish. Many residents, among them the borough president, considered the project a major step toward reviving the community. In earlier years the once-popular island resort area had been blighted by fires and obsolete facilities. The new beach, two hundred feet deep, could now boast of a five-lane boardwalk, adequate restrooms, and covered shelters for protection against the weather.

The New York City WPA also undertook hundreds of smaller renovations throughout the metropolis. One example was the work done in Mt. Morris Park. The children of

The Blue-Collar Projects

Harlem had played there since it was built in 1867, but the park had become dilapidated and unsafe. In 1938 the WPA completely restored it. Somervell's agency performed a similar face-lifting at Baruch Park on the lower East Side.

Besides furbishing these run-down facilities, the WPA laid out some four hundred additional parks and playgrounds. The largest share of these was located in the fast-growing borough of Queens, including, among others, Alley Pond, Cunningham, and Crocheron. While residents enjoyed more open space and wider recreational opportunities, the city collected an annual revenue of nearly $2 million from admission charges on WPA-built swimming pools, beaches, golf courses, tennis courts, and the twenty-thousand-seat Randall's Island stadium.[4]

Constructing new highways, roads, and bridges, as well as repaving existing streets, was a second type of engineering work for which the WPA hired thousands of jobless New Yorkers and spent millions of dollars. For instance, in August 1938 the federal agency employed on these undertakings slightly more than twenty-six thousand men, 95 percent of whom came from the relief rolls.[5] By 1940, if all of the thoroughfares they had surfaced had been laid end to end, the road would have stretched from New York to Denver.

A motorist cruising through the city could easily have spotted WPA crews at their tasks and have driven on streets and expressways the men had recently finished. Again, as in the case of parks, the traveler would encounter the most WPA activities in Queens. There, workers were leveling, patching, and repaving Queens Boulevard and Jamaica Avenue, both of which had been in deplorable shape. In Brooklyn WPA laborers built the South Shore Drive, cleared a wider approach to the Brooklyn Bridge, and added a new eastbound lane to the Williamsburg Bridge, increasing its capacity by 50 percent. The major street project in The Bronx consisted of repaving seven miles of the Grand Concourse from 161st Street to Jerome Avenue. In Manhattan the New York City WPA demolished all of the waterfront structures that blocked the proposed path of the Franklin

D. Roosevelt Drive and then constructed the portion of the expressway between Grand and 14th Streets. The agency also widened and resurfaced First Avenue from 72d to 125th Street and removed old trolley tracks from Madison, Sixth, Seventh, Eighth, and Ninth Avenues and from 34th Street. Much of the scrap metal recovered eventually was used by the army for growing war preparations after 1939.

As whistles signaled twelve noon on 17 June 1937, La Guardia ceremoniously accepted the reconstructed lower level of the Queensborough Bridge from Colonel Somervell. Eighteen months before, relief laborers had begun tearing up the old wood-block paving and replacing it with a five-lane iron grid and concrete roadway. The WPA employees completed the job under the most trying circumstances. The bridge, then the main link between Queens and Manhattan, could not be closed to traffic while they worked, and they had to alter one lane at a time. As one hundred thousand vehicles a day whizzed past, the WPA crews carried on their tasks inches away from racing wheels. It was amazing that not one workman was injured or killed, because many of them lacked previous experience in road building, and their average age of forty-eight years was well above that of all construction laborers. Soon after finishing the lower deck, they began resurfacing the upper level.

Many contemporaries noted the contributions the WPA was making to urban transportation. The Long Island *Press* observed that the roads of Queens had never been in such good shape as they were by 1937 "thanks to the work relief program." *American City* magazine claimed that, as a result of WPA repairs and additions, "community streets are probably in a better condition today than they have been at any time since the advance of motor transport subjected them to the wear of heavily laden trucks, huge buses and millions of passenger cars."[6]

During the years that the New York City WPA concentrated on parks, playgrounds, and roads, it also erected and renovated a variety of buildings for public use. Some of the 391 edifices it raised between 1935 and 1940 were fire and police stations. The Eighteenth Precinct House at Fifty-fourth Street just west of Eighth Avenue was typical. Completed in 1939, it replaced the old precinct headquarters on West Forty-seventh Street, which dated from the Civil War. Hardly a public library in the five boroughs went without WPA plastering, painting, repairs, or additions. At the main branch on Fifth Avenue and Forty-second Street, Somervell's crews installed a new heating system and reroofed the entire building with noncorroding metal.

The buildings that the WPA put up for the Departments of Health and Hospitals contributed directly to the well-being of New Yorkers. There were the baby health stations in dozens of neighborhoods. Costing about fifty thousand dollars apiece to erect, each of these one-story brick structures contained waiting and examining rooms and a small laboratory. The WPA also hired jobless nurses and doctors to staff these clinics, which treated the children of families too poor to obtain care from a private physician. WPA employees completed the nine-floor edifice intended to house the Queens General Hospital. Then, with PWA funds, the city bought the necessary medical equipment, and the hospital, after years of standing idle, began to serve patients. The WPA undertook such extensive repairs at the long overcrowded and neglected Harlem Hospital that whole wings of the building were gutted from cellar to roof and then constructed anew. The hospital also took over an old adjacent hotel, which the federal agency changed into the city's first clinic concerned with detecting and treating outpatients for venereal diseases.[7]

The WPA carried out demolition for the New York City Housing Authority. Usually the effort was part of a multiagency endeavor; that is, the WPA knocked down old-law tenements and other substandard residences so that the Public Works Administration and city development companies could construct public housing on the cleared site. For instance, the WPA completely leveled an area of twelve city blocks in Brooklyn in preparation for the Williamsburg Housing Project built by the PWA. The city got a particu-

A WPA-built and staffed Health Station, March 1939. *Photo by the New York City Department of Public Works Reproduction Section.*

larly good deal out of the arrangement since Somervell turned over to local authorities all the bricks, scrap metal, and lumber recovered from the demolished structures.[8] New York sold the material to private contractors, making a profit that more than covered its sponsor's contribution. By the end of the WPA's career, it demolished fifty-five hundred decaying buildings.

The development of La Guardia Airport was the most expensive and ambitious single project ever handled by the WPA anywhere in the United States. The final cost topped $40 million. It required a little over two years to finish and at the peak of its construction employed nearly twenty-three thousand people. For much of the time operations proceeded around the clock, with the men working in three eight-hour shifts.[9]

Perhaps more than any other accomplishment of the WPA, this one owed its inception to La Guardia. Never doubting for a moment that a bright future beckoned for commercial air travel and transport, he dreamed of building a modern airfield for his city. The mayor, moreover, resented the Post Office's choice of Newark Airport as the eastern terminal for international airmail deliveries. He felt that his community was the logical one to hold that honor. As the New York City WPA began to tackle really big construction projects successfully, La Guardia recognized it as the agency that might realize his objective. In 1936 he proposed the undertaking to Roosevelt, Hopkins, and Somervell. If they would endorse the idea, La Guardia pledged that his administration would contribute more money, supplies, and technical assistance than it had to any previous WPA effort.[10]

On the north shore of Queens lay a small, private airstrip that belonged to the Curtiss-Wright Company. This 105-acre field on the north beach became the nucleus of the new 558-acre municipal airport. The WPA reclaimed over 60 percent of the land from the East River, using fill from the Department of Sanitation's dump on Riker's Island. Since the man-made land was soft and bound to settle over the years, the WPA perched all the hangars and the main terminal on concrete piles descending between 35 and 125 feet below ground. In addition to the four asphalt macadam runways for aircraft, the work relief agency erected a fireproof steel-framed administration center that contained office space, shopping areas, and three restaurants. On either side of the main building they constructed three hangars, each larger than Madison Square Garden. In front of the seven structures, the WPA paved an area designed as parking space for five thousand automobiles. Finally, on the shore the crews built a two story marine terminal to handle sea planes landing in the East River. When the work was finished, airline pilots proclaimed La Guardia field the most modern and safest commercial airport in the country.

On 15 October 1939, before a crowd of 350,000, the elated

A view of La Guardia Airport (at first called North Beach Airport), built by the New York City WPA. *Photo by the New York City WPA.*

mayor dedicated the airport named in his honor. La Guardia informed the throng that the facility was already a financial success. Months before, the nation's three leading commercial airlines—American, United, and Transcontinental and Western—had signed leases for hangar space and had agreed to make New York, rather than Newark, their main eastern terminal. Rumors flew that the Post Office would soon follow suit and switch airmail from New Jersey to the metropolis. Everyone appeared greatly pleased except one young lady from across the river who wore a sandwich board sign declaring "Newark Airport Is Still the Greatest!"[11]

This vast urban building program won praise for the WPA from many sources. In 1938 nine civic and professional groups joined forces to sponsor a nationwide appraisal of the federal agency's endeavors.[12] Their study proclaimed: "If anyone doubts the value of WPA work in the City of New York in terms of permanent improvements to streets, buildings, parks and playgrounds, he has only to open his eyes in almost any part of the city and behold a vision of transformed facilities." The *New Yorker* magazine agreed. An article published in 1940 stated that the community had probably never been in better physical condition, and it noted the paradox in this. For in the prosperous 1920s local government could not afford to give residents the public accommodations and services that the WPA made available to them in the depressed 1930s.

Somervell, in May 1938, asked a number of persons prominent in business and industry to form a committee that would observe the functioning of his administration and advise him on ways to improve its performance. The council, headed by Oswald Knauth of Macy's Department Store, submitted its findings to the colonel the following year.[13] Although the Knauth committee suggested many reforms in the operation, the members never doubted for a moment the tremendous contribution the WPA was making to the city's welfare. They stated that, besides rescuing hundreds of thousands from despair and maintaining their self-respect, the WPA had completed a schedule of construction that was "impressive" in amount, craftsmanship, and durability.

The WPA's public works projects, however, never enjoyed unanimous commendation. They came under fire from the time Roosevelt created the agency, with the heaviest barrage hitting in 1939. On various occasions a portion of the press, building trades associations, and congressional committees demanded investigation and curtailment of WPA projects, especially big-scale undertakings like La Guardia Airport.

Still, even the bitterest critics generally admitted the good quality of what the New York City WPA had created. Somervell could claim with pride that his organization achieved a consistently lower rate of rejections for substandard work by city inspectors than did private contractors. Futhermore, engineers employed by local government judged the WPA paving job on the Queensborough Bridge superior to that done on the Triborough span by private firms using PWA money. During 1939 the decidedly hostile House Subcommittee on Appropriations instructed Allen Stephens and Peter Hein, two engineers on loan from the Treasury Department's Procurement Division, to look into the construction activities of the New York City WPA. After surveying several undertakings, such as a police station, sewers, two new schools, La Guardia Airport, and an edifice erected for the New York World's Fair, the two investigators testified that the workmanship was excellent.[14]

The detractors struck out not at shoddiness but at excessive costs. Using figures supplied by the Building Trades Employers Association, the New York *Sun* charged that the WPA needed double the money to finish the airport that private contractors would have required. Representatives from metropolitan-area construction companies stated that the La Guardia hangars, which they could have put up for twenty cents a cubic foot, cost fifty cents under Somervell's management. As proof of the colonel's overspending, they pointed to a hangar recently completed under contract at Newark Airport for the lesser amount.[15] Engineers Allen Stephens and Peter Hein concurred with these assertions. They told the House Appropriations Subcommittee that they found inflated expenditures not only on the airport but on many other projects as well. For instance, Somervell's men had just completed a school for $782,000, while for five or six schools of essentially the same design the Board of Education paid private contractors, on the average, $441,000. In addition, the WPA job took longer. Overall, the engineers estimated that the work relief organization spent two and one-half times more to build a new structure than did most contractors.

Somervell angrily disputed these figures and questioned the motives that lay behind the arithmetic. The Building Trades Association, after all, looked upon the WPA as a competitor and at the moment was urging Congress to write into the 1939 Emergency Relief Bill a provision forbidding the agency to handle any blue-collar project costing more than twenty-five thousand dollars. The colonel termed ridiculous their claim that they could construct hangars at La Guardia for twenty cents a cubic foot, since the price of materials alone amounted to nineteen cents. He accused Messrs. Hein and Stephens of spending only two days on their investigation and visiting, at most, five or six undertakings, instead of the fifteen that they claimed. Consequently, their report grossly misrepresented actual WPA outlays.[16]

Although Somervell might deny these specific charges, neither he nor any other defender of the WPA believed that it could operate as cheaply as private enterprise or that it should be expected to. Both La Guardia and the colonel admitted that regular building contractors could accomplish roughly the same amount of work as the New York City WPA at 60 percent of the expenditure.

There were many explanations for this difference other than waste or poor management. Unlike private contractors, the WPA had as its prime responsibility employing depression victims, not building parks, hospitals, and airports. Construction firms looked for men who fit the jobs. Somervell and his staff drew the vast majority of WPA laborers from the welfare rolls and tried to tailor the projects to their abilities. When business slackened, companies laid off their older, less-productive workers first. These people, still capable and eager to earn a living but frequently past the prime of life, became federal relief personnel. Thus in 1939 more than half of the New York City WPA workers were over forty; a third had passed forty-four. On the other hand, three-quarters of those on industrial payrolls in the metropolis were under forty-four years of age. This alone might account for the somewhat lesser output of WPA crews (Somervell estimated that they accomplished about 90 percent as much per day as their outside counterparts) and contribute to greater costs. Further, while private management attempted to minimize labor turnover since it hurt efficiency, the WPA encouraged its help to seek other opportunities and vacate their emergency assignments as quickly as possible, even if by doing so they hampered the operations of ongoing projects.

Still another practice of the WPA sacrificed frugality for the higher goal of aiding the destitute. That is, private builders generally suspended activities during the winter when construction expense is the greatest because of frozen ground and foul weather. Knowing that families must eat between December and April, the WPA not only continued its undertakings year-round, but hired additional men during these months to compensate for seasonal layoffs by private employers. Contractors, moreover, reduced their labor bill whenever economically feasible with the use of machinery. This the WPA could not do since money for equipment was almost always scarce and the number of jobless men large. The WPA, therefore, utilized more manpower and less machinery than good management procedures would sanction.[17] As one work relief foreman explained, they were badly hampered in speeding up production and reducing unit costs because they could not use equipment that "any private contractor in his right mind would employ as a matter of course." Congress could have remedied this type of waste only by appropriating much larger sums for the program, thus allowing the WPA to purchase and rent more heavy machinery and initiate additional projects to absorb the personnel displaced by its labor-saving devices.

The compromise between the security and prevailing-wage principles further handicapped the WPA. When organized labor struck against the security wage in 1935, the New York City WPA pacified the AFL by sticking to the fixed limit on total monthly pay but reducing time to the point where a relief craftsman took home about the same hourly wage as those regularly employed. Congress endorsed this procedure and applied it throughout the country in the Emergency Appropriations Acts of 1936, 1937, 1938, and the first half of 1939. This arrangement forced the WPA to use many different foremen and shifts of skilled workers on a single project. Professor Lescohier, in his study of Somervell's agency, made the following appraisal of the effects of this accommodation:

> Crews which have three or four different foremen per month cannot work as effectively as under continuous foremanship. The foremen themselves cannot develop their full interest and skill when they work a week or ten days, turn the job over to someone else, and after a couple of weeks try to pick up from another foreman.[18]

Building trades spokesmen believed that they had the answer to these difficulties: let the WPA farm out its construction to private contractors as the PWA did. The government would get more for its money and still stimulate materials and equipment production while creating jobs. As early as August 1935 a representative of the Building Trades Employers Association made this suggestion to Hugh Johnson. After consulting Hopkins, the general rejected the idea, explaining: "It would be more efficient and probably cost less to do a great deal of construction by contract, but it would employ far fewer people."

At a later date both the Knauth Advisory Council and Professor Lescohier commended Johnson's decision. Although the council was made up of businessmen thoroughly committed to the free enterprise system, it firmly opposed turning construction projects over to the building contractors, who would hire only men already in the field full time and even overtime, rather than spreading opportunities, and who would use more equipment and less labor. Part of the limited funds, moreover, would have to be skimmed off to create a profit for the employer. Lescohier pointed out that the unemployed not hired by the building contractors would still have to be cared for, presumably by home relief. That expense, added to the government's payments to the construction firms, might well cost the community more than the WPA did. Meanwhile, those relegated to home relief would continue to lose their skills and self-confidence and suffer the other deteriorations of enforced idleness. How does one measure such human waste in dollars and cents? Finally, Lescohier concluded that the disparity between WPA efficiency and that of private contractors was likely to diminish in the future because of the improved methods and planning Somervell had introduced in New York.[19]

Besides its extensive building activities, the WPA also engaged in a limited amount of manufacturing. The main enterprises of this type included production of clothing, household linen, toys, and talking-book machines for the blind, and the mending and repairing of school and library

Two hundred sixty-six women were employed in this New York City WPA Sewing Shop in February 1936. Out of textiles processed from surplus cotton, they manufactured women's and children's dresses, which were distributed to families on welfare. *Photo by Art Service Project, WPA.*

books. The agency entered this field in order to create jobs for women, the large pool of unemployed garment workers in New York, and the physically handicapped, none of whom could be used safely or effectively in construction.

The sewing projects actually predated the WPA, having been started originally by private welfare organizations. The WPA, however, tremendously expanded the activity and introduced modern factory techniques. The organization first recruited labor among those laid off by the needles trades and then, when it exhausted that supply, offered places to large numbers of older women and physically handicapped persons on welfare, whom it trained as seamstresses, cutters, pressers, assemblers, and finishers. All told, the sewing shops employed between twelve thousand and fourteen thousand persons, among them two thousand who

In 1937, these women on the New York City WPA Sewing Project were hand finishing dresses manufactured by the project. *Photo by the Photographic Division, Federal Art Project, WPA.*

learned their skill on the WPA and who, by 1942, had left to take jobs in the industry.

From 1935 to the end of 1942 emergency workers manufactured thirty million items that the WPA distributed to families on relief. The articles ranged from layettes to men's suits, from bedding to dresses. For the term beginning in September 1938, 102,000 youngsters received a full back-to-school outfit. The WPA paid careful attention to design and styling, limiting the quantity of garments of a single pattern. They also dispersed identical apparel in widely separated neighborhoods to preclude the possibility that the wearer could be identified as a relief recipient by his clothing. At first Washington purchased all textiles centrally and sent them to the state administrations. This arrangement proved unsatisfactory in New York because it slowed down deliveries, and the fabrics chosen were sometimes unsuitable for the climate and the tastes of urban residents. After 1937 Somervell persuaded his superiors to let him buy locally, where he obtained a better price and more acceptable merchandise.

In 1938 the New York City WPA set up a toy-manufacturing project to turn out wood boats and blocks, games, stuffed animals, and dolls. The production of these items required little skill and was not strenuous; thus Somervell could offer 85 percent of the two hundred positions to crippled, blind, and ailing persons. Each Christmas the WPA dispensed the year's production to hospitals, boys' clubs, nursery schools, settlement houses, and the children of families on relief. In 1939 over two hundred thousand items went out in this way; by 1943, the youngsters of the area had received 1.5 million such gifts.

Although the talking-book project was a relatively small one when measured by its labor force and output, it illustrated particularly well the dual role of the WPA—providing needed commodities and services and simultaneously creating jobs for those rejected by private enterprise. The talking-book machine, a simplified record player, was developed in 1934 by the American Foundation for the Blind, but the organization did not have the money to produce the device itself. Robert Irwin, executive director of the foundation, approached the New York City WPA with the proposal that the work relief agency might manufacture the machines. Washington officials approved the idea and named Irwin to supervise the undertaking. The WPA-built players became the property of the Library of Congress, which lent them to state commissions for the blind, selected libraries, settlement houses, schools, and community centers. Congress furthered the effort with an annual appropriation to be used for making and disseminating talking-book records. Famous actors, authors, radio performers, and other celebrities volunteered to record works of literature and nonfiction. Irwin estimated that of the 120,000 blind men, women, and children in the United States about three-quarters did not read braille. For those individuals the machines and records opened a new world of books.

When Irwin first began directing production, he wanted to extend employment opportunities on the project to the blind, but he had misgivings about their ability to keep up with the pace of sighted laborers. Fortunately, the WPA, not being a profit-making organization, could afford to experiment. Irwin started assigning blind operators, who not only held their own but outshone normal persons at some tasks. For instance, at one point on the assembly line, a tiny screw had to be inserted in the machine. The worker needed the dexterity to do this quickly or he would hold up the whole line. Irwin tried three sighted individuals in the position. Each dropped the screw a couple of times or fumbled before securing it. Ultimately a blind man took the job. His fingers, sensitized by years of distinguishing the tiny dots of the braille alphabet, easily completed the procedure on the first attempt. Eventually, the undertaking used a staff of about three hundred, of whom over one hundred were sightless.[20]

Surveying these blue-collar activities of the New York City WPA, one must conclude that, despite shortcomings, they were a success. To be sure, the projects were expensive and could not match the efficiency, measured in monetary costs, of private enterprise. On the other hand, they rescued from idleness and despair hundreds of thousands of New Yorkers, including many, such as the crippled, the elderly, and the blind, whom outside employers had never given a decent chance even in good times. Indirectly, WPA construction boosted heavy industry by purchasing substantial quantities of steel, cement, electrical equipment, and lumber. The work relief agency, moreover, saved the city from blight and neglect and presented it with facilities it could not afford during prosperity, let alone a depression. An editorial in the Long Island *Press* made this point well. "The plight of Queens would have been tragic had not the New Deal come to its rescue. . . . Queens, like other communities, had men to be kept at work" and many repair jobs to do. The WPA "program was a godsend," the paper claimed. Mayor La Guardia agreed, stating in 1936 that without the help of federal agencies such as the WPA, "there would have been no cities left at this time."[21]

NOTES

1. U.S. WPA for N.Y.C., *Brief Review of Developments in New York City during the Past Two Years*, Report of Brehon B. Somervell to Harry Hopkins (New York, 1937), p. 7; Long Island *Press*, 1 August 1937, ed. sec. p. 1; U.S. WPA for N.Y.C., *The Administration of Work Relief in New York City, August 1936–December 1937*, Report of Brehon B. Somervell to Harry Hopkins (New York, 1938), p. 15; John D. Millett, *The Works Progress Administration in New York City*, (Chicago, 1938), p. 204; U.S. WPA for N.Y.C., *Final Report of the Work Projects Administration for the City of New York, 1935 to 1943* (New York, 1943), pp. 264, 146; U.S. WPA for N.Y.C., *Reports on Public Assistance to the Administrator of the Works Progress Administration for the City of New York*, by Donald D. Lescohier (New York, 1939), p. 155.

2. *New York Times*, 1 October 1939, p. 1; 14 September 1938, p. 32; Brehon B. Somervell to Francis Harrington, 24 February 1938, Papers of the U.S. WPA for N.Y.C., National Archives, Washington, D.C.; Millett, *The WPA in N.Y.C.*, p. 204.

3. *New York Times*, 18 November 1939, p. 17; U.S. WPA for N.Y.C.,

Reports on Public Assistance, pp. 114, 151–52; New York Governor's Commission on Unemployment Relief, *Work Relief in the State of New York, A Report Submitted to Governor Herbert H. Lehman, August 10, 1936* (Albany, N.Y., 1936), pp. 146–47; U.S. WPA for N.Y.C., *Administration of Work Relief*, p. 5.

4. U.S. WPA for N.Y.C., *Final Report*, pp. 157, 159; Long Island *Press*, 26 June 1937, p. 1; Staten Island *Transcript*, 29 June 1937, p. 1; 6 July 1937, p. 1; *New York Times*, 4 July 1937, sec. 2, p. 2; 16 October 1938, p. 46; 18 May 1940, p. 17; U.S. WPA for N.Y.C., *Brief Review of Developments*, p. 9; U.S. WPA for N.Y.C., *Administration of Work Relief*, p. 353; U.S. WPA for N.Y.C., *The WPA in New York City: The Record for 1938* (New York, 1939).

5. From August 1936 to December 1937 the local WPA committed approximately 17 percent of its funds, or roughly $83 million, to road, highway, and bridge projects.

6. U.S. WPA for N.Y.C., *General Statistical Bulletin, 31 August 1938* (New York, 1938), p. 7; U.S. WPA for N.Y.C., *Administration of Work Relief*, pp. 348, 7–8; *Survey Midmonthly* 76 (December 1940): 362–63; U.S. WPA for N.Y.C., *Brief Review of Developments*, p. 13; U.S. WPA for N.Y.C., *WPA in N.Y.C.: 1938*; *New York Times*, 18 June 1937, p. 23; 20 December 1938, p. 52; Long Island *Press*, 1 August 1937, ed. sec. p. 1; *American City* 52 (November 1937): 89.

7. *Survey Midmonthly* 76 (December 1940): 362–63; *New York Times*, 11 July 1939, p. 6; 9 December 1938, p. 2; U.S. WPA for N.Y.C., *Administration of Work Relief*, pp. 9, 15, 237; U.S. WPA for N.Y.C., *WPA in N.Y.C.: 1938*; U.S. WPA for N.Y.C., *Brief Review of Developments*, p. 16.

8. In the late 1930s and the early 1940s the materials went to the War Department for defense purposes instead of to the city.

9. U.S. WPA for N.Y.C., *Administration of Work Relief*, p. 238; U.S. WPA for N.Y.C., *Final Report*, pp. 163, 147, 164; U.S. WPA for N.Y.C., *The WPA in NYC: The Record for 1939* (New York, 1940), p. 41; U.S. Congress, House Subcommittee of the Committee on Appropriations, *Hearings on the Emergency Relief Appropriations Act of 1941*, 76th Cong., 3d sess. (Washington, 1940), p. 793; *New York Times*, 14 April 1939, p. 17.

10. By the time the airport was completed, the city had paid nearly 40 percent of the total cost or about $15 million.

11. New York *Herald Tribune*, 10 September 1937, p. 18; 15 October 1939, pp. 1, 10; *New York Times*, 17 November 1938, p. 17; 1 October 1939, p. 1; 16 October 1939, pp. 1, 21.

12. These included, among others, the American Institute of Architects, the National Aeronautics Association, the American Health Association, the American Engineering Council, the National Education Association, and the U.S. Conference of Mayors.

13. The committee members included Henry Bruère, president of the Bowery Savings Bank; Mary Dillon, president of the Brooklyn Borough

Gas Co.; Paul Nystrom, professor of marketing, Columbia School of Business; E. V. O'Daniel, vice-president of American Cyanamid Co.; T. S. Holden, vice-president of F. W. Dodge Corporation; and others.

14. U.S. Community Improvement Appraisal, *A Report on the Work Program of the Works Progress Administration by the National Appraisal Committee* (Washington, D.C., April 1939), p. 27; *New Yorker*, 17 February 1940, p. 30; "Report of the Advisory Council of the WPA for NYC," in *New York Times*, 14 March 1939, p. 8; U.S. WPA for N.Y.C., *Final Report*, p. 188; Somervell to Harrington, 24 February 1938, Papers of the U.S. WPA for N.Y.C.; U.S. Congress, House Subcommittee of the Committee on Appropriations, *Investigation and Study of the WPA*, 76th Cong., 1st sess. (Washington, 1939), pt. 1, p. 295.

15. The jobs were not really comparable, however, because of the more expensive foundations needed on the soft landfill at La Guardia.

16. New York *Sun*, 10 July 1939, p. 7; 11 July 1939, pp. 1, 2; *New York Times*, 3 May 1939, p. 1; 12 July 1939, p. 18; 4 May 1939, p. 5; 11 June 1939, p. 6; U.S. Congress, House Subcommittee, *Investigation and Study of WPA*, pt. 1, pp. 293, 295, 296, 302–3.

17. About 86 percent of WPA expenditures went directly into the hands of project workers as wages, 10.5 percent into materials, and 3.5 percent into administration.

18. Grace Adams, *Workers on Relief* (New Haven, 1939), p. 341; *New York Times*, 16 February 1939, p. 3; U.S. WPA for N.Y.C., *Administration of Work Relief*, pp. 39, 253, 54; U.S. Congress, House Subcommittee, *Investigation and Study of WPA*, pp. 1266, 1298; U.S. WPA for N.Y.C., *Final Report*, p. 150; Donald Howard, *The WPA and Federal Relief Policy* (New York, 1943), p. 252; Donald Lescohier, "Hybrid WPA," *Survey Midmonthly* 75 (June 1939): 168.

19. C. G. Norman, Building Trades Employers Association of N.Y.C., to Johnson, 16 August 1935; Johnson to Hopkins, 22 August 1935; and Hopkins to Johnson, 4 September 1935, Papers of the U.S. WPA for N.Y.C., National Archives, Washington, D.C.; "Report of Advisory Council," in *New York Times*, 14 March 1939, p. 8; U.S. WPA for N.Y.C., *Reports on Public Assistance*, p. 151.

20. U.S. WPA for N.Y.C., *Administration of Work Relief*, pp. 25, 275; Final Report of the Sewing Project in New York City: A Record of Program Operation and Accomplishments, Papers of the U.S. WPA for N.Y.C., National Archives, Washington, D.C.; U.S. WPA for N.Y.C., *Final Report*, pp. 217, 110, 215; *Survey*, 74 (October 1938):324; *Survey Midmonthly*, 75 (December 1939):379; Corinne Reid Frazier, "WPA Serves the Blind," *Commonweal*, 11 August 1939, pp. 371–72.

21. Long Island *Press*, 1 August 1937, ed. sec. p. 1; *New York Times*, 15 March 1936, p. 31.

6
White Collar and White Apron

Although the WPA concentrated primarily on construction projects, Hopkins and his assistants recognized immediately that a program confined to public works would not meet the needs of thousands of jobless Americans. The relief rolls abounded with persons whose occupational backgrounds varied tremendously, ranging from art to domestic service, from sales to library work. President Roosevelt specified as one of the important objectives of the federal agency preserving the skills of depression victims. Hiring an accountant as a hod carrier or a scientist as a ditchdigger would certainly not fulfill that purpose. Many of the employees on welfare, moreover, were incapable of heavy outdoor labor.

In New York more than anywhere else a government job program had to include white-collar, white-apron, and other nonconstruction positions, since the city's population contained a much larger proportion of professional, clerical, and service workers than that of the average community. The types of people on welfare reflected this fact. As of 1934, one-quarter of them were former white-collar workers, and another 27 percent had been employed in transportation, communication, and trade.

Developing projects that utilized the skills of this highly diverse group of men and women challenged the ingenuity of WPA directors. Hugh Johnson, the first New York City administrator, complained about the headache of trying to "provide work in their crafts for every class of unemployed from puppeteers to lawyers and from eurhythmic dancers to biologists—it's a holy show." Somervell agreed that "putting people to work at tasks they were best fitted to do" was his toughest assignment as WPA chief.

Besides the varied backgrounds of the destitute, many federal regulations complicated the problem of devising acceptable nonconstruction undertakings. They had to be socially useful, but not compete with private enterprise. The WPA also had to guard against projects that might displace municipal civil servants. Further, in 1937 Washington, attempting to spread its limited funds, ordered local offices to keep man-year costs for white-collar labor at a minimum, not to exceed one thousand dollars in most instances. On top of this, there was the tendency of residents and community leaders to prefer tangible achievements—buildings, roads, and parks—to the less visible clerical, research, and service activities. Consequently, Somervell sometimes had to visit city and federal bureaus to drum up business for his clerks, secretaries, and statisticians, something he never needed to do with construction, where sponsors came begging for WPA crews.[1]

Because of these difficulties, the New York City WPA developed its white-collar projects more slowly than its blue. During the first year of its existence, the agency initiated few new service undertakings, but, rather, continued the bulk of those it inherited from earlier programs, adding some personnel. By January 1936 assignments to WPA engineering and construction had soared to over two hundred thousand persons, while white-collar work accounted for a little less than thirty-three thousand, or under 15 percent of the total.

Concerted efforts to enlarge the white-collar and white-apron projects of the WPA began during Victor Ridder's term as administrator and continued with more success under Somervell. By 1937 the latter had increased their number and size to the point where they accounted for almost 30 percent of the WPA labor force and expenditures.[2] The WPA staff somehow devised activities that utilized the skills of five thousand professional and technical people, seven thousand former business managers and proprietors, and fifty-five hundred salesmen, as well as an assortment of other non-blue-collar workers. Obviously, not all of them could perform precisely the tasks they were trained for, but Donald Lescohier, in his 1938 study of Somervell's organization, found that approximately two-thirds of the WPA force labored at jobs sufficiently like their earlier ones that the WPA could honestly claim to be safeguarding their skills.[3]

Serving the health needs of the community afforded the WPA an opportunity to employ a wide range of people who had been forced onto welfare. Under the impact of the depression, the New York City Departments of Health and Hospitals had suffered reduction of budgets and staff.[4] These cuts jeopardized the quality of existing outpatient and hospital care and threatened to make new medical services impossible. Local government averted these possibilities, in part, by assigning relief labor to hospitals and clinics and paying their wages with funds provided by the TERA and later the FERA. By 1934 some two thousand persons from home relief supplemented the regular city hospital crews. When the WPA began in August 1935, it assumed supervision over these workers and expanded their number several fold. Somervell, as of 1937, provided more than four thousand men and women to twenty-six municipal hospitals and another two thousand to projects sponsored by the Department of Health.

These WPA workers included doctors, nurses, pharmacists, dentists, clerks, typists, kitchen help, orderlies, and laboratory technicians. They made it possible for New York to embark on its biggest ventures in preventive medicine. For example, WPA technicians X-rayed the chests of more than four hundred thousand adults and children. Rather than waiting for individuals to develop symptoms of illness or come of their own accord for a checkup, WPA workers in the Health Department set up neighborhood centers and manned mobile X-ray vans. In Harlem they went from door to door, urging residents to return with them to the nearby clinic for an X-ray. By 1937 this extensive coverage had discovered 956 cases of active tuberculosis and over 2,000 other lung ailments requiring treatment.

The WPA applied much the same technique of mass detection and treatment to social diseases. With the aid of WPA doctors, nurses, and clerical help, the Department of Health operated nineteen diagnostic and care centers around the city. During 1936 nearly fifty thousand individuals underwent examination for syphilis and gonorrhea. The following year the case load rose by an additional 25 percent. If someone did not appear for continuing medication, a WPA caseworker went to his home to remind him of the importance of a complete cure. Still other relief employees conducted educational and counseling sessions at the centers, informing patients of the precautions they should take to prevent future contagion.

The WPA assisted the Department of Health in running several diphtheria immunization campaigns during the 1930s. On one project workers got in touch with the mothers of all babies who had reached the age of nine months to tell the women to bring their infants to a doctor or public health station for inoculation. Other relief employees went to public and parochial schools to look for students who had not been immunized. Afterward, registered nurses on the WPA's payroll visited the schools, where they gave injections to those youngsters who had not received them. As a result of these efforts, by 1940 the number of children protected against diphtheria climbed to an all-time high, and the fatalities from the disease dipped sharply.[5]

The WPA also enabled the Department of Health to expand its children's dental program. Federal job-agency dentists worked side by side with those on the municipal payroll to conduct clinics in the public schools. Students from kindergarten through the fourth grade received fillings, cleanings, and extraction of decayed teeth. During 1938 eighty-seven thousand minors were registered in 135 of these public clinics. At the same time, the Adult Dental Care Project served older members of welfare and low-income families. By 1940 work relief dentists had filled one million cavities and pulled three hundred thousand teeth for these adult patients.

Within the hospitals WPA laborers supplemented the efforts of the full-time staff in various capacities. By 1938 work relief barbers had given patients some three hundred thousand shaves and forty-one thousand haircuts; therapists had administered nearly nine hundred thousand massages and shortwave, violet, and infraray treatments; laboratory technicians had run two hundred thousand routine tests; and pharmacists had compounded four hundred thousand prescriptions. The city hospital commissioner estimated that 156 WPA field-workers who aided the 85 permanent members of his department's Division of Investigation saved the community $1 million a year. These interviewers discovered that fifty thousand people who had applied for free care at municipal hospitals were ineligible because they possessed the means to pay for medical services.

The federal works program made possible pioneering developments in recreational therapy in hospitals. One of the New York City WPA's outstanding projects of this sort took place in the children's section of Bellevue Hospital. Consulting closely with psychiatrists, emergency workers helped the disturbed boys and girls to create their own puppets and write and stage plays for them. The doctors believed that the speeches the small patients put into the mouths of their marionettes and the behavior the children expressed through the puppets gave insight into the youngsters' problems. The stage shows also allowed the amateur puppeteers to act out some of their destructive hostility through safe channels. The medical directors at Bellevue liked the results enough to require that all nurses in training there attend classes in recreational therapy conducted by WPA personnel.

Somervell's organization paid unemployed arts and crafts teachers, musicians, and actors, many of whom it trained in group leadership, to entertain and instruct adult hospital patients as well as minors. One grateful inmate of Seaview Hospital on Staten Island described what these efforts meant to him and his fellows in a letter to the colonel:

> Most of us have been confined here for a lengthy period . . . . We are prone to devote too much time to thinking of our troubles . . . are apt to become mentally stagnant. This work you are carrying on comes as a blessing to us, taking us away from the deadly monotony of our daily existence. So for myself, and the rest of the boys of this ward, I thank you.[6]

While many WPA employees served sick people directly, the federal agency also underwrote medical research, some of which produced important advances. The New York City WPA's participation in a study of silicosis, long a scourge of miners, is a prime example. Conducted in cooperation with the Tuberculosis and Health Association and New York Hospital, the project discovered hitherto-unknown lung lesions, permitting early diagnosis and treatment. Many of the sixty WPA employees, as a result of their training in this investigation, found permanent jobs in the health field.

In the judgment of Dr. John Rice, New York commissioner of health, the medical assistance and research projects "permitted a more intensive and adequate health service than could have been provided through the regular departmental personnel. This has resulted in immediate benefit to the community." Dr. S. S. Goldwater, commissioner of hospitals, agreed, but both men also had criticisms of the WPA program. Rice maintained that a number of the people assigned to the projects were inadequately trained or had personality problems that detracted from their effectiveness. Dr. Goldwater thought that some WPA employees performed poorly because they resented earning less than members of the regular hospital staff. He also complained that one could not always count on the WPA. More than once Washington ordered cutbacks in employment, and the local agency complied by suddenly withdrawing large groups of WPA workers from the hospitals.[7]

Like the WPA's health activities, its housekeeping services proved valuable to many sick and disadvantaged persons. Three groups among poor New Yorkers badly needed household assistance: the elderly, the chronically ill, and families in which the mother was temporarily incapacitated. While these community residents urgently wanted domestic help but could not afford it, other city dwellers desperately sought household employment.

In 1935–36, 43 percent of all black families in New York lacked a male breadwinner. More than four out of every ten black homes subsisted on welfare. The female heads of many of these units had supported themselves and their children prior to the crash as domestic servants for the well-to-do in the East Eighties, on Long Island, and in Westchester. With the coming of the depression, their once-affluent employers frequently let them go. Steady household jobs became increasingly scarce. Simultaneously, layoffs in factories, trade, and restaurants drove more and more black women into day labor. By 1935 these people were scrambling for a few hours of work at almost any wage. An article in the *Crisis* called "The Bronx Slave Market" described their daily "shape up" at 167th Street and Jerome Avenue and at Simpson and Westchester Avenues:

> As early as eight A.M. they come; as late as one P.M. they remain. Rain or shine, cold or hot, you will find them there—Negro women, old and young—sometimes bedraggled, sometimes neatly dressed—but with the invariable paper bundle, waiting expectantly for Bronx housewives to buy their strength and energy for an hour, two hours, or even a day at the munificent rate of fifteen, twenty, twenty-five, or if luck be with them, thirty cents an hour.

The less fortunate ones stood until afternoon only to trudge off empty-handed because no one offered to hire them at even fifteen cents an hour.

The WPA's housekeeping project brought together the indigent who needed help and the poor who offered domestic services. The federal agency paid the wages—approximately seventy dollars a month—of between fifteen hundred and two thousand women, almost all of them black. It gave them a one-week intensive training course, conducted by experienced home economists and registered nurses, in marketing, nutrition, practical nursing, infant care, and other domestic skills. The women then went into the households of clients who had been referred to the WPA by such agencies as the Henry Street Nursing Service and the Old Age Assistance Division of the Department of Welfare. For those who required it, the relief housekeepers could help as much as twenty hours a week. In other cases a half-day's labor once a week sufficed. During 1937, for instance, some 425 chronically ill persons, 6,000 temporarily motherless families, and 870 elderly New Yorkers received assistance under this program.

Although the project served real needs of the clients and provided steady work for people who lacked other means of support, it raised some difficulties. First, in relegating so many black women to domestic service, the WPA was accepting the status quo too readily (if it was not guilty itself of racial discrimination). The work relief officials might have used their organization to retrain some of these people for jobs that brought higher status and pay. Roosevelt, however, had defined the role of the WPA primarily as that of conserving skills, not teaching new ones, and therefore the local placement officers tended to assign individuals to the same tasks they had performed previously. Some of the clients, unaccustomed to the role of employer, acted like petty tyrants. Meanwhile, a minority of the WPA workers resented having to take care of the children and clean the apartments of women as poor as themselves. Nonetheless, most of the participants, clients, and workers apparently

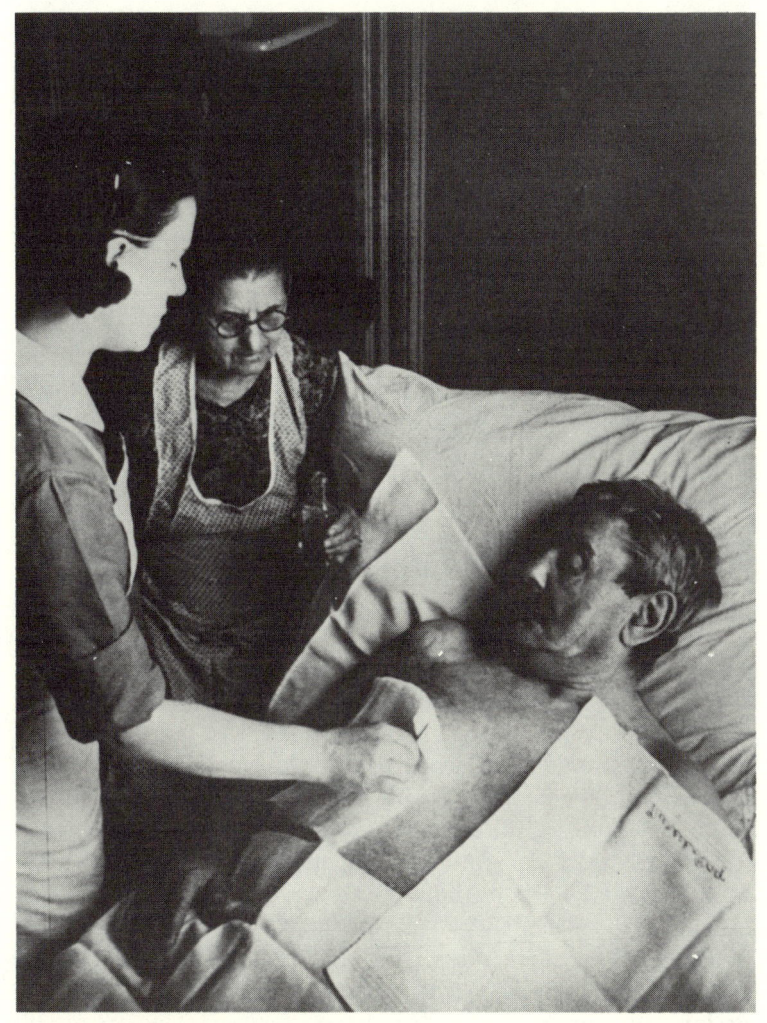

A chronically ill patient being cared for by an employee of the New York City WPA's Housekeeping Project, February 1936. *Photo by the Art Service Project, WPA.*

felt that they benefited. Grateful old people and invalids sent the project numerous letters of appreciation. A couple of typical ones read:

> Your project is a blessing sent to the old, sick and helpless who love that which they can still call their home.
> S—— S——

> Kind friend I wish to thank you for giving me M—— C——, services for five mornings a week when I nede her so Bad for I was very sick. . . . Mable is very Nice and kind and good worker and always chears me upp.[8]

If the sick and elderly benefited from WPA services, so did the inmates of the city jails. New York's commissioner of corrections praised the WPA for supplying teachers for illiterate prisoners, staff for prison libraries, recreation leaders to entertain the inmates, and additional help for the social investigation unit that gathered case histories on each convict for the use of prison doctors and officials.

In addition to these health, housekeeping, and prison activities, the WPA ran a great many clerical-assistance projects. Jobless men and women who had once earned their livings as office help and salespeople now set about filing, indexing, coding, and rearranging records and documents for federal, state and municipal agencies. Some of this WPA work enabled local authorities to serve New Yorkers more quickly and efficiently. For instance, during 1937 and 1938 Somervell's employees installed a complete lot- and block-card index system covering all real estate in Queens, The Bronx, and Staten Island for the municipal Department of Housing and Buildings. According to the department's deputy commissioner, this improvement made it possible to locate an original building plan in the files in three to five minutes, whereas formerly it took one to three days. The increased efficiency that resulted caught one New York woman by surprise. She walked into the Queens office of the housing department with a box lunch under her arm and stated that she wished to see the building plan for her house. When the clerk fetched it almost instantly, she exclaimed: "Ten years ago I called here to see the plan and I didn't have sense enough to bring my lunch with me and it took you a whole day to find it. Now, I've brought my lunch and I've got to take it back home."

The New York City WPA's biggest clerical task, requiring two and one-half years to complete, was indexing the 1920 census. Ever since the passage of the Social Security Act in 1935, the number of requests for proof of age, birthplace, and citizenship had risen mightily. Without an index each inquiry cost the Census Bureau approximately three dollars. The index, finished in the fall of 1940, greatly speeded up the search process, thereby cutting labor expenditure to less than fifty cents a reference.[9]

The WPA assigned individuals with the appropriate educational background to a variety of research projects. Some of these endeavors turned out material that had considerable value for scholars, teachers, scientists, and businessmen. For example, geologists and engineers appreciated the efforts of a WPA team, cosponsored by the Museum of Natural History and New York University, that catalogued the then-unorganized literature on foraminifera. Data on this subject had been so scattered and jumbled as to make it almost inaccessible to scientists. Yet this information was as helpful a tool to the geologist as X-ray pictures to the doctor. The foraminifera gave clues to the conditions that existed deep below the earth's surface, just as the X-ray revealed the bones and organs beneath the patient's skin.

In January 1938 Somervell's administration started the New York Mathematics Tables Project under the sponsorship of Dr. Lyman Briggs, director of the United States Bureau of Standards. This undertaking established a laboratory at 70 Columbus Avenue that by 1942 operated 250 computers tended by WPA employees in two shifts (9:00 A.M. to 5:00 P.M. and 5:00 P.M. to 12:00 P.M.) five days a week. The tables made by this unit were eventually published and, according to a writer in *Science* magazine, proved extremely useful:

> The Mathematics Tables Project . . . has achieved an extraordinary body of calculation and publication. [N]ever before has such an extensive scientific computing laboratory been established. It is kept working to the fullest capacity by confidential demands of the Army and Navy, and by many approved requests of scientists. . . . [T]he war effort . . . only intensified the demand for these and many other tables.

Unlike the catalog of foraminifera literature and the mathematics tables, which were printed and thus reached interested scientists, much potentially useful data compiled by work relief personnel went unnoticed. The WPA had neither the money nor the authority to publish the results of its research projects. If the sponsor of the undertaking did not put up funds for this purpose, the materials simply collected in files. The Census of American Listed Corporations is a case in point. During 1937 the New York City WPA employed forty workers to collate the information reported by American corporations to the Securities and Exchange Commission for the years 1934 and 1935. Soon the personnel had entered on thousands of cross-indexed cards all manner of information about some two thousand companies. A journalist from *Business Week* who visited the office and looked through the material felt certain that industrialists, investors, and economists would find much of interest to them. With the data in the possession of this project one could tell, for instance, if businesses in which the managers had a stock interest did better than companies in which directors had only nominal ownership. Neither the WPA nor the SEC, however, had made any arrangements for publication, and few people knew anything about the work.[10] The output of many other WPA units met a similar fate. To this day, unpublished, typewritten studies and bibliographies compiled by federal emergency researchers abound in the stacks of the New York Public Library on Fifth Avenue and Forty-second Street and in some of its branches in the boroughs.

Along with its worthwhile and potentially useful tasks, the WPA did engage in a few clerical and research projects primarily to pay wages to people who could not be utilized elsewhere. Somervell himself suspected that a few of the bibliographies compiled by his employees were of interest to almost no one. Grace Adams, a social worker who had become very critical of the WPA by 1938, charged that work relief laborers wasted hours on such meaningless undertakings.

The WPA also secured work for the white-collar jobless in the city's libraries. These institutions, generally short of funds and labor even in times of prosperity, had been hard hit by the depression. To weather the crisis they had begun to avail themselves of relief labor as early as 1932. Somervell's agency substantially increased the number of persons assigned to library assistance. WPA personnel augmented the permanent staff in elementary and high school libraries, in many of the colleges, and at nearly every branch of the public library. Alongside the full-time people, they charged books to borrowers, mended broken bindings, reshelved, and catalogued. Because the WPA paid the wages of these supplementary workers, the libraries were able to apply more of their limited budgets to buying books and subscribing to periodicals. The additional staff also permitted libraries to stay open longer each day and on weekends. Moreover, with the WPA aides the New York Public Library initiated new programs and services, such as its popular Open Air Reading Room in Bryant Park and bookmobiles for outlying neighborhoods.[11]

Like the libraries, museums benefited from relief labor. The Museum of Natural History over the years had collected and stored in its basement and closets millions of dollars worth of materials that neither the public nor scientists saw because the institution lacked the staff to arrange, catalog, and properly display the pieces. The workers sent in by the federal agency after August 1935 finally moved

In June 1936, at 11 Bond Street, Brooklyn, one thousand WPA employees were learning how to rebind and repair books. Their first job, upon completion of training, was to repair more than four hundred thousand text and library books for the New York schools in time for the fall term. *Photo by the Art Service Project, WPA.*

these interesting and valuable artifacts out of packing boxes and into showcases. Similarly, WPA employees came to the assistance of the Brooklyn Museum. By 1936 emergency personnel comprised 60 to 70 percent of the labor force of that institution.

Although libraries, museums, and other organizations usually welcomed the work relief help, a few complaints about the WPA inevitably cropped up. An article appearing in the *Library Journal* in 1936 explained why some librarians had reservations about the aid they were getting. According to this account, the introduction of emergency employees was diluting the professional staffs with a certain proportion of "untrained and untrainable people." These incompetents turned out such indifferent work that a minority of the librarians believed they were receiving "five cents worth of results for every dollar of WPA funds spent."

The historian Richard Morris, who supervised the New York Regional Survey of Federal Archives, made similar complaints about the caliber of some of the white-collar people he encountered on the WPA. He had to depend on a pool of WPA typists to prepare reports on the progress of his researchers. Although several of the women were first-rate, many in the pool managed to finish each day only a fraction of the work that a private concern would have expected of its clerical help. His pep talks and prodding only brought "unaccountable absenteeism—eyes went bad, nervous systems collapsed, morale deteriorated."[12]

It is difficult to determine what proportion of the white-collar personnel deserved these criticisms. The closest thing that there is to an overall evaluation of the service program is in a report written late in 1935 by a committee of local business and professional leaders headed by Maj. Benjamin Namm, a Brooklyn department store owner.[13] The Namm Committee inspected 334 clerical and professional projects, condemning 24 of them as either lacking any significant purpose or competing with private enterprise. But the remaining 310, the group felt, were engaged in useful activities worthy of government support. They found that there was "no more—and probably no less—boondoggling in the work relief administration than in private business or in the trades and professions generally."

One can question the competence of some WPA service workers and the usefulness of a few of the projects, but the very real accomplishments of the white-collar and white-apron program deserve to be remembered. The local WPA directors managed to create meaningful tasks for an incredibly varied lot of unemployed, from professionals with Ph.D.'s to cleaning women with minimal education. At the same time, WPA efforts bolstered valuable city services that New York could not have provided out of its own resources. Municipal libraries and museums did not close their doors early or on weekends; rather, they expanded their activities. City hospitals and clinics did not have to turn away the sick who could not pay. Instead, the New York Departments of Health and Hospitals were able to launch drives against communicable diseases, offer enlarged dental programs, develop recreation outlets for patients confined to institutions, and step up medical research. Fewer children died of diphtheria, and the number of undetected tuberculosis and venereal disease cases declined. Invalids, the convalescing, and the elderly who could not afford practical nurses, baby-sitters, and maids received care and help at home.

Still more probably could have been done. Donald Lescohier, in his study of Somervell's administration, estimated that, given the needs of New Yorkers, the federal government could provide useful tasks for an additional fifty thousand service workers for at least ten years.[14] Instead, war brought drastic curtailment of the WPA and was responsible for its eventual demise. When that happened, despite the return of prosperity, the city found it hard, if not impossible, to continue the range of services to residents that the federal government supported during the New Deal.

NOTES

1. U.S. Department of Labor, *Family Income and Expenditure in New York City, 1935–1936,* 2 vols. (Washington, D.C., 1941), 1:11; U.S. WPA for N.Y.C., *Urban Workers on Relief, May 1934,* by Gladys Palmer and Katherine Wood (Washington, D.C., 1936), 1:70, 9, and 2:5, 74, 25, 47, 12, 84, 86, 98, 268, 284; *Reports on Public Assistance to the Administrator of the Works Progress Administration for the City of New York,* by Donald D. Lescohier (New York, 1939), p. 154; Donald Howard, *The WPA and Federal Relief Policy* (New York, 1943), pp. 232, 234; John D. Millett, *The Works Progress Administration in New York City* (Chicago, 1938), p. 121; U.S. WPA for N.Y.C., *The Administration of Work Relief in New*

White Collar and White Apron 163

York City, August 1936–December 1937, Report of Brehon B. Somervell to Harry Hopkins (New York, 1938), pp. 260–63.

2. In the last four years of the WPA the nonconstruction part of the local agency's work rose to one-third of its program.

3. U.S. WPA for N.Y.C., *Final Report of the Work Projects Administration for the City of New York, 1935–1943* (New York, 1943), p. 112; U.S. WPA for N.Y.C., *Administration of Work Relief*, p. 351; Donald Lescohier, "Hybrid WPA," *Survey* 75 (June 1939): 168.

4. The daily census of patients in municipal hospitals rose more than 10 percent between 1931 and 1934, while full-time personnel dropped from 13,092 to 12,416.

5. New York Governor's Commission on Unemployment Relief, *Work Relief in the State of New York, A Report Submitted to Governor Herbert H. Lehman, August 10, 1936* (Albany, N.Y., 1936), p. 82; U.S. WPA for N.Y.C., *Final Report*, pp. 206, 204; U.S. WPA for N.Y.C., *Administration of Work Relief*, pp. 292, 24, 293, 294; Millett, *The WPA in N.Y.C.*, p. 26; U.S. WPA for N.Y.C., *Brief Review of Developments in New York City During the Past Two Years*, Report of Brehon B. Somervell to Harry Hopkins (New York, 1937), pp. 16–17; Final Report of the Defense Health and Welfare Services of the New York City WPA, February 1943, Papers of the U.S. WPA for N.Y.C., National Archives, Washington, D.C.; *Survey Midmonthly* 75 (July 1939):224; New York *Herald Tribune*, 27 July 1937, p. 17; U.S. Congress, House Subcommittee of the Committee on Appropriations, *Hearings on the Emergency Relief Appropriations Act of 1937*, 75th Cong., 1st sess. (Washington, D.C., 1936), p. 302; *New York Times*, 21 October 1940, p. 19.

6. U.S. WPA for N.Y.C., *Final Report*, pp. 204–5; *New York Times*, 21 October 1940, p. 19; *Work* (New York edition), 9 April 1938, p. 3; Goldwater to La Guardia, 22 February 1937, Fiorello La Guardia Papers, New York City Municipal Archives; Edward C. Lindeman, "Recreation Rehabilitates the Shut-In," *Recreation* 31, no. 7 (October 1937): 417–18; *Recreation* 31, no. 7 (October 1937): 452.

7. Rice to La Guardia, 1 September 1936, and Goldwater to La Guardia, 2 September 1936, La Guardia Papers.

8. U.S. WPA for N.Y.C., *Family Income*, 1:4, 6; Ella Baker and Marvel Cooke, "The Bronx Slave Market," *Crisis* 42 (November 1935): 330–31; Final Report of Defense Health and Welfare Services, February 1943, Papers of the U.S. WPA for N.Y.C.; Division of Women's and Professional Projects, Monthly Narrative Report, 20 February–20 March 1937, p. 3, Fiorello La Guardia Papers, New York City Municipal Archives; *New York Times*, 4 September 1938, sec. 2, p. 7; U.S. WPA for N.Y.C., *Administration of Work Relief*, pp. 294–95; U.S. WPA for N.Y.C., *Final Report*, p. 212; U.S. WPA for N.Y.C., *Study and Development of Home Care of Recipients of Old-Age Assistance* (New York, 1937), pp. 30–31, 42–43.

9. *Survey* 74 (September 1938) : 291; *Sunday Eagle,* 30 October 1938, p. 2; *Survey Midmonthly* 76 (September 1940) : 270.

10. Donald Cameron, "Research Projects Aid Schools and Scholars," *American Scholar* 8, no. 2 (April 1939) : 249; Raymond Clare Archibald, "The New York Mathematics Tables Project," *Science* 25 September 1942, pp. 294–96; "Dig Up Rich Data; Can They Use It?," *Business Week* 8 May 1937, pp. 38–41.

11. Proceedings of the State Administrators Conference at the Mayflower Hotel, 21 October 1937, Harry Hopkins Papers, Franklin D. Roosevelt Library, Hyde Park, N.Y.; Grace Adams, "The White-Collar Chokes: Three Years of WPA Professional Work," *Harper's* 177 (October 1938) : 474–84; The Library and Museum Program, Record of Program Operation and Accomplishment, February 1943, Papers of the U.S. WPA for N.Y.C., National Archives, Washington, D.C.; Ruth Wellman, "Open-Air Reading Rooms," *Library Journal,* 15 September 1936, pp. 668–70; *Recreation* 31, no. 5 (August 1937) : pp. 287–88; *North Shore Journal,* 2 August 1937, p. 3.

12. U.S. WPA for N.Y.C., *Administration of Work Relief,* p. 298; Library and Museum Program, February 1943, Papers of the U.S. WPA for N.Y.C.; U.S. Congress, House Subcommittee, *Hearings, 1937,* p. 304; "Can the Librarians Help the WPA?," *Library Journal,* 1 November 1936, pp. 854–56; Richard B. Morris, "Pioneering Days of Regional Archives," pp. 19–20, transcripts from the symposium The Historian and Archives, 23 October 1969, Columbia University, mimeographed.

13. Other members of the Namm Committee included Kenneth Dayton, assistant to the president of the Board of Aldermen; Dr. Neva Deardorff of the Welfare Council; Lee Hanmer of the Russell Sage Foundation; Mrs. Henry Goddard Leach, League of Women Voters; H. J. Kenner, Better Business Bureau; George McCaffrey and W. C. Yeomans, New York Merchants Assoc.; and Lillian Poses of the Trade and Commerce Bar Assoc.

14. Report of the Planning and Advisory Committee on New York City White-Collar Projects (Namm Committee), 14 October 1935, Harry Hopkins Papers, Franklin D. Roosevelt Library, Hyde Park, N.Y.; U.S. WPA for N.Y.C., *Reports on Public Assistance,* p. 159.

7

The Unemployed in the Classroom and on the Playground

The depression might have spelled disaster for public education and recreation in the city of New York, but instead the intervention of the Roosevelt Administration made possible new school construction, the growth of adult education, the development of preprimary schools, and an unprecedented expansion of organized leisure-time activities in the community. Early in the 1930s the situation looked grim. The municipal budget, weighed down by relief costs, could spare little money for school construction or renovation. In 1929 the Board of Education spent $1.01 per one thousand square feet of floor space for the physical maintenance of its plant and equipment, but by 1933 it had to get along with only $.54 for this purpose. The poorest neighborhoods suffered the most. In Harlem many schools were so crowded that they operated on double or triple sessions each day, and half of the elementary schools in that area assigned forty or fifty students to a class. Not a single new school was erected in the black ghetto between 1925 and 1935.

After 1933, however, the picture began to change. The New Deal initiated large-scale federal aid to education and recreation. First through the PWA and later the WPA, Washington created jobs for thousands of construction workers building and repairing schools. From the summer of 1935 until the end of 1937, the WPA in New York City spent over $15 million on labor and materials to renovate three hundred schools, in some cases restoring virtually obsolete structures to the point where they could be used for many more years. Simultaneously, the work relief agency laid out ten modern athletic fields adjacent to high schools and rehabilitated forty-eight elementary school playgrounds. By the close of 1937 the WPA had spent over $2 million in construction on the campuses of the New York city colleges. The following year the WPA built two new elementary schools and had 106 men working on the Hunter College campus being developed in The Bronx.[1]

Of equal importance, although not as visible, were the myriad of nonengineering services that the WPA rendered to education and recreation. Using the large pool of professional, clerical, and domestic workers on the welfare rolls in New York, the local WPA carried out the most extensive school-aid program in the country.[2] During the 1938–39 academic year, for instance, twelve thousand persons labored on WPA education activities ranging from teaching to preparing school lunches, while three thousand worked on varied recreation undertakings.

When the WPA began operations in the community, its directors found the practice of using welfare recipients to aid education already well established. As early as 1931 the Gibson Committee, a nongovernmental, philanthropic agency, pioneered in paying jobless professionals to serve as nursery school teachers and recreation leaders under the supervision of the Board of Education. The organization also hired women to prepare free, in-school lunches for underprivileged pupils. In 1933 and 1934 the Federal Emergency Relief Administration authorized the use of its funds to continue this work as well as to appoint unemployed instructors to teach classes for adult illiterates, workers, and parents.

When the WPA replaced the FERA, the new agency assumed control of the projects already in operation, added personnel to them, and initiated many more endeavors. Federal largess to the schools increased dramatically. As a result, the program reached a lot more people. In the fall of 1937 almost ninety-three thousand students were enrolled in the WPA adult education classes, ten times the number receiving instruction during the last year of the FERA.[3]

WPA instructors in New York City earned on the average $95.44 a month. This was only about one-third of the salary of a high school teacher on the Board of Education payroll, but it represented an improved economic status for most of the emergency workers, since 96 percent of them had been taken off home relief. Perhaps this wage differential was justified in part by the fact that the WPA staff as a whole had less previous teaching experience and formal education than the regular faculty.[4]

Several things accounted for the less-impressive credentials of the relief instructors. First, the WPA did not require its people to have four years of college and possess a teaching certificate. Some "previous training and/or practical experience in the field to be taught" were sufficient. Secondly, the school system, when instituting cutbacks during the early 1930s, presumably held on to the most qualified teachers and laid off the less effective ones. Therefore the certified personnel on welfare were either instructors dropped by the city or young college graduates for whom no positions existed. Since many of the WPA employees were neophytes in the profession, the Board of Education tried to prepare them for their assignments by giving them a four-week crash course in teaching methods. Once they began meeting classes, the work relief educators also attended in-service training sessions conducted by old-timers.[5]

President Roosevelt's Advisory Committee on Education, which undertook a thorough study of the WPA school projects, reported that, while some teachers held substandard qualifications, overall they proved to be dedicated and able in the classroom.[6] Apparently, many of the pupils thought so, too. From time to time students enrolled in the courses wrote to the Board of Education or the mayor to praise their instructors. Typical was a note addressed to La Guardia by a member of a WPA Spanish class, which said: "Our teacher, a Spaniard who has lived for many years in Cuba, is hard working, capable, and a source of inspiration to us in our efforts to master Spanish."

The WPA set as one of the prime objectives of its educational program bringing opportunities for learning to people who had never been adequately served by the public school system. Chief among these were adults, especially the poor and members of minority groups. By the spring term of 1938 two hundred thousand urban residents, seventeen years of age or older, were registered for thirty-five thousand classes taught by fourteen hundred WPA instructors. Courses in elementary English and English for the Foreign Born attracted the largest enrollments. During 1938 more than fifty thousand illiterate New Yorkers attended these WPA classes.

For some this was their first chance to master reading and writing. Such was the case of Alice Bryant, who in 1936 entered a literacy class held daily from noon to 2:00 P.M. at the Union Baptist Church on 145th Street in Harlem. Although she was a great-great-grandmother, Bryant knew only the alphabet. Born a slave in 1849, in Hanover County, Virginia, she spent her childhood working in the fields. She recalled that on the plantation "if they caught me with a book in my hands, I was whipped." Now, at eighty-seven years of age, she wanted to be able to read the newspapers and "find out what's goin' on."

Other community residents had never learned to read or write English because they migrated to the United States as adults. Frequently, their struggles to earn a living occupied them so completely that they had no time to study their adopted language. The Board of Education estimated that people of this sort accounted for the preponderance of the

Unemployed in Classroom and on Playground 169

approximately three hundred thousand illiterates in New York in the mid-1930s. Encouraged by conveniently located, free instruction, immigrants and aliens signed up for WPA English for the Foreign Born and Citizenship classes. When the WPA offered such a course on the lower East Side in the spring of 1938, so many people appeared that the agency quickly began a second section for students past their eightieth birthday. Most of the octogenarians resided in two homes for the aged in the neighborhood and spoke only Yiddish. William Goldstein, at 103, was the oldest student in the class. By far the youngest person in the room was the teacher, Sylvia Lehr, twenty-four years old. Graduated from Hunter College in 1935, she had been unemployed until the WPA created this job for her. Why did her pupils come? Well, one explained, "I just want to learn a little English before I die."[7]

November 1936, a WPA instructor teaching a class in English for the Foreign Born in Brooklyn. *Photo by the Photographic Division, Federal Art Project, WPA.*

Alan Buxton, who also taught a class in English for the Foreign Born, came to the WPA in circumstances similar to Sylvia Lehr's. The son of a struggling Jewish family, he worked his way through City College. Every evening until eleven and all day Saturday he was employed as a salesclerk in a women's wear store. For his thirty-four hours a week he earned nine dollars. That provided him with money for books and supplies and allowed him a budget of thirty cents a day—a dime for the subway to school and home again, fifteen cents for lunch, and a nickel for miscellaneous expenses. He was graduated in June 1937 and certified to teach in the elementary schools. He soon discovered, however, that there were no teaching jobs available. For months he looked for work, watching the help-wanted advertisements, taking one civil service exam after another. He did well on them, placing near the top of the list on several, but he was told there would be a long wait before any positions opened. Finally, he applied for home relief, not because he wanted the public assistance, but because it was the route to a WPA job.

Nearly forty years later, Alan Buxton remembered the unpleasantness of applying for relief. Technically, he did not qualify because he still lived at home, and his father was working. Friends, who were members of the Workers Alliance, told him how to get around this. He moved in with another family temporarily (they set up a cot for him in the hall) and told his caseworker that he could no longer expect support from his parents. A social worker arrived early one morning to check on his story, and after further investigation, he was certified as destitute. Next he made his way to the Brooklyn borough headquarters of the WPA to request placement. "The offices were poor and shabby. Everything was makeshift. Bare light bulbs hung from the ceiling. It was depressing to go there; it seemed part of the welfare system," he recalled.

At last he received his assignment. In January 1938 the WPA hired him to teach English to a class of thirty-five students at the Eastern District Evening High School in the Williamsburg section of Brooklyn. It was a great feeling to conduct a class of his own. His students did not know what he had gone through to step into that room; they respected him as a teacher. The ninety-five dollars a month the WPA paid him was the most money he had ever earned. "It kept me in clothing and it made me feel respectable," he remembered.

His students were immigrants from Poland, Lithuania, and a half dozen other European countries. Most of them were working people and very eager to learn English so that they could become citizens. The brightest in the class were the Jewish-German refugees, who had recently fled from the Nazi regime. Many of them had been in business or the professions. Buxton met his pupils for three hours a night, Monday through Friday, in a room made available by the Board of Education. The supplies he used were also issued by the board, except for the textbook, which had been specifically developed by the WPA to assist adult pupils in learning to read and write English.[8]

The adult education project did not confine itself, by any means, to instructing the foreign born. WPA teachers offered a full range of academic topics normally covered in high schools, such as history, literature, foreign languages, science, and mathematics. They also taught a wide variety of vocational subjects, including homemaking, sewing, typing, bookkeeping, accounting, and business management. Still other adult education offerings aimed at aiding people to enjoy their leisure hours by developing their talents, interests, and hobbies. In this category fell the classes in art, music, dancing, puppetry, and public affairs.

Many adults took full advantage of the varied WPA fare, returning for course after course. Although individuals had their own particular reasons for enrolling, the popular response generally is not hard to understand. Without jobs to fill the bulk of their waking hours, people during the depression found time weighing heavily upon them. Attending WPA classes got them out of the house, provided social contacts with other students, offered a kind of free entertainment, and allowed the unemployed person to feel that he was accomplishing something useful until he could again secure work. Thus, the WPA adult classes helped these persons weather the psychological strain of enforced idleness.

Praise for the achievements of the WPA in this field came from many sources. The National Education Association commended the program for notably furthering "the movement of adult education in the United States." *Current History* magazine called the New York City undertaking perhaps the most interesting one in the country and an outstanding accomplishment of the New Deal. The periodical continued: "It is mass education for that part of the population past high school age, and it is paradoxical that America could afford it only in the years of economic depression." An article in the *Monthly Labor Review* noted that WPA adult classes had attracted large numbers of blacks and had made important progress in reducing the rate of illiteracy among them. But the most eloquent testimonial issued from the students. In 1943 when Washington liquidated the WPA, hundreds of protest letters from immigrants struggling with their newly acquired English poured in to Mayor La Guardia's office. The two following are typical:

> In my twenty-nine years of living in America, never have I realized the importance of learning English. Not a word was I able to understand until I started attending the WPA Daytime Citizenship Classes.

> Dear Mr. Mayor,
> You must keep our WPA citizenship classes. We want to be good citizens for our sons in the army. Please stop taking our teachers away.[9]

While recognizing the educational and humanitarian achievements of this school program for adults, one can discern that some of the government officials who supported and sponsored the projects had other objectives as well.

The rise of aggressive totalitarian regimes abroad in the 1930s produced a resurgent national consciousness in America and a desire to draw its people together. Heightened patriotism manifested itself in growing interest in American art, folklore, music, literature, and history.[10] Negative manifestations included the investigations of Martin Dies's House Committee on Un-American Activities and the proliferation of loyalty oaths for government employees in the late 1930s and early 1940s. In this context, especially after World War II began, the English literacy and citizenship classes were frequently touted as the best way to assimilate and indoctrinate potentially dangerous foreigners. The following statement by an educator involved in the New York projects illustrates this kind of thinking:

> The potential threat of sabotage to a city's vital services can be effectively reduced through the proper approach to and handling of aliens. . . . This is where the Citizenship Education Program sets in.
>
> The objective of the program is simple. It is set up to aid national unity. . . . It offers the alien an opportunity to demonstrate his loyalty to this country by becoming an active part of the American way of life. It teaches him English, the duties and responsibilities of citizenship and precisely how he can best fit into American community activities.

If the WPA, regardless of its motives, opened the classroom to more adults than ever before, it also invited in a larger number of pre-elementary school youngsters. At the start of the decade, day-care centers hardly existed. In 1932 there were approximately three hundred nursery schools in the entire nation, almost all of them privately controlled. By 1937 the New York City WPA, in cooperation with the Board of Education, was operating fourteen play schools attended by some 580 children between the ages of two and five years. As of 1943, these nurseries had expanded to twenty-eight in number and accommodated 950 pupils. The day-care program accepted children of low-income working mothers and youngsters from families on relief. In the early 1940s the offspring of men in the armed forces also became eligible. For the poorest parents the schools cost nothing. Those a little better off might pay up to $1.25 a week. This money helped to buy additional toys and equipment for the nursery.

The typical WPA nursery ran from 8:30 A.M. to 5:30 P.M. to accommodate the working mother. At the start of the day a registered nurse examined the children as they arrived, sending home any who exhibited signs of contagious illness. Then the instructors led the youngsters through a program that included individual play, indoors and out-of-doors, organized games, storytelling, arts and crafts, and an afternoon nap. At midmorning and afternoon

Children at play at a New York City WPA nursery school, Recreation Center at 48 Henry Street, May 1936. *Photo by the Art Service Project, WPA.*

the children received fruit juice, milk, and cod-liver oil, while at noon they ate a hot lunch designed to be nutritious and to introduce toddlers to a more varied diet than they might receive at home.

Day care did not intend to replace the mother's role with institutionalized child rearing—quite the opposite. Play schools for the young were seen as strengthening the family. For this reason, a program of parent education accompanied the nursery school. WPA teachers urged the mothers and fathers to attend evening sessions devoted to discussing the development of their offspring. At the night meetings, the instructors came to know the parents well and sometimes helped to solve family problems by securing desired services. For example, nursery teachers arranged for one mother who had taken ill to get domestic assistance from the WPA housekeeping project and expedited the efforts of another to obtain some laboratory tests for her child.

Proponents of early childhood education believed that these WPA nurseries filled many additional needs. Obviously they provided reliable baby-sitting for the mother who had to work because she was the sole breadwinner for the family. They also freed women on home relief to take vocational training that might make them employable. For instance, a young mother, registered in the WPA's Household Training Course (hoping the experience would get her a job as a waitress), enrolled her two-year-old son in a WPA day-care center. "He's learning lots there with the other children, and they give him a good lunch, and it's only twenty-five cents a day. He's getting along fine," she said. Furthermore, advocates of day care claimed that the nursery school experience instilled self-confidence in the child, improved his or her health through good diet and rest habits, and allowed teachers and nurses to spot emotional and physical disorders early so that they could be treated.[11]

Besides expanding adult and early childhood education, the WPA gave the New York schools a chance to concentrate more effort on remedial instruction. The board had long recognized that there were thousands of elementary and high school pupils in the community who read below their grade level and could barely add and subtract. This was due, in part, to overcrowded classrooms that made it impossible for the teacher to offer a student much individual help. The city, however, lacked funds to change the situation until the WPA supplied the labor to undertake special tutoring. For the 1937–38 academic year, the federal agency employed nearly two thousand men and women to coach sixteen thousand primary and fifty-five hundred secondary students in reading and arithmetic. Also, during 1936, 1937, and 1938 WPA teachers ran small summer classes to assist youngsters who had failed subjects in the previous fall and spring semesters.

WPA personnel helped the schools identify and educate youngsters with physical handicaps. The lipreading project, by means of audiometer, tested the hearing of nearly every child in the municipal schools and discovered over one hundred thousand cases of impairment. The relief personnel referred approximately thirty-five thousand of these boys and girls for treatment and instructed about three thousand of them each month in lipreading so that they could function better in the classroom and in social situations. While the partially deaf child usually attended school, the epileptic, crippled, or invalid frequently did not. The Board of Education, prior to the 1930s, employed some teachers to work with these pupils in their homes, but the educational system never had the money to hire as many people as were required. By the fall of 1937, the WPA had placed 103 new instructors on this service, and, as a result, 350 more bedridden students than formerly obtained tutoring.

Although WPA employees did not start the child-nutrition project, they manned it for seven and one-half years. The Board of Education initiated the lunch program in 1930 when teachers spotted a growing number of children coming to classes without breakfast or a noonday meal. With voluntary private contributions, the school system bought lunches for these youngsters. In 1933 the federal government first began to aid the program. Eventually, the WPA assumed responsibility and, by the 1937–38 academic year, had hired 2,300 women who cooked and served free hot meals to 115,000 pupils daily.[12] When the WPA ended, the precedent of feeding hungry children was too well established to be dropped, and the La Guardia Administration agreed to cover the wages of the personnel who had been on the national payroll.[13]

Besides the education projects, the WPA conducted a host of recreational activities in schools, settlement houses, parks, orphanages, prisons, and on the city streets. At their peak, the New York recreation projects hired some six thousand men and women to supervise leisure-time activities that

July 1936, a group of children from Public School 41 visiting Inwood Park, where they were studying nature under the direction of Margaret Evans, a WPA instructor. This was part of a day-camp project operated by the Recreation Unit of the New York City WPA. *Photo by the New York City WPA.*

attracted over twelve million urban residents. The majority of those assigned to recreation jobs were white-collar unemployed without previous experience as social directors or counselors. To prepare them for their work, the WPA sent them to its Recreation Training School, where they learned a smattering of arts and crafts, puppetry, folk singing and dancing, and how to referee games.

Many of the recreation workers ran after-school centers. At the start of the decade, the Board of Education, faced with depression cutbacks, had to curtail almost all after-school activities. This reduction particularly hurt youngsters in slum areas, which lacked alternative, adult-supervised diversions. The mayor's commission on the causes of the 1935 race riot in Harlem commented on the wandering, neglected youths in the black ghetto. At 3:00 P.M. schools released thousands of children who had nowhere to go but the streets until their parents returned from jobs at six or seven o'clock. La Guardia's investigators found an "appalling" lack of playgrounds and recreation centers in the neighborhood.[14] With the assistance of federal work relief labor, however, the after-school programs began to function again. By 1937, 114 schools kept their doors open from three o'clock to ten on weekdays and for eight hours on Saturday. A staff of 375 regular teachers, augmented by 2,000 WPA instructors, led a program consisting of sports, handicrafts, dancing, and other arts. During the 1937–38 semesters, between 100,000 and 118,000 New Yorkers attended the centers daily. The Board of Education gave the WPA credit for involving youngsters in community recreation on a scale never before achieved.

Much of the WPA-generated recreation took place on city streets. With the cooperation of the police, WPA crews closed to traffic selected blocks and avenues in congested neighborhoods. Then they set up portable sports equipment and organized ball games, contests, and arts and crafts projects. Relief actors presented free outdoor performances; musicians gave concerts and played for street dances and festivals. The deputy police commissioner praised these efforts, saying: "The Works Progress Administration Street and Play Center Projects . . . have provided the bureau with a constructive program for the underprivileged and neglected youth of this city."[15]

As well as placing recreation directors in the schools and on the streets, the WPA also assigned personnel to playgrounds. When Alan Buxton's class in English for the Foreign Born ended in the summer of 1938, he was transferred to a playground in upper Manhattan. There his job consisted of checking out sports equipment, organizing games, and protecting the smaller youngsters from the bullying of the larger ones. He had a black WPA supervisor who came once a week to see how he was doing. On one occasion Buxton was eager for the weekly visit because a problem had arisen. His charges had tossed a ball through the windows of the neighboring apartment building once too often, and the landlord had called the police. An officer came to the playground and threatened "to beat the hell" out of Buxton if it happened again. Buxton related the story to his supervisor, who decided they should go to the station house to lodge a complaint. On their way, his supervisor commented to him: "What a chance we have—a colored guy and a Jew going in to complain against a New York cop!" In fact, no action ever was taken against the threatening officer.

Besides Buxton's individual problem, the education and recreation projects exhibited certain larger shortcomings that reduced their overall effectiveness. First, some of the local school administrators did not make as much use of welfare labor as they might have because they believed that the WPA was an emergency agency that the national government intended to curtail at the earliest signs of returning prosperity. Why put effort into developing new ventures when federally supported personnel might be withdrawn in a few months? Second, the conditions of WPA employment were not conducive to the highest teacher morale and performance. The work relief instructor had no chance for tenure or promotion. Indeed, like all WPA employees, the teacher or recreation director lived with the constant threat of layoffs and dismissals. Alan Buxton remembered the insecurity. "We knew that the WPA depended on continued Congressional appropriations. It could be phased out at any time." Also, the regular Board of Education employees "looked down on us." "They did not consider us full-fledged teachers," Buxton recalled. That is why, when in the fall of 1938 the Department of Sanitation offered him a job as a clerk, at a lower wage than he was earning on the WPA, he took it. At least it was a civil service position that offered some security.

Despite these drawbacks, the WPA contributed greatly to education and diversion in depression-struck New York. As a result of federal intervention, new schools were built and repairs made. Relief teachers instructed groups that had never been adequately served before, among them adult illiterates, the foreign born, and preprimary youngsters. The fields of adult and nursery school education expanded tremendously. The child from a low-income family received a free school lunch, the bedridden youngster was taught at home, and organized recreation brightened the life of many a city resident. In short, one can concur with the judgment of the President's Advisory Committee on Education: "An educational offering of major significance has been made available to the poor and needy."[16]

NOTES

1. New York Governor's Commission on Unemployment Relief, *Work Relief in the State of New York, A Report Submitted to Governor Herbert H. Lehman, August 10, 1936* (Albany, N.Y., 1936), p. 79; The Mayor's Commission on Conditions in Harlem, A Report on Social and Economic Conditions Responsible for the Outbreak of March 19, 1935, Submitted by Oswald Garrison Villard, chairman of the Educational Subcommittee, Fiorello La Guardia Papers, New York City Municipal Archives; U.S. WPA for N.Y.C., *The Administration of Work Relief in New York City, August 1936–December 1937*, Report of Brehon B. Somervell to Harry Hopkins (New York, 1938), pp. 353, 13, 10; U.S. WPA for N.Y.C., *Reports on*

Public Assistance to the Administrator of the Works Progress Administration for the City of New York, by Donald D. Lescohier (New York, 1939), pp. 258–59.

2. Between August 1935 and the end of 1937, the WPA spent more than $33 million on white-collar personnel services for the New York City Board of Education.

3. U.S. Advisory Committee on Education, *Educational Activities of the Works Progress Administration*, by Doak S. Campbell (Washington, D.C., 1939), p. 42; U.S. WPA for N.Y.C., *Administration of Work Relief*, pp. 350, 33; *School and Society*, 5 November 1938, pp. 594–96; U.S. WPA for N.Y.C., *Final Report of the Work Projects Administration for the City of New York, 1935 to 1943* (New York, 1943), pp. 192–93; Hopkins to All State FERA Administrators, 19 August 1933, Harry Hopkins Papers, Franklin D. Roosevelt Library, Hyde Park, N.Y.; FERA Letter A-26, 23 October 1933 and E-31, 25 July 1934.

4. As of 1940, among the 1,670 instructors on the N.Y.C. WPA, 431, or approximately 26 percent, had taught prior to their relief employment. Two hundred nineteen others held college diplomas, and 392 had completed one to three years of college. Another 302 were mechanics qualified by experience to teach vocational courses. U.S. Congress, House Subcommittee of the Committee on Appropriations, *Hearings on the Emergency Relief Appropriations Act of 1941*, 76th Cong., 3d sess. (Washington, D.C., 1940), p. 800.

5. Hopkins to All State Administrators, 25 July 1935, WPA Bulletin no. 19; U.S. WPA for N.Y.C., *Final Report*, p. 194; John D. Millett, *The Works Progress Administration in New York City* (Chicago, 1938), pp. 111–12; *New York Times*, 23 September 1936, p. 2; U.S. Advisory Committee, *Educational Activities of WPA*, p. 139; U.S. WPA for N.Y.C., *General Statistical Bulletin*, 31 August 1938, p. 7; U.S. WPA Bulletin no. 18, 23 July 1935.

6. In September 1936, President Roosevelt appointed an Advisory Committee on Education to make a study of federal aid to public schools. The group included prominent educators and social workers, such as Frank P. Graham, Katherine Lenroot, and Luther Gulick. The body published its findings in 1939, the report being written by two school administrators—Dr. Doak S. Campbell, dean of the Graduate School of Education of George Peabody College for Teachers, and Dr. Frederick H. Blair, superintendent of schools of Bronxville, N.Y. This report contained perhaps the most objective evaluation of the WPA education program ever compiled.

7. U.S. Advisory Committee, *Educational Activities of WPA*, pp. 4, 152; Letters protesting the end of WPA classes in 1943, Fiorello La Guardia Papers, New York City Municipal Archives; *Current History* 48 (May 1938): 58–59; New York *Herald Tribune*, 8 December 1936, p. 12; 24 June 1938, p. 21; U.S. WPA for N.Y.C., *Educational and Recreational Programs of*

182   THE NEW DEAL AND THE UNEMPLOYED

the U.S. Works Progress Administration in Cooperation with the Board of Education of the City of New York (New York, 1938); *Survey* 74 (September 1938): 288.

8. Interview of Dr. Alan Buxton by the author, 22 November 1976, Paramus, N.J.

9. U.S. WPA for N.Y.C., *Education and Recreation Programs; New York Sun,* 7 February 1938, school page; U.S. Advisory Committee, *Educational Activities of WPA,* pp. 70–71; U.S. Congress, House Subcommittee of the Committee on Appropriations, *Hearings on the Emergency Relief Appropriations Act of 1937,* 75th Cong., 1st sess. (Washington, D.C., 1936), p. 298; *Current History* 48 (May 1938): 58–59; "Negroes Under the WPA, 1939," *Monthly Labor Review* 50 (March 1940): 636–38; Caterina Cugganta and Mary Malonink to La Guardia, January 1943, La Guardia Papers, New York City Municipal Archives.

10. For a discussion of resurgent cultural nationalism, see Alfred Kazin, *On Native Ground* (New York, 1942), and Charles Alexander, *Nationalism in American Thought, 1930–1945* (Chicago, 1969).

11. "Citizenship Education for Aliens," *American City* 57 (September 1942): 79; U.S. Advisory Committee, *Educational Activities of WPA,* p. 110; *New York Times,* 28 February 1943, p. 46; U.S. WPA for N.Y.C., Record of Program Operation and Accomplishment of Nursery Schools and Parent Education and Cumulative Report for Nursery Schools and Parent Education, October 1933–December 1936, Papers of the U.S. WPA for N.Y.C., National Archives, Washington, D.C.; *Literary Digest,* 11 September 1937, p. 20.

12. City funds were used to buy the food, and the Home Making Division of the Board of Education selected the menu.

13. New York City Board of Education, *All of the Children,* Thirty-ninth Annual Report of the Superintendent of Schools for New York City, 1936–37, p. 33; New York City Board of Education, *All of the Children,* Fortieth Annual Report of the Superintendent of Schools for New York City, 1937–38, pp. 104, 107; *New York Times,* 30 September 1936, p. 20; *New York Herald Tribune,* 4 August 1937, p. 13; 11 June 1938, p. 8; U.S. WPA for N.Y.C., *Final Report,* p. 211.

14. *Survey* 74 (September 1938): 295; U.S. WPA for N.Y.C., The Recreation Program: Record of Operation and Accomplishment, Papers of the U.S. WPA for N.Y.C., National Archives, Washington, D.C.; U.S. WPA for N.Y.C., *Administration of Work Relief,* pp. 29, 31; Mayor's Commission on Conditions in Harlem, La Guardia Papers.

15. N.Y.C. Board of Education, *All of the Children,* Fortieth Annual Report, pp. 104, 107; *Survey* 74 (September 1938): 295; Byrnes MacDonald, deputy police commissioner, to La Guardia, 27 August 1936, La Guardia Papers, New York City Municipal Archives.

16. Interview of Dr. Alan Buxton, 22 November 1976; U.S. WPA for N.Y.C., Recreation Program, Papers of the U.S. WPA for N.Y.C.; U.S. Advisory Committee, *Educational Activities of WPA,* pp. 152, 157.

8

Unemployed Artists and the WPA

Along with clerks, teachers, and construction workers, artists felt the impact of the depression. Middle-class families gave up the luxury of attending concerts and plays in favor of buying food and paying rent. Museums and galleries, facing curtailed municipal budgets and dwindling private patronage, bought fewer paintings. Publishers became reluctant to take a chance on any but established authors. In New York City, long the mecca for creative talent from all over the country, the situation of the artist was particularly grave. In 1933 one-half of the legitimate theaters were dark, more than 50 percent of the actors were jobless, and the American Federation of Musicians announced that twelve thousand of its fifteen thousand members in the city were unemployed.

The Roosevelt Administration responded to the desperate plight of creative artists by initiating the first substantial aid to them in American history. Government projects to employ these citizens began with the FERA, expanded under the CWA, and reached a zenith with the WPA. To the critics who objected that the state had no business squandering money on aspiring dancers and thespians in the midst of our worst depression, Hopkins replied, "Hell! They've got to eat just like other people."

Although the arts program started primarily as a means of helping talented individuals weather the depression, the New Deal projects, before they ended in the early 1940s, accomplished several other significant things as well. They brought music, painting, and drama into the daily lives of more Americans than had enjoyed these arts in any previous decade. Many in WPA audiences, even in supposedly sophisticated New York, had never attended a professional show before. Unable to afford tickets to the Metropolitan Opera or Broadway offerings, they flocked to the free and low-priced entertainment that the government provided.[1] The projects also launched gifted young people into careers in the creative and performing arts. This impact was especially pronounced in the case of black writers, composers, actors, and painters, quite a few of whom gained their first recognition while on the federal payroll. Moreover, Washington's plunge into sponsorship of the arts was affected by and, in turn, influenced the resurgent cultural nationalism of the thirties.

Charles Alexander in *Nationalism in American Thought, 1930–1945* points out that artists in the depression years displayed "a heightened social awareness, a renewed interest in national values and traditions, and a yearning for a uniquely American statement." There was a "'rediscovery' of America in literature, the visual arts, and music." According to the literary critic Alfred Kazin, this patriotism was neither "blind" nor "parochial." Many writers and other creative intellectuals called for far-reaching reforms, perhaps even a revolution along Marxian lines. At the same time, in a world beset by economic collapse and menacing fascism, they sought reaffirmation in the country's past and the virtues of its people in all their heterogeneity.[2]

These currents of thought also affected the directors of the WPA arts projects. They set out to play more American music and perform more native drama than had hitherto been offered; to compile a record of native crafts; to write about the cities and counties, the ethnic groups and occupations that made up the United States; and to find, index, and preserve its historical documents. By doing these things the WPA further stimulated national consciousness, bringing an appreciation of the American scene to an ever-widening audience.

New York affords a particularly good vantage point for viewing the operations of the federal arts projects. There the WPA had the largest pool of unemployed talent to choose from. Consequently, the New York agency hired the most people, ran the biggest events, and spent the greatest sums of money. For example, in 1938 40 percent of all WPA painters lived in New York. This situation in all of the arts prompted one historian to say of the federal program: "New York City was the tail that wagged the dog."

If the experiment accomplished the most in New York, it also encountered some of its most difficult problems there. A good part of the city's intellectual and creative circles had been thoroughly radicalized by the depression. The artists and writers hired by the WPA frequently brought their Marxist persuasions along. At times this colored the plays they performed, the murals they painted, and the books they wrote. Inevitably, the question arose as to how much freedom of expression a tax-supported arts program could tolerate. Some project members accused the Roosevelt Administration of censorship, while critics of the New Deal constantly asserted that Hopkins and the president had allowed the Communists to take over the WPA and propagandize the nation at government expense.

Because Hopkins and his assistants realized that running projects for people in the creative arts presented certain unique problems, they organized a separate administrative setup for those endeavors. In the summer of 1935 they placed the program for artists, musicians, writers, and actors within a special Federal Project number 1, divided into four parts: the Federal Art Project, the Federal Music Project, the Federal Writers' Project, and the Federal Theatre. This organization was run by regional supervisors, all with some background in the respective arts, who reported directly to the capital rather than to the state administrators. In January 1936 two historical inventories were also placed under Federal Project number 1. Arts activities did not require a local sponsor, as construction and white-collar endeavors did, since Hopkins and his associates suspected that in many parts of the country there existed no authorities willing to contribute funds to cultural pursuits.

In New York this arrangement meant that the first three heads of the local WPA—Johnson, Ridder, and Somervell—prior to 1939 exercised little control over the arts units. The only exception was a brief period in the winter of 1936-37 during which Hopkins temporarily put the colonel in charge of making personnel cuts as an economy measure. Otherwise, each of the parts of Federal Project number 1 had its own New York regional administrator independent of the New York City WPA chief.[3] This was probably fortunate since, according to the head of the city artists' project, Somervell did not like or understand artists, and they distrusted him.

The WPA Federal Theatre in New York City was extremely active. In November 1938 it employed more than four thousand local residents, all but 15 percent of whom had come from the relief rolls. They included actors, stagehands, playwrights, and costume and set designers. These people were divided into such diverse units as children's and marionette companies; Negro, Yiddish, and German drama groups; the radio division; traveling caravans that gave free shows in the parks; the WPA circus; four vaudeville troupes; a Gilbert and Sullivan repertory theater; the dance project; and the "Living Newspaper."[4]

Much of the vitality of the Federal Theatre reflected the personality and beliefs of its national director, Hallie Flanagan. A former drama professor at Vassar and creator of its experimental workshop, she believed that the theater ought to be "a social and educative force" as well as a source of entertainment. As her first New York regional director she chose a man who shared her views, Elmer Rice. Rice was a Pulitzer Prize-winning playwright with such social protest works as *The Adding Machine* and *Street Scene* to his credit.

The "Living Newspaper" embodied many of the ideas of Hallie Flanagan and Elmer Rice. They conceived of it as a way to dramatize current social problems with techniques inspired by film newsreels like "The March of Time." Using charts, projections, loudspeakers, sudden spotlights and total blackouts, actors, stage sets, and illustrative skits, the Federal Theatre attempted to present issues such as depressed agriculture, slum housing, or public versus private ownership of electric power in a manner both fascinating and instructive.[5]

The New York Federal Theatre chose *Ethiopia* as its first "Living Newspaper" production. The directors decided on this topic because it was much in the headlines in 1935 and because one of the earliest groups of unemployed actors that welfare sent to the WPA was a stranded African troupe. Many of the members spoke no English, but they could "beat drums, sing and shout in the courtyard of Haile Selassie." The script was rapidly completed, rehearsals proceeded, and the curtain was to go up in January 1936.

Washington, however, began to have second thoughts about the total artistic freedom it had allowed its tax-supported thespians. The State Department feared a drama that portrayed Italy's aggression against Ethiopia might be considered an unfriendly gesture by Mussolini. Bowing to pressure from the diplomats, Hopkins's assistants ordered changes. Rice, incensed at what seemed to him unwarranted censorship, resigned and *Ethiopia* was never staged. Discouraged by this early fiasco, but not willing to abandon the idea of social documentary theater, Hallie Flanagan appointed Philip Barber, Rice's thirty-three-year-old assistant, to fill the vacant post. Barber announced that the WPA would immediately proceed with a second "Living Newspaper" dealing with the plight of agriculture.

On 14 March 1936, *Triple-A Plowed Under* opened. It dramatized the farm problem in the 1920s and 30s, ending with the Supreme Court's rejection of the Agricultural Adjustment Act and the renewed troubles that that decision produced. In the next few years the New York WPA presented *Injunction Granted,* showing the treatment of labor by the courts from a prounion position; *Power,* which explored the shortcomings of private utilities companies as opposed to the beneficial role of the TVA; and *One-Third of a Nation,* an exposé of the deplorable housing conditions in the city and the attempts to improve them through such federal legislation as the Wagner-Steagall Housing Bill.

These shows aroused much enthusiasm. John Gassner, in an essay on the modern American stage, claimed that the " 'Living Newspaper' gave rise to the one original form of drama developed in the United States." The theater critics for the *New York Times, Daily News,* and *Post* all commended *One-Third of a Nation.* Even when they did not like the message, reviewers sometimes hailed the "Living Newspaper" productions as good theater. Thus a *Life* magazine staff member dubbed *Power* "WPA Public Ownership Propaganda" but said that it was "exciting and unique."[6]

When this *Life* journalist called *Power* "WPA Public Ownership Propaganda," he raised an important issue: Did the New Deal improperly use the arts projects as vehicles to popularize the administration's policies? The answer appears to be somewhat complicated. There is no evidence that government officials encouraged the work relief personnel to write or produce any particular play. Nor were actors, directors, scriptwriters, or any other employees hired or fired because of their loyalty or opposition to Roosevelt and his program. However, during the depression, the majority of artists, both on and off the projects, tended to be liberal or radical. Therefore, they staged dramas that either backed New Deal reforms or advocated more far-reaching change.

Should Hopkins and his assistants have stepped in and censored those works that engaged in pro-New Deal or radical propaganda on the grounds that an arts program supported by the money of all the people must be neutral and avoid special pleading? Again, there is no easy answer. When, in fact, Washington did stop productions, as in the cases of *Ethiopia* or *The Cradle Will Rock,* it aroused anguished cries from the WPA artists that their First Amendment freedoms were being curtailed. On the other hand, one can certainly understand the anger of critics of the WPA who resented having their taxes used to propagandize for causes they disliked and to glorify a presidential program, while making those who opposed it look like selfish reactionaries. The popularity of these productions—they generally drew large audiences and enjoyed long runs—only heightened the fears of Republicans and anti-New Deal Democrats.

Regardless of the difficult political questions raised by the "Living Newspaper," it trained a number of talented people who later went on to distinguished careers on Broadway and in films. Joseph Losey, coauthor of *Injunction Granted,* became a leading director in the British movie industry during the 1960s with such highly acclaimed motion pictures as *The Servant, Accident,* and *The Go-Between* to his credit. Howard Bay, who designed the set for *One-Third of a Nation,* subsequently created the scenery for Lillian Hellman's *Little Foxes,* starring Tallulah Bankhead. Bay and Arthur Arent, who wrote the script for *Power,* both won Guggenheim Fellowships after their WPA years.

Reviving and adapting classical dramas got the WPA in far less trouble than did producing documentaries. During the 1936–37 season, John Houseman, one of the theater project's most gifted members, produced a French farce entitled *Horse Eats Hat.* The play was translated by Orson Welles, who also directed and starred in the comedy. Other members of the cast included Joseph Cotton and Arlene Francis, while Virgil Thomson created the musical score. The drama critic of the *World-Telegram* called the offering "a feast for the True Classicist." Fresh from this success, Welles and Houseman proceeded to Marlowe's *The Tragical History of Dr. Faustus,* with Welles playing Faustus. Some reviewers disliked Welles in the part, but almost all commended the production.

When the Welles-Houseman team left the classics for contemporary American drama, however, their relationship with the government turned stormy. The New York Federal

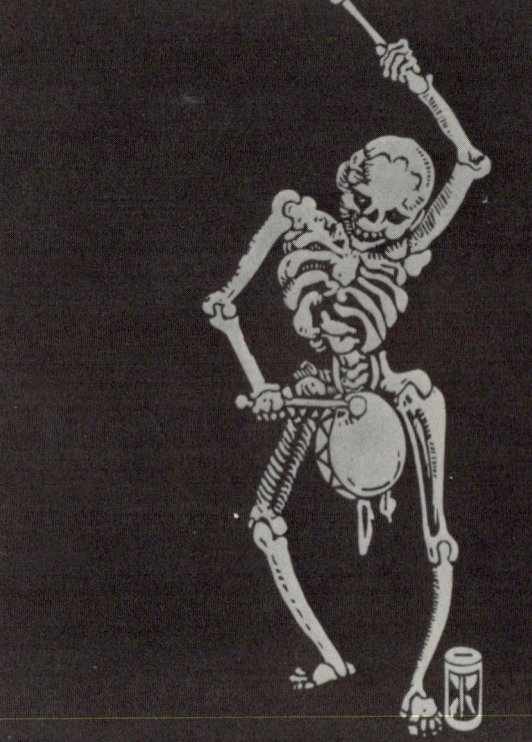

A poster designed by the artists of the WPA Poster Unit to advertise the opening of the Federal Theatre production *The Tragical History of Dr. Faustus*, starring Orson Welles. *Photo by the Photographic Division, Federal Art Project, WPA.*

Theater agreed to stage Marc Blitzstein's *The Cradle Will Rock,* a folk opera about a steel strike. The Roosevelt Administration, increasingly sensitive to the attacks on the WPA from conservatives, decided to be cautious. They would hold back the controversial musical until after Congress had voted the work relief appropriation, and orders arrived from Washington that no new shows could start until after 1 July 1937. Welles, terribly upset, flew to the capital to try to win an exemption from the ruling. When he failed to do so, Welles and Houseman left the WPA, rented a theater down the street, and opened *The Cradle Will Rock* as the first offering of the Mercury Theatre, which for several years thereafter was regarded as the most creative acting group on the American scene.[7]

A scene from the Federal Theatre production *The Tragical History of Dr. Faustus.* It shows Dr. Faustus (Orson Welles) announcing his decision to sell his soul for certain powers to the two magicians, Valdez (Bernard Savage) and Cornelius (Myron Paulson). *WPA Federal Theatre Photograph.*

Despite the row over *The Cradle Will Rock,* the Federal Theatre generally showed itself much more willing to take chances on new ventures than were commercial producers. One case in point involved T. S. Eliot's *Murder in the Cathedral.* The verse-drama had been running in a small house in London, where it received highly favorable reviews, but the financial backers of Broadway shows regarded it as a "difficult" piece unlikely to have much appeal. In the spring of 1936 the WPA presented *Murder in the Cathedral* and proved the over-cautious private investors wrong. The play enjoyed a long run during which over forty thousand people paid admission to see it. Not only did the gamble on the drama turn out well, but also the one on its star, Harry Irvine, who earned unanimous praise from the critics. He had been rejected for parts consistently by commercial managers because a slight tremor of his hands convinced them that he was too old for the stage.

While the Federal Theatre presented much adult fare, it did not neglect the youngsters. Prior to the depression perhaps one in thirty New York children under sixteen years of age had ever seen a professionally acted show. By 1937 WPA thespians had appeared at least once in the majority of public elementary schools, and about one-half of the city's pupils had attended these events. During the 1938 fall semester forty thousand students saw productions of *Macbeth, Twelfth Night, She Stoops to Conquer,* and *An Enemy of the People* when a WPA troupe toured the metropolitan high schools. The Children's Drama unit, staffed in large part by retrained vaudevillians, also presented works like *Hansel and Gretel* and *Pinocchio* in downtown theaters, where tickets sold for as little as five cents.[8]

The WPA arts projects came into being at a particularly opportune time for black performers. After a decade of promise and excitement during the Harlem Renaissance, black theater had fallen upon hard days. The Lafayette, at Seventh Avenue near 131st Street, which had attracted large audiences of whites and blacks in the 1920s, shut its doors in the early 1930s, leaving the ghetto community without a

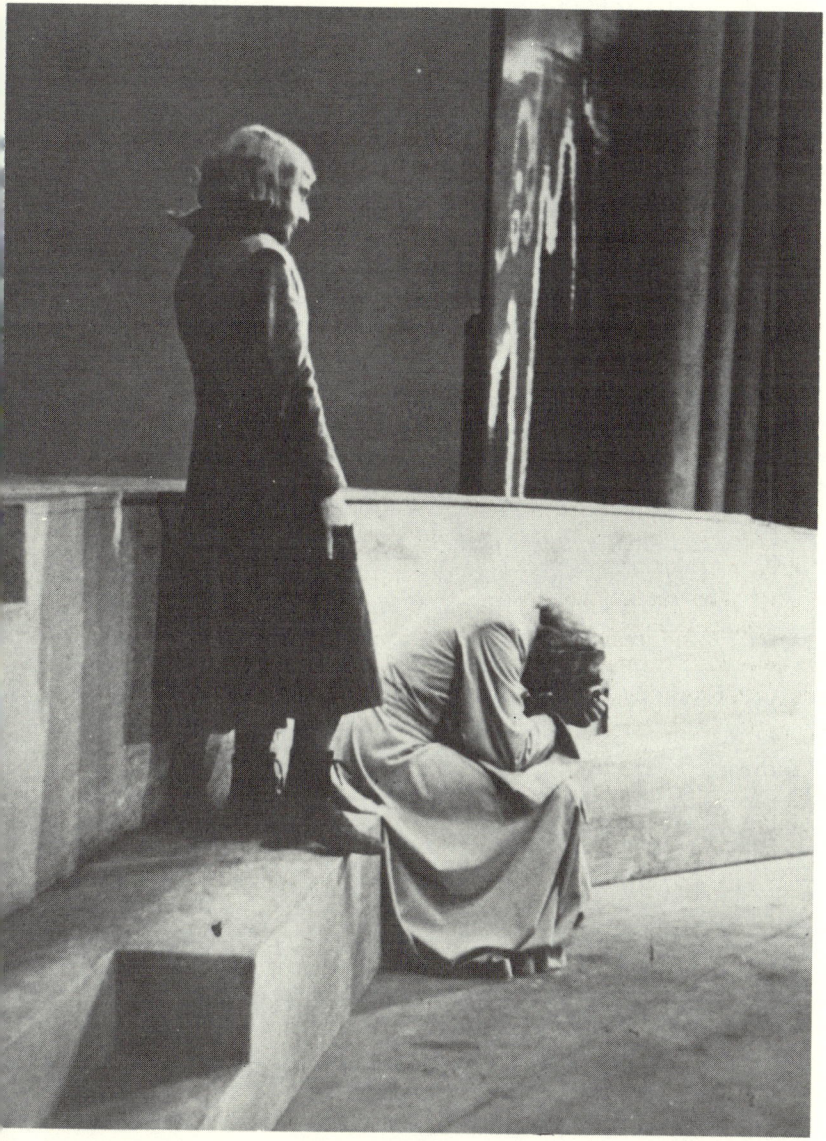

A scene from T. S. Eliot's *Murder in the Cathedral*, produced by the Federal Theatre Project in New York in 1936. *WPA Federal Theatre Photograph.*

single playhouse. Nor did Broadway give black actors much of a chance. Since the closing of *Porgy* and *The Green Pastures* at the beginning of the 1930s, there had not been a single successful show using an all-black cast.

In 1935 Rose McClendon, a veteran of the black stage, organized a committee of black actors to try to remedy the situation.[9] This group approached Hallie Flanagan with the idea of funding a black theater project in Harlem, and she readily assented. Soon the Lafayette players began rehearsing *Walk Together Chillun* by the black playwright Frank Wilson. It was one of the first WPA productions to open in New York. By 1937 black actors, retrieved from the welfare rolls, had offered eight shows to overflow crowds, the most acclaimed being an all-black *Macbeth* adapted from Shakespeare by Orson Welles.

The WPA, both at the Lafayette and in downtown houses, presented many new plays by and about blacks. These included *Haiti,* which dealt with the historic struggle of the island's blacks to throw off French slavery, and two works by Paul Green, *Unto Such Glory* and *Hymn to the Rising Sun.* In addition, the WPA began to develop black directors, such as Gus Smith, and set designers, like Perry Watkins. As Edith Isaacs of *Theatre Arts* stated, "No American theatre project . . . has meant more to Negro players . . . than the Federal Theatre did." It left behind in the minds of all involved with the stage "a fresh consciousness of what [the black] could really do, given the opportunity."

The WPA recognized the importance as performers or spectators of other minorities as well. Federal support did much to enliven Yiddish theater. The Jewish language unit presented an adaptation of *King Lear,* Clifford Odets's *Awake and Sing,* and Sinclair Lewis's *It Can't Happen Here,* as well as many classical Yiddish plays. Still another WPA company performed in German.

Whatever the project achieved was accomplished in the face of severe handicaps. WPA regulations were often in conflict with good theater practices. The prevailing-wage arrangement prevented actors from giving more than six performances a week or rehearsing more than four hours a day. That limitation could be crippling when a new play was in preparation. On top of that, actors who were in the casts of shows about to open frequently left to take outside jobs or were dropped from the rolls in personnel cutbacks. As a result, WPA productions remained in rehearsal longer than commercially backed theatrical events. Lincoln Kirstein, who was associated with the WPA for one week, handed in his resignation to Hallie Flanagan, saying: "How do you stand it? Requisitions, time sheets, inadequate rehearsal space, inferior pianos and *temperament*." Under these conditions it is not surprising that some of the WPA presentations were poorly chosen, badly staged, and amateurishly acted. What is more amazing is how many of them were hailed as first-rate.[10]

The history of the Federal Writers' Project closely parallels that of the drama unit in many respects. Like the theater program, it was created primarily to help individuals forced onto relief by the depression—in this case novelists, poets, playwrights, and journalists. In New York City, especially, stranded literary people abounded. There were writers, such as Maxwell Bodenheim and Anzia Yezierska, who had achieved recognition and fortune in the 1920s but who were now broke. Many journalists were jobless because their newspapers had folded. One writer had been sleeping in the subways prior to his WPA assignment; another, who had not eaten for three days, fainted when he received his first WPA check. In addition, the city harbored numbers of young people, like Lionel Abel, Ellen Tarry, Kenneth Fearing, and Ralph Ellison, who had just begun writing careers or dreamed of doing so when hard times set in.

Henry Alsberg, a newspaperman who had been a foreign correspondent for the *Nation* and an editorial writer for the New York *Post,* headed the Federal Writers' Project nationally. The first New York regional administrator, Orrick Johns, was a journalist, too.[11] Apparently, he talked his way into the post by arguing that, as a Communist, he would be able to understand and handle radicalized writers and their militant unions.

Alsberg wanted his writers to concentrate their efforts on the richly diverse national scene. The American Guide series appeared to be an excellent way to achieve this objective and at the same time create jobs for thousands of writers on welfare, including rank amateurs, literary hacks, and talented professionals. In each of the states and in New York City, project employees set to work collecting everything they could find on the history, topography, economy, population, art, and legends of their respective regions. Once they gathered their data, they compiled it into a set of guidebooks that, taken together, were intended to serve as a Baedecker for America. Alsberg hoped that these books would also shed light upon the roots from which the United States had grown, reveal its democratic tradition, stress the lifestyles and speech of its ordinary people, and point out the contributions of its minorities.[12]

In New York City, between 1935 and 1939, the local project spent the majority of its time on the American Guide series. The researchers and writers uncovered so much material that they decided to prepare two volumes on the community instead of one. The first, entitled *New York Panorama* (526 pp.), was published by Constable in 1939.[13] The book consisted of twenty-six essays covering the city's past, its people, commerce, art, literature, and so on. Random House brought out the second, called *New York City Guide* (680 pp.). It was reissued in 1970 by Octagon Press. This volume contained descriptions of each of the neighborhoods and their major points of interest.

Allan Angoff worked on the New York guides. He supervised a staff of junior and senior journalists who gathered information for the section on historical monuments and landmarks. Each morning he handed out assignments, such as finding out everything—visiting hours, physical description, history—about the Poe Cottage in The Bronx. When the researcher had done this, he handed in an essay about

Walter Winchell, at NBC Radio, reading from *New York Panorama*, the first of two guidebooks on New York City produced by the Federal Writers' Project. *Photo by the Photographic Division of the Federal Art Project, WPA.*

the particular place of interest. Many of these compositions, Angoff thought, were quite poor, some almost unintelligible. The low quality of the work did not surprise Angoff, since in the early days elevator operators, clerks, salesmen, and other unqualified individuals talked their way onto the project. Then he and other supervisors covered for the incompetents because these people needed the jobs. "One just hoped they'd somehow disappear," Angoff recalled. Mixed in with these nonwriters were highly talented persons. One day in 1936 Angoff heard that a transferee from the Chicago writers' unit was joining his group. The name of the as-yet-unpublished author was Richard Wright. It was the minority of skilled writers and editors who eventually reworked and edited the material into readable form. These men and women included Richard Wright, John Cheever, William Rollins, Jr., and Charlotte Wilder (sister of Thornton Wilder).

The guidebooks, including the two New York ones, received generally favorable reviews when they first appeared, and critics ever since have regarded them as important in the history of American letters. Charles Alexander in *Nationalism in American Thought, 1930–1945* says of them:

> In this vast compendium of historical, geographical, cultural, and economic information, the nation was introduced to itself in uniquely comprehensive fashion. Far from Chamber of Commerce brochures, they embodied a literal rediscovery of America, part of the national turning inward in search of assurance during the Depression years.

To Alfred Kazin the guides represent "an extraordinary contemporary epic." He goes on: "The WPA Guides became something more than a super-Baedeker: [they] became a repository as well as a symbol of the reawakened American sense of its own history."

While the guides contained many sections devoted to minorities in each community, the Writers' Project also decided to produce monographs featuring particular ethnic groups. The WPA had special units working on New York's Jews, Italians, Irish, and Poles. The first study they finished, *The Italians of New York*, was published in English by Random House in 1938. It contained material on the heritage, customs, and achievements of the 1,070,000 Italian-Americans of the city. The following year the book appeared in Italian, and Arno Press reprinted the English edition in 1969. In 1939 a book dealing with the Jews, *The Landmanschaften of New York*, was published in Yiddish. When the project ended, manuscripts on the Irish, Poles, and an additional one concerning the Jews were nearly completed.

The federal writers also stimulated interest in black studies. The black unit began for the dual purpose of hiring unemployed black authors and shedding light on the history of Afro-Americans, a topic that up to that time had been largely neglected. In New York approximately thirty staff members worked in this division, including at one time or another some of the leading black literary figures. Ralph Ellison, who later wrote *The Invisible Man,* served his apprenticeship on the black-studies project. Claude McKay, the West Indian-born writer, was a colleague of Ellison's. He had achieved fame during the twenties with his poems and his best-selling novel, *Home to Harlem* (1928). His job on the WPA in the thirties fed him, and he was able to use some of the data gathered by the black unit in his last book, *Harlem: Negro Metropolis* (1940).

Although the New York WPA never produced a work on the black during the lifetime of the organization, it did utilize information collected by the black-studies group in the New York City guides. Since the demise of the federal agency, moreover, at least two books have drawn upon this source material. Roi Ottley, who supervised the undertaking, was laid off in the extensive cutbacks of 1939. Fearing that the records of his black project would be mislaid and forgotten, he took them with him. He retained possession of the papers long enough to enable him to write *New World A-Coming,* published in 1943, which received the Houghton Mifflin "Life in America" annual award. When he had finished with the WPA documents, he presented them to the Schomburg Collection of the New York City Library, where they are still held. Later Ottley collaborated with W. J. Weatherby in editing some of the unfinished manuscripts and gathering them into a volume entitled *The Negro in New York: An Informal Social History,* finally issued by the New York Public Library and Oceana Press in 1967.

The New York writers did not confine themselves to studies of the metropolis and its people. They turned out several works in the field of natural history, such as *Who's Who in the Zoo,* first issued in 1937 and reprinted in 1969; *Birds of the World* (1938); *Reptiles and Amphibians* (1939); and *American Wild Life Illustrated* (1940), which became a best-seller, quickly exhausting an edition of twenty-five thousand. It was reissued with a different format in 1954. The WPA treated an entirely different subject in *The Film Index: A Bibliography,* published by H. W. Wilson and Co. (1941). All told, by the early 1940s the employees of the local project completed and found commercial outlets for twenty books.[14]

When the directors of the WPA originally drew up the plans for a writers' project, they discussed whether to allow some authors to work individually on their own novels, short stories, plays, and poetry. Ultimately, they decided against permitting this since they felt that the quite limited hours that the organization required of its personnel would leave the writers plenty of free time to pursue outside interests. Although this remained the official position of the Federal Writers' Project throughout, Henry Alsberg secretly told a few members of the New York agency that they might stay home to engage in creative writing. Edward Dahlberg, Maxwell Bodenheim, Claude McKay, Harry Roskolenko, Anzia Yezierska, and Richard Wright were among the elite who exercised that privilege now and again. Apparently, Richard Wright made the most of his opportunity. During these years he won a prize for a short story that was later published as a part of *Uncle Tom's Children* and began his most famous novel, *Native Son.*

The Writers' Project, of course, had its share of problems. There were the malingerers and people with no writing skill who weren't worth the wages they received. There were also a number of alcoholics on the New York project. Inadequate job quotas and the repeated cutbacks caused fear and insecurity, which, according to Allan Angoff, lowered employee morale. Charges of Communist intrigue and domination attached to the project from beginning to end. The radicalism was almost inevitable. As Charles Alexander points out, "In one way or another, perhaps a majority of American writers during the thirties were influenced by theories of economic determinism, class struggle, capitalist decadence and proletarian revolution." Further, the Marxists divided into factions, most falling into either the Stalinist or Trotskyist camp.

The battles among the leftists kept the New York WPA in a turmoil. The Stalinists constantly attacked the Trotskyists in a Communist paper called *Red Pen,* which circulated among project members. The Trotskyists countered with their pamphlets. Harry Roskolenko, a poet belonging to the latter group, years later was still hurling bitter accusations against the pro-Soviet ranks. He asserted that Communist supervisors "flooded the Project with half-authors who had published only in their own minds." These incompetents used their government jobs "to write propaganda leaflets summoning the workers . . . to various ramparts." Moreover, they "wanted physical domination of the Writers' Project to sponsor Stalin, Red picnics, proletarian literature, full-assed and half-assed proletarian dancers and to fire all the Trotskyists and other dissenters."[15] With the office so full of intrigue, one wonders how they managed to finish any books at all.

The music program represented a third division of Federal Project number 1. Nikolai Sokoloff, its national administrator, had achieved wide recognition in the field as organizer and, for fifteen years, leader of the Cleveland Symphony. For his New York regional director, Sokoloff chose Chalmer Clifton, a composer who taught classes on conducting at Columbia University. Clifton had founded the American Orchestral Society, which in the twenties prepared young players in New York for concert careers.

During the fall of 1935 the Federal Music Project placed some two thousand New Yorkers on its payroll. In order to be hired, the musician on welfare had to pass qualifying auditions held by a board of six examiners—half drawn from the agency's supervisory staff, the rest from outside critics and performers. Approximately eight hundred of the original employees worked as music teachers in the public schools, settlement houses, WPA music centers, and many other institutions. The remainder were assigned to symphony orchestras, chamber music ensembles, military bands, dance orchestras, and choirs.

Besides providing for indigent musicians, the WPA specified as one of its objectives bringing music into the lives of more Americans. It proceeded to do this in many ways. In New York the project ran an extensive education program. During 1938 forty-four thousand children and adults received free instruction weekly in playing musical instruments, singing, and composing. The project also opened a concert hall called the Federal Music Theatre on West Fifty-fourth Street. There audiences could hear, at a top price of fifty-five cents a ticket, performances featuring the music of Beethoven, Tchaikovsky, Brahms, Sibelius, Wagner, and others. James Agate of the Sunday *London Times* described one of these concerts:

> We saw an elegant theatre half full of a wholly attentive audience with its gaze fixed upon a stage bare as one thought only Russian stages can be bare. The band of thirty contained two women, one of whom was the leader (concertmistress). I thought it played about as well as the best English amateurs.

The Music Project placed its ninety or so most talented performers in the New York City WPA Symphony Orchestra. After hearing them in rehearsal, Sir Adrian Boult, the British musical director, stated that they "play with fine precision and accuracy." In 1939 this group gave a series of six programs at the City Center Theater. Each event packed the house, and many people had to be turned away. Equally popular were the weekly Sunday-evening concerts held at Carnegie Hall season after season. At every performance a famous musical personality appeared as guest conductor or soloist without pay. Among the notables featured were Sir Thomas Beecham, Fritz Reiner, Otto Klemperer, and Ronald Hayes.[16]

The enthusiastic response of the New York public to these programs indicated that there was a large potential audience for classical music that had gone untapped because concert tickets cost more than many could afford. V. F. Calverton in *Current History* made this point when he proclaimed: "Music has been financially confined to the Classes and not to the masses. Thanks to the WPA Music Project (and also the radio) that is no longer the case."

The WPA, however, did not offer only classical music. On 8 June 1937 the federal agency inaugurated "The People's Night Club" in Central Park. More than three thousand couples came to while away the night to the tunes of a WPA swing band. The energetic youths vied to outdo each other as they danced the Shag, the Lindy, Flea Hops, the Westchester, and the Peabody. Between numbers the delighted New Yorkers set up a mighty cheer: "Ray for Roosevelt." The evening reached a high point when Paul

The Knickerbocker Dance Orchestra, a unit of the WPA Federal Music Project, playing for a free public dance at the Central Park Mall. *Photo by the Art Service Project, WPA.*

Whiteman dropped in and led the band in a few selections. From then on the WPA repeated the free dances every Tuesday and Thursday night on the Central Park Mall. Those who could not make it in person could listen to the music over the municipal radio station. Or if one liked the pace faster and hotter, one could travel uptown to Harlem, where on the same evenings a black jazz band played for a street dance between 150th and 151st.

In addition to bringing music to ever-larger audiences, the WPA attempted to encourage American talent. Apparently, native composers felt that such an effort was badly needed. They complained that their creations were largely ignored by the European-born directors who led most of the major symphony orchestras in this country. Roy Harris, for instance, accused "foreign conductors and soloists" of "denying American creative musicians the right to speak to the American people."

Soon after the project began, Nikolai Sokoloff announced that if American composers submitted their works to a national audition board, suitable ones would be performed by WPA musicians. The agency kept this promise. During the 1935–36 season, approximately one-fifth of the music played by the local project was written by Americans. In 1939 the New York unit gave premiers to nine new American compositions, and each year during National Music Week the WPA devoted a substantial portion of its activities to promoting native music, whether folk, jazz, or symphonic. All of this led Olin Downes, *Times* music critic, to observe that no other musical organization had given as much attention to American composers as the New York City WPA.[17]

The WPA initiated a rather unique experiment, designed to bridge the gap between the contemporary artist and the public, known as the Composers' Forum Laboratory. Each Wednesday a different composer was invited to present his creations to a live audience at the Federal Music Theatre. The evening started with the distribution of a printed sheet containing facts about the featured individual and his music. Next, a work relief orchestra, sometimes conducted by the composer himself, played the piece. Afterward came a discussion, with the composer replying to questions and comments from those in attendance. Aaron Copland, Roy Harris, Virgil Thomson, Daniel Gregory Mason, and Marc Blitzstein were among those who presented their works. Ferde Grofe, composer of the *Grand Canyon Suite,* because of these forums and other WPA activities, predicted:

> When many of our sturdy schools and bridges and public buildings have passed with the weight of years, some of the music brought to public performance by governmental intervention in a relief emergency may still be played and sung by generations of Americans. The dawn of a music culture identifiably America's own . . . is already discernible on the horizon.

The WPA aided young performers even more directly than it did composers. Some musicians received their first chance to learn conducting while on the federal payroll. Others, comparatively new to ensemble playing, gained experience and polish. The work relief apprenticeship led to desirable outside positions for quite a few. Twenty-year-old Frank Gullino, for one, had studied the violin since he was eight, but in 1935 he could not find work as a musician. After approximately a year with the WPA Symphony, however, Gullino tried out for the Metropolitan Opera Orchestra, was hired, and became the group's youngest member.

As with all of the subdivisions of Federal Project number 1, the Music Project extended its help to talented blacks as well as to whites. WPA orchestras frequently featured selections of contemporary black composers such as William Grant Still, Clarence Cameron White, and Julian Work. The New York unit contained a number of all-black groups, including the Melody Singers, the Art Singers, an instrumental trio, and several jazz bands. An all-black cast performed Verdi's opera *Il Trovatore,* and black musicians held supervisory and teaching jobs alongside Caucasians.

While the Music Project generally escaped the charges of

A performance of the WPA Composers' Forum Laboratory at the Federal Music Theatre on West Fifty-fourth Street in New York. Aimed at encouraging native talent, this unit of the Federal Music Project presented the works of both established and unknown American composers. *Photo by the Photographic Division, Federal Art Project, WPA.*

Communist infiltration flung at its sister units, it shared some of their other problems. The small nonrelief quota (eventually cut to 5 percent of total personnel) made it difficult to attract enough qualified concert masters, directors, and soloists. The WPA allotted inadequate funds for purchasing new music for its orchestras and arrangements for its dance bands, which limited their repertories unnecessarily. And rapid turnover of members, especially after 1939, when Congress imposed an eighteen-month maximum on WPA employment, hurt the performance of work relief musical groups.[18]

The New York artists' program differed from its counterparts—the drama, writing, and music projects—in the continuity of its leadership. As early as the time of the Gibson Committee, Audrey McMahon began to organize assistance for painters. She remained in charge of these efforts in the community through the TERA, FERA, CWA, and WPA periods, staying with the last agency until its demise in 1943. McMahon proved to be a tough, aggressive executive, ready to do battle for her artists against all adversaries. Somervell, after a few encounters, dubbed her "the Iron Woman." She held a degree in art from the Sorbonne; during the twenties she had edited *Parnassus* and become head of the College Art Association. When Hopkins began to plan a Federal Art Project in 1935, he solicited her advice, as well as offering her the post of national administrator. McMahon turned this down but agreed to head the New York office.

The top job went instead to Holger Cahill, an authority on folk art, a respected critic, and a museum technician who had served on the staff of the Museum of Modern Art. Cahill and McMahon, although their personalities sometimes clashed, had the same basic objectives. They shared a passionate concern for destitute artists. They also saw the emergency situation as an opportunity to encourage new talent, increase the nation's awareness of art, and give full expression to whatever was unique in American artistic development.

Their project in New York began with approximately eleven hundred people and briefly reached a peak of almost three thousand. The most talented and experienced easel painters were allowed to create their own canvases at home or in their studios. The top individuals in the Mural and Sculpture Divisions labored on assignments for such clients as hospitals, libraries, schools, and airports. Those with less skill became members of the poster unit, the Index of American Design, the art teaching staff, or were placed as assistants to muralists and other craftsmen.

A large portion of today's prominent artists once worked for the New York WPA. Some of them had achieved con-

Sculptors of the Federal Art Project at work. *Photo by the WPA Federal Art Project.*

siderable recognition prior to their federal employment: Arnold Blanch, Don Freeman, Emil Ganso, Yasho Kuniyoshi, Edward Laning, Raphael Soyer, and Harry Sternberg had all sold at least one painting to the New York Metropolitan Museum. Others, little known when they joined the project, gave the WPA credit for encouraging their careers. Joseph Solman, president of the Federation of Modern Painters and Sculptors from 1965 to 1967, claimed that he and his friends in the easel division, Ilya Bolotowsky, Mark Rothko, and Louis Harris, "found the WPA indispensable for our development as artists." Herman Rose, whose paintings now hang in many New York galleries, stated flatly: "I do not know if I could have even continued to be an artist if not for the WPA."[19]

Besides employing painters and sculptors, the WPA attempted to bring the artist and the public together. One way was education. Before the program ended, it had given free art lessons to some two million municipal residents, who attended classes held at museums, settlement houses, schools, and WPA-operated centers. The agency ran its own galleries, where it displayed the creations of its personnel. During the summers, the project participated in outdoor festivals, such as the ones held in Washington Square Park. In addition, WPA posters, prints, oils, and sculpture adorned hundreds of public institutions in the community. All that a nonprofit organization needed to do to acquire the objects was pay for the materials used in their construction.

Murals, above all, fitted into the scheme of producing art for the masses. New York project members painted over two hundred of them in places such as airports, hospitals, libraries, and housing developments, where thousands would see them daily. Many of the people employed by the Mural Division took their inspiration from the Mexican school of the twenties and thirties (especially Diego Rivera and Jose Clemente Orozco). They frequently imitated both the Latin style, with its bold impressionistic images, and the social message. WPA mural painters often chose themes that honored minority groups, celebrated the working class, chronicled American history, and protested against economic injustice. At times, left-wing sentiments incorporated in paintings aroused a storm of controversy, such as that over Ben Shahn's murals at the prison at Riker's Island.

Opinion on the esthetic worth of these murals still varies. Holger Cahill, reminiscing about his organization many years later, concluded that much of the work was inferior because American artists lacked a tradition of mural painting. At the time, however, a number of the efforts were cited for excellence. The New York Architectural League voted a gold medal, its highest annual award, to James Michael Newell for his series of frescoes, *The Growth of Western Civilization*, on the walls of the library of Evander Childs High School in The Bronx. At the 1939 World's

Artist James Michael Newell at work on his series of frescoes *The Growth of Western Civilization* at Evander Childs High School, 800 East Gunhill Road, Bronx, New York. *Photo by the Federal Art Project, WPA, New York City.*

Fair first prize for the best outdoor painting went to Philip Guston for his mural on the front of the WPA exhibition hall.

The WPA murals that have probably been viewed more than any others by New Yorkers over the past thirty years (though few people know of their origin) cover the walls and ceiling of the lobby adjoining the third-floor reading room in the New York Public Library on Fifth Avenue and Forty-second Street. Executed by Edward Laning, in a style that owes more to Rubens than Rivera, they depict the story of the recorded word from Moses receiving the Tablets of the Law through Mergenthaler and the Linotype.[20]

Although the majority of New York artists in the thirties, many of whom joined the militant Artists' Union, took the position that during a depression art should be representational in style and socially crusading in content, a minority had begun to experiment with abstraction. Left-wingers generally looked upon this innovation as "escapist" and indifferent to the suffering of the masses, but, to the credit of the WPA, it did not insist that its employees adhere to any line. In fact, a number of its New York artists, such as Stuart Davis, Byron Browne, and Ilya Bolotowsky, painted nonrepresentational oils and murals.

Probably the best-known American abstract artist, Jackson Pollock, first tried his wings in the new style while on the New York WPA. Pollock had been painting in the American landscape genre of Thomas Hart Benton. Then for about a week he did not show up at the project headquarters. Burgoyne Diller, his supervisor, went to his home to find out what was wrong. When Diller arrived, Pollock told him, "I can't do this stuff that I'm doing for you any more. I've given it up." Instead, Pollock showed Diller some abstract expressionist work he had started. The WPA executive immediately responded, "Well, that's alright. Paint as you want to. We're not going to tell you how to paint." This attitude prompted one historian of the WPA arts program to say that "the artist during his employment on the Federal Art Project enjoyed a freedom of expression that was almost unprecedented in the history of art."

As with the Federal Theatre, the Art Project came at a particularly opportune time for black Americans. In the 1920s the work of black artists was just starting to gain access to professional galleries and be recognized by the informed public. The depression, however, threatened these hopeful beginnings. Private patronage, which diminished for white painters, all but disappeared for blacks.

Alain Locke, who first called attention to the emergence of the black art movement known as the Harlem Renaissance, attributed its survival in the thirties to the WPA. He stated:

> All, indeed, would have been disastrously nipped in the bud but for the timely intervention of the Federal Art Projects. The generous inclusion of the Negro artist in these programs has not only saved the very existence of creative art among us, but . . . has been responsible for the production of the present flowering of the younger Negro art.

James Porter in his *Modern Negro Art* makes much the same observation: "Young talents are being recruited constantly to the ranks of the Negro artists. Most of them have been given their first chance to work on equal terms with white artists through the WPA Federal Art Projects."

As of July 1937, the New York project had 3 black supervisors and employed 115 black artists. These included Charles Alston, Palmer Hayden, Gwendolyn Bennett, Ronald Joseph, and Robert Pious. Through the subject matter of many of their paintings and murals, these artists furthered the awakening interest in black history and culture. In addition, the WPA ran an outstanding free school in the black community. The Harlem Art Center, under the direction of Gwendolyn Bennett, operated out of a building at 125th Street and Lenox Avenue from 1937 to 1941. There a staff of black and white artists conducted classes, both day and evening, for adults and children. Porter says of the center that the training it offered "was the equal of several professional art schools in New York City."[21]

Another undertaking of the Federal Art Project, the Index of American Design, reflected the renewed interest in the country's heritage. Charles Alexander refers to it as "one of the most brilliant manifestations of American nationalism in the 1930's." Former illustrators, commercial artists, and others not talented enough to create original paintings and sculpture set to work compiling a pictorial record of native decorative, practical, and folk arts from the colonial period to 1890. These people tracked down such handmade items as ship figureheads, tobacco-store Indians, weather vanes, and old Western guns in antique shops, back-country farmhouses, and museums. They made watercolors or drawings of the items, accompanying each with a data sheet that told something about the background of the piece and its craftsman. When the Art Project ended in 1943, twenty thousand of these plates—seven thousand of which were done in New York—were deposited in the National Gallery of Art. Every year since then art historians, teachers, designers, and others have consulted this index, and at least two books have been published using a portion of the archive—Edwin O. Christiansen, *The Index of American Design* (1950) and Clarence Hornung, *Treasury of American Design* (1972).

Like its sister projects, the art program suffered from problems that hampered its production. Quota cutbacks frequently threatened to leave half-finished murals without their painters. Edward Laning, for instance, was on the verge of receiving a pink slip in the midst of his New York Public Library assignment, and only his vigorous protest and Audrey McMahon's special intervention saved him. Even when individuals did escape being laid off, the insecurity took its toll. According to McMahon, "a horrifying uncertainty as to the duration of Project employment . . . seeped down to the artists and was vastly detrimental to their efforts and morale." The Communist-backed unions also interfered with hiring and firing and tried to influence artistic style and content. Holger Cahill stated: "I know there were a lot of things very shoddily done on the New York Project. One of the reasons for that was that there was so much left-wing activity up there. It was really scandalous."

Despite these shortcomings, Barbara Rose in *American Art Since 1900: A Critical History* calls the WPA a "unique but crucial chapter in American art." It allowed the artist to paint full time, giving him a sense of professionalism he had never known before. Young novices were supplied with the materials and opportunity to develop their own craftsmanship and style. The group activities created an esprit de corps among artists, especially in New York, that lasted well into the forties, and the exhibitions, classes, and murals aroused a new consciousness of art in the country.[22]

A woodcut, *Bar and Grill*, designed and executed by Eli Jacobi, who was employed on the Federal Art Project in New York City. *Photo by the Federal Art Project, WPA, New York City.*

The last-organized and smallest unit of Federal Project number 1, the historical surveys, again illustrate the heightened interest in the nation's past that was so prevalent in the thirties, and the WPA contribution to stimulating an appreciation of America's heritage. Luther Evans, an unemployed history and political science professor, became head of the Historical Records Survey, which undertook to locate, preserve, and inventory important state, county, and municipal documents. The Survey of Federal Archives, directed by Philip Hamer, on loan from the National Archives, sought to do the same thing with United States government papers housed outside of Washington.

Early in 1936 the two projects got underway. Employees of the Historical Records Survey began to invade the cellars of county courthouses, the subbasements of city halls, storerooms attached to churches, and old warehouses. There they frequently found long-neglected, poorly arranged, decaying documents. They generally started their labors with such necessary tasks as cleaning and sorting the papers. Then they took inventory of what they had uncovered. In New York City the Historical Records Survey eventually published a guide to manuscript depositories in the urban area, including the hitherto almost-untapped source of church-held records.

The New York Historical Records Survey, with the aid of Columbia University historian Clifford Lord, also turned out a two-part work entitled *Executive Orders Numbered 1–8030, 1862–1938*. The first volume consisted of an introduction by Lord discussing the increasing importance of the executive order, followed by abstracts of the orders arranged chronologically. The second book contained an index by subject matter of the orders included in volume 1. Persons other than historians apparently thought that this work was badly needed. A member of the New York Bar Association stated that such a source was "indispensable" to anyone interested in presidential authority from a judicial, legislative, or administrative point of view.

The Survey of Federal Archives in New York meanwhile proceeded under the guidance of Richard Morris, an assistant professor at the City University. Morris and his staff of about two hundred found the papers of the United States Government just as deplorably stored as those of the state and municipality. At the old Customs House, which held the largest collection of federal records in any single building outside Washington, they discovered the bulk of the noncurrent papers in a subbasement shared with discarded furniture, a steam plant, and an emergency boiler. Many of the documents had simply been dumped in two huge piles, nicknamed by the WPA personnel Mounts Vesuvius and Aetna. This became the first attack area as the WPA workers sorted, arranged, and catalogued the contents of those heaps.

Subsequently, the survey explored other locations that yielded forgotten records very worth preserving. Among the holdings of the District Court of the Southern District of New York were documents about the undeclared war with France between 1798 and 1801, papers concerning the Embargo before the War of 1812, and cases that shed light on the operations of the blockade and blockade-runners during the Civil War.[23]

What, then, may one conclude about the myriad of activities referred to collectively as Federal Project number 1? Certainly, this first experiment with government-sponsored arts and scholarship had its weaknesses, which made it very vulnerable to attacks by conservatives. The performances of WPA orchestras and theater companies were at times amateurish. Some of the murals and plays abounded in leftwing propaganda. A certain proportion of the personnel were misfits and incompetents who had somehow convinced interviewers that they could write, paint, or act. Communists and their followers engaged in office intrigue and tried to establish control over hiring, firing, and other policy decisions.

Nonetheless, the arts projects represent the most daring and humanizing segment of the New Deal unemployment relief efforts. For the first time in America's history, the federal government concerned itself with the welfare of artists, writers, musicians, actors, and scholars, not only supporting those who had already established their reputations, but encouraging young people with promise, as well. The works that these individuals on the government payroll produced served to enrich American life during the depression with music, color, and drama, reaching parts of the population previously barely touched by the arts. The WPA program, furthermore, combined with the cultural nationalism prevalent in the thirties to arouse a new interest in American history, literature, crafts, music and the diverse ethnic, racial, and religious groups that made up the United States.

NOTES

1. When admission was charged at WPA events, it generally ranged from fifteen to fifty-five cents.

2. Jane D. Mathews, *The Federal Theatre, 1935-1939* (Princeton, N.J., 1967), p. 23; William F. McDonald, *Federal Relief Administration and the Arts* (Columbus, Ohio, 1969), pp. 585-86; Robert Sherwood, *Roosevelt and Hopkins*, 2 vols. (New York, 1948), 1:71; Charles Alexander, *Nationalism in American Thought, 1930-1945* (Chicago, 1969), p. xi; Alfred Kazin, *On Native Ground* (New York, 1942), p. 488.

3. A single administrator, Paul Edwards, acted as business manager for all parts of Federal Project no. 1 in the New York region.

4. McDonald, *Federal Relief Administration*, pp. 383, 399, 400, 524; Alexander, *Nationalism in American Thought*, p. 5; Jacob Baker to All State Administrators, WPA Bulletin no. 7, 2 August 1935, Harry Hopkins Papers, Franklin D. Roosevelt Library, Hyde Park, N.Y.; U.S. WPA for N.Y.C., *Final Report of the Work Projects Administration for the City of New York, 1935 to 1943* (New York, 1943), p. 229; Arthur Macmahon et al, *The Administration of Work Relief* (Chicago, 1941), p. 253; Audrey McMahon, "A General View of the Federal Art Projects," in *The New Deal Art Projects: An Anthology of Memoirs*, ed. Francis V. O'Connor (Washington, D.C., 1972), p. 56.

5. Moreover, this kind of production suited the needs of work relief. The scripts were written by authors and newsmen on the WPA payroll, creating jobs for these people and saving royalties that would have to be paid otherwise. Also documentary drama, filled with crowd scenes and bit parts, utilized lots of actors, some of whom were not overly talented.

6. Hallie Flanagan, *Arena* (New York, 1940), pp. 45, 54, 120, 70–71, 65–67; Elmer Rice, *The Living Theatre* (Westport, Conn., 1972), pp. 149–53; U.S. WPA Federal Theatre, Summary of Activities to September 1938, A Report to Hopkins by Hallie Flanagan, p. 6, Papers of the U.S. WPA for N.Y.C., National Archives, Washington, D.C.; McDonald, *Federal Relief Administration*, pp. 508, 553; Mathews, *Federal Theatre*, pp. 62, 63–66, 69; *New York Times*, 28 January 1936, p. 15; 14 February 1936, p. 22; John Gassner, ed., *A Treasury of the Theatre from Henrik Ibsen to Arthur Miller* (New York, 1956), pp. 780–81; Brooks Atkinson, *New York Times*, 2 May 1937, sec. 11, p. 1; 30 January 1938, sec. 10, p. 1; New York *Daily News*, 18 January 1938, p. 16; New York *Post*, 18 January 1938, p. 6; *Life*, 22 March 1937, pp. 22–23.

7. Flanagan, *Arena*, pp. 217–21, 202–203; Mathews, *Federal Theatre*, pp. 299, 170; New York *World-Telegram*, 28 September 1936, p. 12; Edith Isaacs, *Theatre Arts* 21 (March 1937): 184–85.

8. "Unemployed Arts: WPA's Four Arts Projects: Their Origins, Their Operation," *Fortune* 15 (May 1937): 108–17; Hiram Motherwell, "Uncle Takes the Stage," *Survey Graphic* 26 (April 1937): 213; Irving Kolodin, "Footlights, Federal Style," *Harpers* 173 (November 1936): 622; *New York Times*, 23 May 1937, sec. 2, p. 8; E. V. Wyatt, "The Federal Theatre Project," *Catholic World* 149 (August 1939): 599; McDonald, *Federal Relief Administration*, pp. 560–62.

9. Members included Gus Smith, Harry Edwards, and Edna Thomas.

10. Bronx *Home News*, 30 June 1937, p. 15; Flanagan, *Arena*, pp. 62–64, 199; Mathews, *Federal Theatre*, pp. 115, 303–4; Edith Isaacs, "The Negro in the American Theatre," *Theatre Arts* 26 (August 1942): 519–21; McDonald, *Federal Relief Administration*, pp. 570–71; Rice, *The Living Theatre*, pp. 154–55.

11. Many directors followed in his wake, the New York Writers' Project having one of the highest rates of turnover among its supervisors of any part of Federal Project no. 1.

12. Anzia Yezierska, *Red Ribbon on a White Horse* (New York, 1950), pp. 137–44; Orrick Johns, *Time of Our Lives: The Story of My Father and Myself* (New York, 1937), pp. 344, 342; *Nation*, 31 October 1936, p. 510; Jerre Mangione, *The Dream and the Deal: The Federal Writers' Project, 1935–1943* (Boston, 1972), pp. 155, 53–54; "Unemployed Arts," pp. 108–17; McDonald, *Federal Relief Administration*, p. 665.

13. All royalties from publishers went either to the WPA to cover costs other than wages or directly to the U.S. Treasury, not to the writers.

14. WPA Writing Services, Record of Program Operation and Accomplishment, February 1943, Papers of the U.S. WPA for N.Y.C., National Archives, Washington, D.C.; Mangione, *Dream and the Deal*, pp. 359, 103, 49–50, 256, 257, 260–61; Interview of Allan Angoff by the author, 20 November 1976, Teaneck, N.J.; Alexander, *Nationalism in American Thought*,

p. 45; Kazin, *On Native Ground*, p. 501; New York *Herald Tribune*, 4 January 1938, p. 17; McDonald, *Federal Relief Administration*, p. 728; Report of Paul Edwards, administrator for the N.Y.C. Arts Program, 29 March 1939, Papers of the U.S. WPA for N.Y.C., National Archives, Washington, D.C.

15. McDonald, *Federal Relief Administration*, pp. 697, 703–4; Mangione, *Dream and the Deal*, pp. 245, 124; Yezierska, *Red Ribbon on White Horse*, p. 168; Alexander, *Nationalism in American Thought*, p. 29; Interview of Allan Angoff, 20 November 1976; Harry Roskolenko, *When I Was Last on Cherry Street* (New York, 1965), pp. 155, 152.

16. The Music Program: Record of Operation and Accomplishment, February 1943, Papers of the U.S. WPA for N.Y.C., National Archives, Washington, D.C.; McDonald, *Federal Relief Administration*, p. 599; New York *Times*, 10 April 1938, p. 22; 18 July 1937, sec. 10, p. 5; 18 June 1939, sec. 9, p. 5; Earl V. Moore, "Men, Music, and Morale," *Musical America* 25 April 1942, pp. 5, 41.

17. V. F. Calverton, "The Cultural Barometer," *Current History* 49 (October 1938): 45; New York *Sun*, 9 June 1937, p. 9; Alexander, *Nationalism in American Thought*, pp. 78–80; McDonald, *Federal Relief Administration*, pp. 623–24, 597, 635; New York *Post*, 3 May 1937, p. 8; New York *Times*, 25 June 1939, sec. 9, p. 5; 19 June 1936, p. 17; 26 April 1936, sec. 2, p. 7.

18. "Unemployed Arts," pp. 108–17; New York *Times*, 10 July 1938, sec. 9, p. 5; 23 February 1936, sec. 10, p. 8; 10 January 1937, sec. 10, p. 7; 6 May 1937, sec. 10, p. 5; 25 June 1939, sec. 9, p. 9; 17 October 1937, sec. 11, p. 7; Moore, "Men, Music, and Morale," p. 41; New York *Herald Tribune*, 19 May 1936, p. 20; McDonald, *Federal Relief Administration*, p. 613; Music Program, February 1943, Papers of the U.S. WPA for N.Y.C.

19. Reminiscences of Holger Cahill, 1957, Columbia University Oral History Research Office, New York, pp. 503–4; McDonald, *Federal Relief Administration*, pp. 383–84; O'Connor, *New Deal Art Projects*, pp. 50, 54, 56, 125, 130; New York *Herald Tribune*, 14 May 1936, p. 17.

20. The Art Program in N.Y.C.: Record of Program Operation and Accomplishment, February 1943, Papers of the U.S. WPA for N.Y.C., National Archives, Washington, D.C.; U.S. WPA for N.Y.C., *The WPA Federal Art Projects: A Summary of Activities and Accomplishments* (New York, 1940), p. 2; New York *Herald Tribune*, 9 April 1936, p. 14; 27 August 1938, p. 13; O'Connor, ed., *New Deal Art Projects*, pp. 118, 116, 100–1, 107–8; Alexander, *Nationalism in American Thought*, p. 74; Barbara Rose, *American Art Since 1900: A Critical History* (New York, 1967), pp. 126–27; Reminiscences of Holger Cahill, p. 291.

21. O'Connor, ed., *New Deal Art Projects*, pp. 205, 223, 232, 239; Reminiscences of Holger Cahill, pp. 548, 549; McDonald, *Federal Relief Administration*, pp. 424, 411–13; Alain Locke, *The Negro in Art: A Pictorial*

Record of the Negro Artist and the Negro Theme in Art (New York, 1940), pp. 10, 130–35; James A. Porter, *Modern Negro Art* (New York, 1969), pp. 127, 130.

22. Alexander, *Nationalism in American Thought*, p. 73; O'Connor, ed., *New Deal Art Projects*, pp. 177, 178–79, 184–85, 191, 195, 106–7, 57; U.S. WPA, *Index of American Design Manual*, WPA Technical Series, Art Circular no. 3 (Washington, D.C., 1938), pp. 1–3; Calverton, "Cultural Barometer," pp. 94–95; McDonald, *Federal Relief Administration*, pp. 448, 453, 455; *New York Times*, 12 November 1972, sec. 2, p. 72; Reminiscences of Holger Cahill, p. 537; Rose, *American Art Since 1900*, pp. 127–28.

23. McDonald, *Federal Relief Administration*, pp. 754–55, 805, 820–22, 823; Reminiscences of Luther Evans, 1966, Columbia University Oral History Research Office, New York, pp. 111–15; Historical and Cultural Records Surveys and Inventories: Record of Program Operation and Accomplishment, February 1943, Papers of the U.S. WPA for N.Y.C., National Archives, Washington, D.C.; U.S. WPA for N.Y.C., *Final Report of the Work Projects Administration for the City of New York, 1935 to 1943* (New York, 1943), p. 232; Richard B. Morris, "Pioneering Days of Regional Archives," pp. 14–15, 17, 21–24, 28–29, transcripts from the symposium The Historian and Archives, 23 October 1969, Columbia University, mimeographed.

9

The WPA under Attack

Despite the roads, schools, and airports it built, the contributions it made to the arts, and the white-collar services it performed in New York and elsewhere, the WPA never won overwhelming public approval. When it began in 1935, the majority of Americans seemed ready to accept it as a short-term emergency measure. The handful of conservative Republicans in Congress and the big business leaders who denounced a federally operated job program were for the most part isolated. From 1937 on, however, the critics of the WPA grew both in number and in vociferousness until, by 1939, the New Deal's relief and work efforts had become its most controversial undertakings. A Gallup poll conducted in that year asked a broad cross section of people to name the Roosevelt Administration's "greatest accomplishment" and the "worst thing" it had done. The respondents mentioned the relief experiment more than anything else in answer to both questions.

How can one account for this mixed response? First and foremost, the WPA worried many citizens because they saw it as an extremely expensive way to support depression victims and one that led inevitably to deficit spending and unbalanced budgets. While the president and his liberal advisers might talk about pump priming, the majority of Americans in the 1930s, especially businessmen, still believed in frugal government that lived within its means. This was demonstrated by the results of a 1939 Roper poll in which Americans with different incomes were asked if they favored reducing federal spending to the point where the budget was balanced. Sixty-one percent indicated that they did. To be sure, the well-to-do exhibited more enthusiasm for retrenchment than the poor, but in every class, including the unemployed, the majority supported a balanced budget. Further, when asked specifically about WPA appropriations, less than one-quarter of the sample felt that the government should spend as much in 1939 as it had in the previous year. When Colonel Somervell sent a questionnaire about his agency to local businessmen, he received the same kind of response, with a majority replying that they did not know much about the WPA except that it spent a lot of money.[1]

The WPA also suffered from conflicting ideas about what its program represented. New Dealers like Hopkins and his assistant administrator, Aubrey Williams, believed that every able-bodied person who wished to work had the right to a job. If private enterprise failed to supply employment, then it became the responsibility of government to do so. As a practical matter, they were never fully able to put this philosophy into effect because limited appropriations compelled them to confine job offers to those on the relief rolls, and often not even all of them were employed. The New Dealers, in any event, saw the people that the WPA did hire as legitimate laborers, not as welfare clients.

It seems unlikely that the majority of congressmen or the public shared these advanced views. Many historians writing about the thirties have pointed out that the depression forced a grudging acceptance even among Republicans of a larger role for the federal government. At the same time, much of the laissez faire thinking of the Hoover era hung on.[2] Conservatives generally agreed that people should not be allowed to starve. If local resources failed, Washington might have to contribute funds for relief, but that was quite different from recognizing an obligation on the part of the state to supply every citizen with a job.

If one saw the WPA solely as an emergency relief effort (the only terms on which it was acceptable to conservatives), then it followed that Washington should raise only the amount absolutely necessary to prevent suffering and should return responsibility for welfare to the states and localities as soon as economic recovery permitted. And the WPA was not justified in spending its scarce dollars on expensive projects like Federal Project number 1 when, for the same money, many additional destitute families might be aided. Furthermore, work relief employees, who were recipients of federal alms, should not complain about what the government saw fit to give them. This attitude was well illustrated by the public response to strikes against the WPA. In 1939 when the skilled workers in New York staged a walkout, 74 percent of the city's residents polled by the American Institute of Public Opinion thought that the participants should be discharged. In explaining their stand, the persons interviewed often commented that the WPA is "a form of charity and the workers should be glad of what they get."

Although the depression probably weakened somewhat the traditional American belief that the United States is a land of opportunity where anyone who really tries can find work, it far from killed that notion. Since more than 50 percent of those who lived through the 1930s did not experience joblessness firsthand, many of these fortunate individuals tended to hold the men and women on the breadlines responsible, at least in part, for their own plight. The unemployed reliefer, they suspected, was a bit of a chiseler who preferred being a parasite on the public to going out and earning his own way. In a survey conducted in 1936 one-quarter of the people asked thought that welfare clients removed from the rolls would have an "easy time" obtaining work. In August 1937, 55 percent of those polled stated that "many persons on WPA . . . could get jobs if they tried."

Apparently, many congressmen shared these sentiments. After listening to his colleagues' insinuations that the WPA was filled with "bums" making a career out of work relief, Sen. Robert Wagner of New York indignantly protested: "The overwhelming majority of these people are fine American citizens, anxious to earn a living, but denied the opportunity to do so in private employment." Wagner's assertion was correct judging from the personnel on the New York City WPA, 97 percent of whom had been regularly employed in private industry prior to the depression. Indeed, they averaged ten years of experience at their former occupations. Of the remaining 3 percent who had never held an outside position, better than half were under twenty-five and thus had reached maturity since the 1929 crash.

Whatever the reality, the public cherished its traditional notions about opportunity and never really accepted the idea of government as employer of last resort. Thus the moment the worst of the depression seemed over, there were expressions of sentiment for terminating the federal job program. One can see this trend in the New York press. Newspapers that in 1935 were willing to admit that some depression victims deserved made-work positions had changed their opinion by 1937. The *Daily News* editorialized:

> Started from the highest motives, and operated with the greatest generosity, by high minded people, the WPA was all right for a while. But now it appears to be running away with itself; to be building up an army of not too competent people who feel they have a vested right to go on working for the Government.

The *Herald Tribune* echoed the same thought: "[M]ost of the abler 'clients' are being drained away to private employment; most of the sounder projects are coming to completion, and most of the arguments originally used to justify the work relief scheme are losing their force."

The press not only reflected disenchantment with the WPA; it helped create it. Papers hostile to the New Deal published many articles designed to prove that the projects were valueless and the personnel lazy. An item appearing in the New York *Sun* in 1936 was fairly typical. Headlined "Today's Boon-Doggle," it stated: "The ability of WPA corporals and sergeants . . . to originate fresh time-wasting jobs for those who toil or loaf in the ranks has been a constant source of wonder, and now comes an assignment at the craft school project, . . . which even when listed among the boon-doggles, should receive some sort of award. . . . [T]he project supervisor assigned one of the workers to count the threads in a square inch of muslin."[3]

Conditions on the New York City WPA during its opening phase also contributed to the unfavorable image of the organization and its workers. In the early days men had been hired at breakneck speed and assigned or misassigned to projects almost haphazardly. The planning of tasks and the overall program were still in a primitive stage, so that, at times, labor reported to sites before material and equipment arrived. As a result, the public saw knots of men standing about idly. Also, jobs took too long to complete. Streets and car tracks remained torn up for months, inconveniencing motorists and pedestrians. Many urban residents, therefore, concluded that the WPA was hopelessly inefficient and that shovel leaning was the favorite pastime of its employees. This impression lingered on long after Somervell's reforms had greatly improved performance.

When in 1939 merchants and property owners on Austin Street in Forest Hills, Queens, heard that seven blocks of the business thoroughfare were to be widened by work relief employees, many thought "the job would take months and cause traffic delays and other inconveniences." Only direct contact with the hundred men who completed the alteration in one month changed the minds of people in the neighborhood. The president of the Austin Street Association, a club of local proprietors, recalled: "The work progressed so rapidly that merchants . . . asked me who the contractor was. They did not believe it could be a WPA project. Men have to rest sometimes, but I haven't seen a man lean on a shovel since the whole thing started."

Increased efficiency did not make everyone applaud the WPA, however. Rather, the more construction the agency finished, the louder became the objections of building contractors, who feared government competition, and the unions of skilled workers worried that the WPA might be training common laborers in carpentry, masonry, and other crafts. By 1939 these forces had joined hands to try to convince Congress that the WPA should not be permitted to handle any undertaking costing more than twenty-five thousand dollars.

Another type of disgruntlement with the WPA arose from limited appropriations. President Roosevelt never requested, nor did Congress ever vote, enough money to hire all of the healthy unemployed. In New York City professional workers on the WPA earned approximately one hundred dollars a month and skilled laborers around ninety, but other equally deserving and competent people remained on home relief, where a family of five survived on sixty dollars. Understandably, the differences caused bitterness and envy among the home relief clients and prompted charges of unfairness in the government's policies. The *New York Times* in 1938 said: "The present national relief system cannot be permitted to continue indefinitely. [It has] set up a class division among the persons on relief. Those on the Federal work program are treated well; those who are left to depend purely on local funds often receive a mere fraction of what WPA workers receive." The editorial writer did not suggest larger national contributions as a remedy, however, but advocated returning the whole welfare management to the states.

Worrying more about those who held WPA jobs than those denied positions, Republicans and conservative Democrats repeatedly expressed apprehension that the New Deal was building a gigantic vote-getting machine among work relief laborers. Their fears grew particularly acute in the 1938 congressional elections when Roosevelt was attempting to purge a number of antiadministration Democrats. Aubrey Williams was quoted in the *New York Times* as advising WPA employees to "keep our friends in power." In Pennsylvania and Kentucky the WPA was accused of freely interfering on behalf of the president's favorites. Conservatives in New York pointed to the announcement of the Workers Alliance, the biggest union of the unemployed, that it intended to collect fifty thousand dollars from project personnel to aid candidates who favored larger relief appropriations and to fight economizers. One of its prime targets, as well as one of Roosevelt's, was John J. O'Connor, Democratic chairman of the House Rules Committee. O'Connor, an outspoken critic of the WPA, lost in the primary to a liberal, James Fay. Refusing to retire from the battle, O'Connor then ran as a Republican against Fay for the disputed Sixteenth District seat. Throughout the campaign, O'Connor charged that the WPA was putting its manpower at the disposal of his rival.[4]

In fact, Somervell had done no such thing. He posted notices at all project sites reminding employees of the strictly neutral character of the federal agency. WPA rules forbade personnel to solicit contributions while on the job or to engage in any political activity during working hours. No WPA supervisor or foreman could run for or hold any elective office, make public speeches, obtain signatures on petitions, watch polls, or be a member of a political committee. The colonel justified this curtailment of the rights of the administrators on the grounds that their power to hire, fire, promote, or demote could intimidate those under them if the supervisors showed the slightest hint of partisanship. The WPA, however, felt that it had no authority to keep the rank-and-file relief employee from participating in politics as long as he did this on his own time. Undoubtedly, quite a few WPA men and women saw O'Connor as an enemy and chose to contribute to and vote for Fay, who was subsequently elected.

Finally, from 1936 on Roosevelt faced mounting opposition from Capitol Hill. James Patterson in *Congressional Conservatism and the New Deal* argues that much of the president's problem was caused by a split between rural and city interests. As the urban character of the administration's programs became more pronounced—for example, the bulk of WPA funds and jobs went to cities, with New York generally topping the list—Democrats representing rural constituencies, especially Southern ones, joined hands with small-town Republicans in attempts to obstruct many of the president's legislative proposals. The congealing of this conservative coalition was hastened by the court-packing fight and the 1937 recession, which seemed to indicate that Roosevelt could not beat the depression. The failure of Roosevelt's attempt in 1938 to purge antiadministration Democrats, together with the increased number of Republicans who won seats in Congress that year, further strengthened the conservative forces. In matters of work relief, particularly, this conservative, rural bloc felt safe in asserting its independence of the White House. The acute economic crisis of the early thirties no longer threatened its agricultural areas, and as far as it was concerned the emergency was over. It was now time to curtail aid to the urban poor.

The opening skirmish in the conservative campaign against the WPA came in July 1938 when J. Parnell Thomas, the ranking Republican on the House Committee on Un-American Activities, chaired by Martin Dies of Texas, announced that the group would launch an investigation of the Federal Writers' and Theatre Projects. Thomas, sure of what he and his colleagues would find even before calling witnesses, stated that the WPA authors and actors were "not only . . . serving as a branch of the communist organization but also one more link in the vast and unparalleled New Deal propaganda machine."[5]

In August the Dies Committee began to hear the testimony of current and former WPA employees, most of them from New York City. One after another they charged that Federal Project number 1 was a hotbed of Communism. A woman named Hazel Huffman, previously a member of the New York drama project, claimed that Communists dominated the WPA through their front group, the Workers Alliance. Those who refused to join the Workers Alliance or cooperate with it were in danger of being fired or demoted, and many of the plays presented by the Federal Theatre were clearly propaganda pieces for Communism. Among the examples she cited were George Bernard Shaw's *On the Rocks* and Sinclair Lewis's *It Can't Happen Here*. A blond actress from New York, Sallie Saunders, accused the Workers Alliance and some of the WPA directors of encouraging "social equality and race merging," as evidenced by interracial dating among some of them. This presumably was further proof of Communist domination.

According to the committee witnesses, subversion thrived in the literary unit as well. Edwin Banta, a self-confessed Communist who was employed by the WPA, asserted that the party controlled over 40 percent of the writers in the New York branch, while the Workers Alliance dictated which individuals should be hired or fired. A young project supervisor named Ralph De Sola followed Banta to the stand and said much the same thing. He then gave the congressmen the names of many of his colleagues who he believed were Communists.

As the hearings continued through the fall, each new accusation receiving wide coverage in the press, Washington officials maintained an almost total silence. Hallie Flanagan, eager to go before the committee and refute what she felt were lies and half-truths, was instructed to make no public statements. Later, in her history of the Federal Theatre, she speculated on why Hopkins and his advisers took such a course. There were rumors floating around the capital that the administration had decided to end Federal Project number 1, and especially the drama unit, before 1940 because it had become a political liability. Flanagan rejected that explanation and suggested that the leaders believed that the wisest policy was to say nothing in hopes that the storm would soon blow over.

By November, when the Dies Committee seemed as active as ever in its drive to expose radical infiltration, the WPA executives could ignore the hearings no longer. It was arranged that Hallie Flanagan and Henry Alsberg would testify before the congressmen. The committee called them for questioning on 6 December 1938. Each admitted that there probably were some Communists working for the projects and that there had been many labor disturbances, particularly in New York. Flanagan, however, reminded the committeemen that the WPA was not permitted to deny anyone a position because of his political views or associations. Both directors denied that they were Communists and contradicted many of the allegations made by previous witnesses. The Dies group, nonetheless, stated in its report to the House of 3 January 1939 that a "rather large number of employees" on the theater and writers' projects were either Communists or fellow travelers, and that other workers felt compelled to join the Workers Alliance in order to keep their jobs.[6]

At the time of the hearings and ever since, critics of the committee have maintained that the congressmen considerably exaggerated the extent of Communist influence in Federal Project number 1. No doubt there were Marxists among both rank-and-file employees and supervisors. Allan Angoff, who worked on the New York Writers' Project, recalled that "there were Communists, conservatives, Trotskyites, Cannonites, old-time Republicans and Democrats." Some of the writing and some of the productions of the drama unit, moreover, inevitably reflected the views of New York's radicalized intellectual community. One ought to be skeptical, however, about quite a few of the witnesses and their more extreme statements.

Several of those who testified held grudges against the WPA because they had been dropped for lack of talent or for other reasons. Hazel Huffman had repeatedly tried without success to win a promotion on the New York Theatre

The WPA under Attack

Project for her husband, Seymour Revzin. Edwin Banta had a history of emotional disturbance, including confinement in a mental hospital. Responsible professional organizations like Actors' Equity contradicted the claims that the Workers Alliance controlled the productions and their members. Actors' Equity stated that 90 percent of those associated with the New York WPA Theatre belonged to it, while 10 percent were either unaffiliated or belonged to the Workers Alliance. Sworn affidavits from personnel directors on all divisions of Federal Project number 1 denied that lists of available jobs were given to Workers Alliance officials; and the officials were also not consulted about appointments.

Regardless of the reliability of the Dies Committee findings, they did much to strengthen the opponents of the WPA. During the 1939 congressional debates on the work relief program, lawmakers quoted from the hearings again and again. Citing the testimony of Sallie Saunders, Congressman Clare Hoffman of Michigan called for liquidating the Federal Theatre on the grounds that it promoted social equality between blacks and whites. Sen. Robert Reynolds of North Carolina, also referring to the Dies revelations, wished to consign the WPA Theatre "to the ashcan of oblivion" because it was "being used by clever Communists to spread . . . their doctrine of destruction of American institutions."

In the same week that the Committee on Un-American Activities filed its report with the House, the president asked Congress for a supplemental appropriation of $875 million to enable the WPA to maintain its rolls until 1 July 1939. The timing could not have been more unfortunate. In open defiance of Roosevelt, Capitol Hill passed a measure granting $150 million less than the president's request. This was done despite the protests of urban liberals, such as New York's Vito Marcantonio and Emanuel Celler in the House and Robert Wagner in the Senate. Behind the move stood a coalition of Southern Democrats, headed by Congressman Clifton Woodrum of Virginia, and rural Republicans, such as John Taber of upstate New York. Not only did they insist on economizing, but they also adopted a provision—presumably aimed at the Workers Alliance among others—making it illegal for anyone to solicit campaign contributions from work relief employees. The best that the liberals could do was write a clause stating that if the president found that an "emergency" had arisen, he might ask Congress for new funds before 1 July.

Roosevelt signed the measure and then immediately took advantage of the loophole the liberals had left him. He reminded the lawmakers that the appropriation they had just adopted threatened the livelihood of one million men and women who in turn supported more than four million dependents. In light of these "simple and alarming facts," the president declared that an emergency existed and asked the legislators to provide a supplemental fund of $150 million at once. New York civic leaders and local government officials backed Roosevelt with pleas to Congress, and the city's unemployed took to the streets of Manhattan shouting "Give the Senate Home Relief, We Want Jobs." Such demonstrations may have strengthened the president's hand, but they did not succeed in convincing the congressional majority to grant Roosevelt the funds he wanted. Early in April the lawmakers relented to the point of granting $100 million of the $150 million FDR sought. Evidently convinced that he could do no better, the president signed the measure. For the first time he had failed to wring from Congress the full amount he requested for the WPA.[7]

New York felt the consequences soon enough. The economizing of the conservatives required the removal of approximately thirty thousand men and women from Somervell's payroll between April and the end of June. The chances that most of the discharged would find outside employment seemed minimal. Jobs were still so scarce that when the city Health Department announced openings for twelve laboratory helpers at $18.46 a week, four thousand women waited on line all night to apply the following morning.

The clash between the executive and legislative branches over the funds for the period January to June 1939 produced more than forced layoffs. Some of the congressmen felt that Roosevelt had applied undue pressure for the extra $150 million. Therefore, they listened sympathetically to Clifton Woodrum when he called for an investigation of the WPA. Why should the organization spend such prodigious sums, the economy-minded congressmen wondered. Perhaps an inquiry would uncover waste, graft, and mismanagement, which, if eliminated, could save millions. At any rate, if the chamber conducted its own probe, in the future Capitol Hill would not have to rely blindly on the president's estimates of the WPA's needs. In March 1939 the House voted by the lopsided margin of 352 to 27 to authorize Woodrum's Subcommittee on Appropriations to examine the work relief setup from top to bottom.

On 17 April the hearings commenced, and almost immediately the proceedings took on the aspect of a witch-hunt. Disgruntled building contractors, ex-WPA employees who had been fired for various reasons, self-confessed former Communists, and lobbyists filled the air with accusations to which most of the committeemen listened quite uncritically. On the other hand, Woodrum and his colleagues frequently contradicted or cut short the testimony of witnesses, such as the leaders of the Workers Alliance, whose views they disliked. Somervell, who wished to refute many of the charges relating to the New York City WPA, was not invited to appear, although the committee did accept a written statement from him.

During the first weeks the investigation concentrated primarily on proving that Communists controlled the Workers Alliance. The subcommittee called the Alliance's national officers, President David Lasser and Secretary-Treasurer Herbert Benjamin. Lasser stated that he had belonged to the Socialist Party until 1938. Benjamin admitted his Communist Party membership readily, but both men denied that they aimed to foment strikes among WPA workers or had any intention of preaching to them the overthrow of the government. Later Mrs. Frankie Duty, a black woman who had recently resigned from the Communist Party and from her post as second vice-president of the Workers Alliance of Greater New York, took the stand. She claimed that twenty of the twenty-five members of the union's executive board in the city were "Reds."

Next came a string of witnesses who alleged that the left-wing union ran Federal Project number 1. Ralph De Sola, who had earlier appeared before the Dies Committee, swore that 65 to 70 percent of his fellow supervisors were members of the Workers Alliance. These men, he asserted, used their positions to slip radical ideas into the books produced by the WPA. Oscar Gall of Brooklyn, a discharged managing editor, delivered the same message. The government, he said, was doing little more than "conducting a school for communist writers." If the Workers Alliance had infiltrated the writers' unit, it "absolutely dominated" the Theatre Project, claimed Charles Walton, a drama director for the New York City WPA. Many of the plays staged had been "clever propaganda for communism," he told the committeemen, and to emphasize the danger he reminded them that "the theater for centuries had been used to sway public opinion. Voltaire once wrote a play that started the French Revolution."

Col. Francis Harrington, who succeeded Harry Hopkins as national administrator of the WPA when the latter became secretary of commerce, tried to counter these broad accusations by telling the committee that he felt the charges against the Workers Alliance had been "considerably exaggerated." The organization, he stated, had never made any improper demands upon him.[8]

Regardless of the true character of the Workers Alliance, by 1939 the congressmen had little reason to fear the group's power over the WPA staff. The left-wing union was dissolving into warring factions. Beginning in the fall of 1938 it experienced repeated defections by affiliates who resented the Stalinist bias of most of the leadership. Henry Rourke, former paid organizer for the New York WPA, led a secession of eleven locals from the older body. These joined with four small independents to form the rival Unemployed and

Project Workers Union, of which Rourke became president. Raymond Meisnere, a lawyer employed by the New York WPA, took another thousand white-collar workers out of the alliance and established a second competing association. A third new union, the Chauffeurs, Auto Mechanics, Truck Masters and Gas Attendants, also began wooing members away from Lasser's ranks. All of these signs of weakness and disunity, however, the Woodrum Subcommittee chose to ignore.[9]

Having proved to their own satisfaction that much of the WPA was in the grip of Communists, the congressmen focused on other alleged shortcomings in the work relief setup. One of the subcommittee's investigators uncovered an instance in which Somervell had allowed a sewing project to hire jobless needle-trades workers, recommended by the International Ladies' Garment Workers Union, without insisting that the persons first apply for welfare. Further, engineers on loan from the Treasury Department and spokesmen for the New York Building Trades Employers Association accused the WPA of inefficiency and waste that raised construction costs well above those on comparable jobs done under private contract.

In letters to Woodrum and statements to the press Somervell refuted these charges as best he could. He explained that an exception to the usual rules was made for the ILGWU people because the union had been supporting its jobless members from its own treasury, and, therefore, organized garment workers seldom applied for public assistance. Nonetheless, their poverty and need for employment was just as great as those on welfare. The colonel admitted that, for reasons that he listed, it cost the WPA more to put up a structure than most building contractors expended, but he challenged the specific figures mentioned before the subcommittee.

In addition to listening to scores of witnesses, the subcommittee perused the data provided by WPA statisticians. Woodrum and his colleagues found one bit of information particularly disturbing. In the big cities, especially New

York, labor turnover on the WPA lagged badly. Forty-two percent of those on Somervell's rolls had been there for at least three years.[10] Could it be that wages were too high and the hours too few? Were the workers really trying to secure outside employment, or had they come to regard their emergency positions as permanent?

At first Roosevelt ignored the House investigation and proceeded with his own plans to make the administration of work relief more effective. On 25 April he submitted a message to Congress in which he explained that he intended to group together in one organization all bodies engaged in public works. This new unit, named the Federal Works Agency, would oversee the operations of the Bureau of Public Roads, the public buildings branch of the Procurement Division of the Treasury Department, the United States Housing Authority, the Public Works Administration, and the WPA, the initials henceforth to stand for Work Projects Administration.[11]

Soon after the reorganization announcement, Roosevelt informed Capitol Hill of the sum he desired to support the WPA for the 1939–40 fiscal year. He asked the lawmakers to appropriate $1.477 billion, which was one-third less than the total spent in the preceding twelve months. One can speculate as to why the president suggested such a marked reduction. Perhaps he believed that the economy, stimulated by European war preparations, would absorb a major portion of the jobless. On the other hand, viewing the hostility and growing power of the conservative bloc, he may have decided that he could not hope to get more from Congress and should avoid a losing battle.

If the latter was the case, the chief executive's words gave no hint of surrender. His message praised the achievements of the WPA and criticized its detractors. He declared that "a vast amount of worthwhile work remained to be done" and that expenditures on public works produced "permanent, tangible additions to our national wealth," as well as stimulating purchasing power. Noting briefly the probe of the Woodrum Subcommittee, he expressed the hope that it would be "guided along constructive lines and not focused on criticism of isolated projects, obscuring the real value of the overall program." Roosevelt chided the economy bloc for slashing his earlier requests and urged Congress to accept his figures this time, leaving the status of the WPA untouched except for the administrative changes he had completed.

The Woodrum Subcommittee showed itself in no hurry to comply with the president's wishes, continuing the hearings for another two months. Finally, on 14 June 1939, it presented a bill to the House for debate. The measure left no doubt that this time the conservatives intended to curtail the WPA. The bill proposed granting the WPA $125 million less than the president had requested. But that was just the beginning. The WPA was prohibited from constructing any building that cost in excess of twenty-five thousand dollars, and the agency was not to retain any worker for more than eighteen months. At the expiration of that time, the employee must be dropped and his position given to another person who was on welfare. The original worker could eventually be reinstated only if no qualified replacement could be found. Further, all WPA personnel would henceforth work a minimum of thirty hours a week. That requirement, of course, put an end to the prevailing-wage formula followed since 1936. As for Federal Project number 1, it was to disappear. The art, music, writing, and history programs might continue if local sponsors willing to cover a portion of their expenses came forward, but the measure specifically denied any government funds for operation of a drama project.

Some right-wing members of the House felt that the subcommittee bill did not go far enough. John Taber led a handful of old-line Republicans who made it clear that nothing short of the liquidation of the WPA would satisfy them. Most of the conservative bloc, however, seemed pleased with Woodrum's proposals. Meanwhile, the liberals made a frantic effort to modify the restrictive bill. Samuel Dickstein of New York City attacked the provisions reducing funds for the WPA and eliminating Federal Project number 1. Congressman Celler predicted that the twenty-five-thousand-dollar limit on buildings would hamstring almost all WPA construction in New York and thus idle as many as twenty-seven thousand blue-collar laborers. The Brooklyn congressman persuaded the House to raise the figure to forty thousand dollars but was defeated in his attempt to have no ceiling so long as the sponsor contributed half the sum.

Some of the most heated debate involved the mandatory firing of destitute persons after a year and one-half to make way for other jobless individuals. Even before the subcommittee introduced its bill in June, the president, La Guardia, and WPA officials had warned Woodrum and his colleagues not to adopt a provision that threatened to rob the work relief agency of administrative flexibility, disrupt the program, and inflict hardships on depression victims. On the House floor many liberal congressmen, including such members of the New York delegation as Dickstein, Celler, Marcantonio, and William Sirovich, argued against the proposal. Woodrum accused them of misplaced sympathies, proclaiming:

> If the government were undertaking to give a job to every person out of work . . . what these gentlemen say about the inhumanity of taking people off the rolls would be eminently true, but the program has never called for doing more than giving a job to about one in every three or four entitled to it.
>
> What . . . about the hundreds of people standing in line in New York City who would like to have some of the benefits of the government program that you will not let get on . . . because you want to perpetuate the people already there?

Woodrum's belated concern for the New Yorkers who had not received help from the WPA might have been more convincing if he had not earlier joined in almost every conservative attempt to reduce spending on work relief. Genuine friends of the unemployed proposed bigger appropriations for the WPA, not dismissing some needy individuals to make way for others. The majority, nonetheless, apparently shared the Virginian's view since they defeated an amendment to scuttle the controversial section by a vote of 153 to 83. The only softening of the provision that the New Dealers in the House achieved came when that body agreed to James Fay's suggestion that veterans be exempt from the layoffs.[12]

The liberals fought their last rearguard action for Federal Project number 1, including the Theatre Project, and on this they did not even have the help of the WPA leaders or Roosevelt. Sometime during the Woodrum investigation, if not sooner, Harrington and his advisers decided to abandon the nationally run arts units, hoping to protect the rest of the agency's endeavors from the conservative assault. On 23 May 1939 Harrington told the subcommittee that he intended to secure "local sponsorship for as many of the projects as possible, thus eliminating their operation as federally sponsored projects." An assistant of Harrington's informed Hallie Flanagan regretfully but firmly: "There isn't going to be a fight [to save] Federal Theatre." Jerre Mangione of the Writers' Project, after having dinner with the president and Mrs. Roosevelt in the spring of 1939, also received the impression that the chief executive's mind was occupied by defense preparations, not by battling with Capitol Hill on behalf of Federal Project number 1.

On 16 June 1939 Congresswoman Mary Norton (New Jersey, Democrat) proposed that the House rescind the abolition of the Theatre Project. She was immediately backed by members of the New York City delegation. Sirovich made an impassioned plea for all of Federal Project number 1, proclaiming that it had "created a cultural revolution in America" and had brought the "American artist and the American audience face to face for the first time." Celler read a telegram signed by virtually every leading drama critic that praised the New York City Theatre Project and urgently recommended its continuation.[13] But when it came to a vote, the Norton Amendment went down to defeat, 56 to 192. The House then passed the Woodrum bill and sent it on to the Senate, where liberals still hoped that they might be able to undo the conservative mischief.

In many respects the bill that began to take shape in the Senate was an improvement over the House version. The upper chamber restored the $125 million cut, removed the mandatory thirty-hour week for WPA employees, dropped the layoff provision, and raised the ceiling on permissible cost of building projects from forty to seventy-five thousand dollars. However, one amendment, adopted over the objections of liberals, including New York Senators Wagner and James Mead, increased the burden on cities and states with big WPA programs by requiring that the local sponsor raise at least 25 percent of the money for work relief undertakings.[14]

The most intense fight on the Senate floor came over Federal Project number 1. For weeks previously, friends of the arts had besieged the members with pleas, especially for the drama project. La Guardia pointed out that its demise would leave three thousand New Yorkers jobless. Thirty prominent show business people signed a petition praising the Federal Theatre and requesting continued national support for it. Among the names appearing on the declaration were those of Helen Hayes, Eddie Cantor, Moss Hart, Richard Rogers, Burgess Meredith, Katharine Cornell, and Katherine Hepburn. Lionel Barrymore spoke on the radio in behalf of the WPA thespians, and Tallulah Bankhead flew to Washington to intercede with her uncle, Sen. John Bankhead of Alabama. But her kinsman proved balky. When Miss Bankhead said to the Senator, "Uncle John, of course, you'll vote to do something for unemployed actors," he replied, "No, I don't think I will. These city fellows in Congress never vote to do anything for our farmers."

On 28 June Robert Wagner introduced an amendment providing that the arts projects, including the Federal Theatre, remain under national sponsorship. He suggested that

1 percent of the WPA appropriation, or roughly $17.5 million, be earmarked for their use. After much debate, during which Senators Mead, Wagner, and other New Dealers attempted to refute charges of waste, Communist domination, and poor selection of plays, the lawmakers decided to approve Wagner's proposal but with the funds reduced to three-quarters of 1 percent. Later that day the chamber passed its considerably altered version of the Emergency Relief Bill and requested a conference with the House.[15]

The legislation that emerged from the conference committee retained some of the liberalized Senate provisions but basically resembled the House bill. This is not surprising, considering that the majority of the participants were conservatives from rural states and districts. The measure followed the Senate in giving Roosevelt the full amount of money he had requested. The House members also readily agreed to the 25 percent sponsor's contribution called for by the Senate and reluctantly compromised over the building limit. The seventy-five-thousand-dollar ceiling of the Senate bill and the forty-thousand-dollar limit specified by the House became a fifty-two-thousand-dollar maximum in the final draft. On the rest of the Senate modifications the congressmen refused to budge. The thirty-hour week remained, and the mandatory eighteen-month layoff as well.

Finally, the conference group took up Federal Project number 1 and the Theatre Project. Woodrum had announced before he entered the meeting that "he was going to put the government out of show business if it was the last thing he ever did." Apparently, he and his colleagues meant it. A Senate participant in the joint committee later described what happened to Hallie Flanagan:

> Never before have I seen such a united and determined attitude. . . . They were all determined to eliminate the theatre project. [This] was the last concession made by the Senate conferees and that concession was made only as the last resort in order to secure an agreement. It really

seemed that if the Senate refused to yield . . . we would have the entire two and one-half million WPA relief workers thrown out of employment.

Thus the death sentence on the drama project and all federally sponsored undertakings remained. The writing, music, art, and history programs might continue if they acquired local backers willing to pay one-quarter of their cost.

When the conference committee's report reached the two chambers on 30 June, it was too late for the friends of the WPA to do more than register their bitter disapproval. Celler pointed out that not one New York City legislator had participated in the final decisions, and yet that community would suffer greatly. "The rule of the day," he warned, "will be mass layoffs, with springboard jumps back to home relief." The Brooklynite's remarks did not faze the conservatives. Woodrum proclaimed, "Congress for the first time has vigorously moved into this picture and asserted its legislative prerogatives." If he had any regrets at all, it was over allowing the other arts endeavors to continue with local sponsors. In the end the liberals in the House and Senate voted, along with the conservatives, to accept the committee bill. They had little choice. To reject the measure would mean the demise of the WPA, since the new fiscal year began the next day.

The last-minute timing also tied the president's hands. As Roosevelt put it:

> Obviously I cannot withhold my signature and thereby stop work relief for the needy unemployed.
>
> The bill contains, however, a number of provisions which will work definite hardship and inequality on more than two million American citizens—about eight million if we count their families—people who through no fault of their own are in dire need.

Though earlier he had not intervened to save the Federal

Theatre, the chief executive now condemned its liquidation as "discrimination of the worst type" because it "singles out a specific group of . . . people for a denial of work in their own profession." He ended his message with the hope that Congress in the future might remove the objectionable features of the law.[16]

The repercussions of what the conservatives had done hit New York immediately. The eighteen-month provision of the Emergency Relief Act forced Somervell to discharge during July and August of 1939 nearly fifty-nine thousand people, or approximately 45 percent of his total personnel. The law did not allow him to take into account an individual's age, sex, relative need, or past performance. Among those dismissed that summer, 16 percent were over fifty-five years old. Nearly one-quarter of the men and women dropped supported four or more dependents with their WPA wages.

Ellen Tarry, who had been on the Writers' Project since 1936, received her pink dismissal slip that summer. "Half of my Alabama relatives were here visiting the 1939 World's Fair. And suddenly I found I no longer had a job," she recalled. Jacob Kainen had worked for the Graphics Division of the Art Project since 1935, except for one three-month layoff during the summer of 1937. When he was fired on 31 August 1939, he was earning $95.44 a month. Suddenly the income was gone. That eighteen-month rule was "the worst problem the artist had to face," he remembered. You could return to the project, Kainen explained, but "the procedures for doing so were strenuous and demeaning." First, he declared himself a pauper and was reaccepted for welfare. Then, he waited in a home relief center day after day, week after week, "sitting on a hard bench in a dreary waiting room together with other unemployed persons and homeless derelicts." He watched the blackboard on which a clerk occasionally listed a job opening. Finally, the words he was waiting for appeared, "graphic artist, WPA, 110 King Street." He "made a mad dash for the exit and took the first streetcar" to the project headquarters. It never occurred to him to take a taxi; they were foreign to his world, and, besides, he did not have the money. On 13 December 1939 his "persistence in waiting in home relief offices" paid off; the WPA rehired him at $87.60 a month. He was safe for another year and one-half.

During the first week of July a thirty-five-year-old unskilled laborer, earning $60.50 a month on the WPA, received his notice of discharge. He had been a subway worker prior to the depression, but his chances of reemployment in that field were slim. If he did not find any job and was reaccepted for home relief, he would, as a single man, collect at best thirty-four dollars a month. A thirty-six-year-old steam fitter, with three dependents to support, faced an equally uncertain fate. He had been a chauffeur in the 1920s. When first placed on work relief, he performed unskilled labor. He took advantage of the training the WPA offered, however, and became a plumber's helper, then a steam fitter's assistant, and finally a steam fitter. He was earning $93.50 a month when the WPA dismissed him in July 1939. Home relief maintained a family of four on less than sixty dollars a month. That was his future unless he found a job.[17]

What happened to the people dropped because of the eighteen-month rule? When the WPA inquired eight months later, it discovered that only 14 percent of those laid off in New York had found outside jobs, and in many instances they earned less than they had on work relief. Nearly half had returned to the WPA after months of economic struggle; the remainder were still unemployed, and most were not even getting home relief. They were unlikely to get back on the WPA since the small appropriation for 1939–40 necessitated personnel cutbacks. The New York agency's employment quota fell from 140,000 in June to under 110,000 in September 1939.

Besides the hardships inflicted on those discharged, the eighteen-month rule played havoc with ongoing projects. Construction almost ground to a halt as carpenters, plumbers, and masons were released. By 1939 there were few skilled laborers on home relief, and Somervell often could not find qualified replacements. The production costs of the sewing unit almost doubled in the fall as inexperienced recruits assumed the tasks of trained operatives and foremen. New secretaries and clerks fumbled with unfamiliar WPA clerical procedures. Almost 100 percent of the child-nutrition staff had to leave. WPA doctors rushed frantically to give medical examinations to thousands of women on welfare to permit them to be assigned to the vacant food-handling positions.

Summer school classes suffered dramatically, since nearly 80 percent of the WPA teachers were dismissed in the middle of the term. Social workers could not find enough suitable people on home relief to take over the courses, and by the time the dismissed instructors qualified for reinstatement, the session was over. Eight prominent educators published a statement urging at least temporary suspension of the eighteen-month rule for the sake of the students.[18] Somervell sympathized but saw nothing in the law that empowered him to intervene.

Despite all of the disruptions the rotation provision caused, it brought some New Yorkers benefits that had been long delayed. Thousands who had been waiting on home relief for years had almost given up hope of receiving WPA assignments. Now Congress opened the door to them, even if it meant depriving others. By 7 July Somervell had placed fourteen thousand of these people on projects, and city relief officials were referring new applicants at the rate of one thousand to fifteen hundred daily. Perhaps William Hodson, municipal welfare commissioner, expressed the most balanced view of the operations of the eighteen-month rule. He stated that the rotation principle itself was not a bad one if the government could not provide work for all of the jobless, but "the trouble was that Congress invaded the area of wise administrative discretion and fixed an arbitrary time for accomplishing the result which did not square with the needs of the people, the needs of the projects, or the capacity of the relief administration to absorb those in need."[19]

The layoffs did not anger the AFL building trades unions so much as the loss of the prevailing-wage formula for which they had fought so hard in 1935. By requiring skilled as well as unskilled employees to work thirty hours a week for their checks, Congress in effect was lowering the hourly rate of WPA carpenters, masons, electricians, and others well below the union scales paid by private contractors.[20] The labor leaders declared that if their men accepted the new government terms, they would undermine wage standards throughout the construction industry. Therefore, five days after Roosevelt signed the act, the New York Building and Construction Trades Council of the AFL struck the WPA. Thomas Murray, president of the council, explained that the walkout was not aimed at the local agency but was intended to force the legislators to repeal the obnoxious provision.

Somervell and Murray differed in their assessments of the events that followed. The union head claimed that "practically all" of the more than thirty-two thousand skilled building trades workers on the government program were staying away from their jobs. The colonel placed the total on strike at about eleven thousand. He did admit, however, that the absence of these men required him to halt operations on two schools and La Guardia Airport in the first weeks of July. Furthermore, the walkout, occurring simultaneously with the mass layoffs decreed by the eighteen-month rule, produced a critical shortage of carpenters, electricians, plumbers, iron workers, and brick masons. By 1 September nearly thirty construction sites stood idle for want of these laborers.

Although the strike temporarily hurt the WPA, the AFL did not have a chance of winning its point. Too many forces opposed both the work stoppage and the prevailing-wage principle. The more radical labor groups, such as the Workers Alliance, gave the walkout only token support. They responded this way, in part, because of Somervell's get-tough policy, which included turning over the names of all demonstrators to the Woodrum Subcommittee. Also, they were more disturbed by the eighteen-month clause, which was decimating their ranks, than by the prevailing-wage question. Besides, many unskilled and intermediate WPA laborers resented the privileged position of the skilled people, who had been working as little as twelve hours a week prior to July 1939. A Gallup poll conducted in August 1939 found that 53 percent of all WPA employees applauded the new provision that required a standard thirty hours for everyone. If the WPA personnel approved the measure, the public favored it still more. In the same survey 67 percent of the people interviewed said that relief laborers should work full time, and 74 percent felt no sympathy for the AFL protest then underway.

In Congress even many of the liberals who had voted a prevailing-wage clause into the 1936, 1937, and 1938 appropriations acts, had decided that the idea operated badly in practice. A committee headed by Sen. James Byrnes of South Carolina made a study of skilled laborers on the WPA and discovered that 63 percent of them worked for outside contractors on their time off. These individuals were not only taking scarce jobs from other unemployed men; they also accepted below-standard remuneration since they had a guaranteed monthly income from the WPA. This evidence seemed to undermine the AFL's argument that the WPA must support the prevailing wage in order to protect union scales in private industry. In addition, Woodrum and his colleagues had convinced a majority on Capitol Hill that the abbreviated work week made WPA positions too attractive.

Although Roosevelt disliked many features of the 1939 act, he favored the thirty-hour week. The president, moreover, condemned the walkout, asserting at his press conference on 14 July: "You cannot strike against the government." In line with Roosevelt's thinking, Somervell and Harrington decided to give the strikers no quarter. The colonel declared that he would fire anyone absent from his job for five consecutive days. In the face of this ruling, many of the workers stayed out for four days but buckled under on the fifth and returned to their tasks. Others remained away, gambling that the colonel would relent and that their protest would eventually succeed. Their calculations proved erroneous. By 1 October, when the strike petered out, Somervell had discharged almost nineteen thousand for failure to report.

The directors of the WPA chose to break the walkout in this fashion because they believed that the thirty-hour workweek, unlike most of the provisions of the new law, benefited the agency. Somervell had long complained of the effects of the prevailing-wage formula. Foremen and skilled laborers worked so few days a month that there were numerous shifts of supervision and crews on any given job. This increased labor costs, cut down on efficiency, and destroyed the participants' sense of responsibility and accomplishment. In addition, figuring the correct hours and rates of compensation under the prevailing-wage arrangement was a complicated, time-consuming process, requiring the WPA to keep an excessively large staff of payroll clerks. Harrington stated a year after the thirty-hour rule went into effect that, despite the strike, the change was "the greatest single improvement in the operation and administration of the program . . . since its inception."[21]

If the walkout over the prevailing-wage formula crippled the construction activities of the New York City WPA temporarily, two other provisions that the conservatives wrote into the 1939 law threatened to hamper the building projects permanently. These were the fifty-two-thousand-dollar ceiling on structures and the requirement of the 25 percent sponsor contribution. Since construction cost in the urban area was higher than anywhere else in the country, just about any school, community center, hospital, or police station was likely to exceed the permissible figure. Moreover, as La Guardia pointed out, it was difficult for New York to raise one-quarter of the money for projects because the municipality was supporting approximately eighty thousand able-bodied residents on home relief who would have been on the WPA if Congress had appropriated a more adequate amount for that agency. Fortunately for the city, however, the president had approved all of the undertakings comprising the 1939 building program prior to 1 July. Roosevelt's attorney general ruled that the law could not be put into effect retroactively. Somervell's organization could thus finish the work in progress and would not feel the impact of the new restrictions until it drew up its plans for 1940.

Three thousand New York actors, stagehands, playwrights, and directors won no comparable temporary reprieve. By act of Congress, on 30 June 1939, thirty-two units of the Federal Theatre in the metropolis ceased to exist. These included the Gilbert and Sullivan Company, the WPA circus, the dance group, the marionette theater, and the classical troupe that played in the high schools. Three productions then on Broadway—*Pinocchio, Life and Death of an American,* and *Sing for Your Supper*—went dark that night. At the last performance of *Pinocchio* the puppet, instead of becoming a real boy, died, while the actors chanted "So let the bells proclaim our grief/ That his small life was all too brief." Then cast and crew marched from the Ritz Theatre on West Forty-eighth Street carrying placards that read "WANTED—REPRESENTATIVE CLIFTON A. WOODRUM FOR THE MURDER OF PINOCCHIO."

La Guardia and Somervell reached an accord that saved the other sections of Federal Project number 1 from the same fate. The mayor agreed to become their official sponsor and pledged that the city would assume one-quarter of their expenses. On 1 September 1939, the date that the legislators had set for ending nationally operated endeavors in the arts, the colonel integrated the forty-one hundred employees engaged in writing, music, painting, and historical research into his organization, placing them under the management of his white-collar and professional division.[22]

All of these changes decreed by Congress made 1939 a vital turning point in the career of the WPA. The conservatives had gained the upper hand over federal unemployment policy. Liberals might succeed in deflecting some of the shafts aimed at the program, but, beginning in that year, the disaffected majority on Capitol Hill laid down the ground rules. The results of their intervention nearly wrecked the WPA and caused untold suffering among the urban residents dependent on it. Although one might debate whether abolishing the prevailing-wage principle hurt the administration of work relief, it is impossible to see the rest of the Emergency Relief Act for 1939–40 as being anything but harmful to the job program. The eighteen-month provision led to the greatest mass layoff in the history of the WPA, forcing the removal of people without regard to need, age, sex, or diligence. It disrupted educational, health, and other important services that low-income New Yorkers were receiving, as well as halting, for a time, construction on La Guardia Airport, schools, and other undertakings. Further, the inadequate appropriation that Roosevelt recommended and that Congress passed deprived thousands of poverty-stricken Americans of any government work at all. The future of WPA public construction looked grim because of the imposition of an unrealistically low ceiling figure. Urban finances, already strained, had to stretch still further to cover one-quarter of the cost of work relief projects. And the Federal Theatre disappeared entirely, leaving three thousand New York professionals stranded.

NOTES

1. Donald Howard, *The WPA and Federal Relief Policy* (New York, 1943), p. 105; *Fortune* 19 (March 1939): 132–35; *New York Times*, 2 October 1938, p. 1.

2. For a discussion of persistent conservative thinking in the thirties, see such works as James Patterson, *Congressional Conservatism and the New Deal* (Lexington, Ky., 1967); idem, *The New Deal and the States*

The WPA under Attack

(Princeton, N.J., 1969); and Bernard Sternsher, introduction to *Hitting Home*, ed. Bernard Sternsher (Chicago, 1970).

3. *New York Times*, 19 July 1939, p. 4; Michael E. Schiltz, *Public Attitudes toward Social Security, 1935-1965* (Washington, D.C., 1970), pp. 155-56; U.S. *Congressional Record*, 76th Cong., 1st sess., 1939, 84, pt. 7: 7980; U.S. Congress, House Subcommittee of the Committee on Appropriations, *Hearings on Work Relief and Relief for Fiscal Year 1940*, 76th Cong. 1st sess. (Washington, D.C., 1939), pp. 23-24; New York *Daily News*, 20 April 1937, p. 25; New York *Herald Tribune*, 5 May 1937, p. 26; New York *Sun*, 9 January 1936, p. 21.

4. U.S. WPA for N.Y.C., *Final Report of the Work Projects Administration for the City of New York, 1935 to 1943* (New York, 1943), p. 265; New York *Herald Tribune*, 23 June 1939, p. 1; *New York Times*, 12 July 1939, p. 18; 18 November 1939, p. 20; 25 November 1938, p. 22; 29 June 1938, p. 1; U.S. *Congressional Record*, 76th Cong., 1st sess., 1939, 84, pt. 7: 7346, 7974; U.S. Congress, House Subcommittee of the Committee on Appropriations, *Hearings on the First Deficiency Appropriations Bill*, 74th Cong., 2d sess. (Washington, D.C., 1936), p. 121; U.S. Congress, House Subcommittee of the Committee on Appropriations, *Investigation and Study of the WPA*, 76th Cong., 1st sess. (Washington, D.C., 1939), pt. 1, p. 353; William E. Leuchtenburg, *Franklin D. Roosevelt and the New Deal* (New York, 1963), pp. 269-70; New York *World-Telegram*, 22 August 1938, p. 1; 1 November 1938, p. 1; 4 November 1938, p. 20.

5. Aubrey Williams to Somervell, 11 October 1938, Papers of the U.S. WPA for N.Y.C., National Archives, Washington, D.C.; Patterson, *Congressional Conservatism*, pp. 331-336; *New York Times*, 27 July 1938, p. 19.

6. U.S. Congress, Special House Committee for the Investigation of Un-American Activities, *Investigation of Un-American Propaganda Activities in the United States*, 75th Cong., 3d sess. (Washington, D.C., 1938), 1: 775-829, 859-860, and 2: 981-1017, 1021-26; *New York Times*, 16 September 1938, p. 1; Hallie Flanagan, *Arena* (New York, 1940), pp. 335-36, 338-44; Jerre Mangione, *The Dream and the Deal: The Federal Writers' Project, 1935-1943* (Boston, 1972), pp. 315-20; Report of the Special House Committee on Un-American Activities—Pursuant to H.R. 282, *Investigation of Un-American Activities and Propaganda*, 75th Cong., 4th sess. (Washington, D.C., 1939), p. 31.

7. Mangione, *Dream and the Deal*, pp. 153, 310; Jane D. Mathews, *The Federal Theatre, 1935-1939* (Princeton, N.J., 1967), pp. 206, 207, 228; U.S. *Congressional Record*, 76th Cong., 1st sess., 1939, 84, pt. 7: 7234-35, 8084-86; 84, pt. 1: 240-41, 323-26, 314-15, 327-28, 331, 887; New York *World-Telegram*, 5 January 1939, pp. 1, 13; 9 January 1939, p. 1; 14 January 1939, pp. 1, 4; 27 January 1939, p. 1; 28 January 1939, p. 1; 7 February 1939, pp. 1, 30; New York *Herald Tribune*, 29 January 1939, pp. 1, 16; 12 April 1939, p. 1; *New York Times*, 29 January 1939, p. 3; *Work*, (national edition), 11 February 1939, p. 1.

8. U.S. WPA for N.Y.C., "The Number of Employees Working for the N.Y.C. WPA, 1939," *General Statistical Bulletin,* January–June 1939 (New York, 1939); *New York Times,* 2 April 1939, p. 1; 6 April 1939, p. 20; 26 April 1939, p. 15; 5 May 1939, p. 25; 7 June 1939, p. 1; 2 May 1939, p. 1; New York *Herald Tribune,* 2 April 1939, p. 5; 10 February 1939, p. 5; 12 March 1939, p. 1; 19 April 1939, p. 9; New York *Post,* 13 March 1939, p. 2; 27 March 1939, p. 20; U.S. Congress, House Subcommittee, *Investigation and Study of the WPA,* 1: 107, 136, 110, 1290.

9. The most crippling defection came in 1940, after the House investigation, when David Lasser quit as president of the Workers Alliance and started the American Security Union, which barred Communists, Nazis, and Fascists from membership.

10. Leaflet of Chauffeurs, Auto Mechanics, Truck Masters, Gas Attendants Union, November 1938, Fiorello La Guardia Papers, New York City Municipal Archives; *New York Times,* 20 September 1938, p. 2; 2 October 1938, p. 45; 3 October 1938, p. 16; 12 July 1939, p. 18; 7 June 1939, p. 7; New York *Sun,* 11 July 1939, pp. 1, 2; New York *Herald Tribune,* 6 June 1939, pp. 5, 10; 4 May 1939, p. 18; U.S. Congress, House Subcommittee, *Investigation and Study of the WPA,* 1: 991, 293, 995–1000, 1298, 10.

11. New York *Herald Tribune,* 26 April 1939, p. 10; Roosevelt used the authority granted to him in the Federal Reorganization Act of 1939 to effect these changes. In May 1939 he appointed John Carmody to head the Federal Works Agency, and Harrington continued in command of the WPA, now under the title of commissioner of the Work Projects Administration.

12. New York *Herald Tribune,* 28 April 1939, pp. 1, 13; U.S. *Congressional Record,* 76th Cong., 1st sess., 1939, 84, pt. 7: 7165, 7167, 7241–44, 7341–45, 7352, 7361–63; U.S. Congress, House Subcommittee, *Investigation and Study of the WPA,* 1: 359.

13. Among the signers were Brooks Atkinson of the *New York Times;* Burnes Mantle, *Daily News;* Sidney Whipple, *World-Telegram;* John Gassner, *Forum;* Paul Peters, *Life;* and Arthur Pollock, Brooklyn *Daily Eagle.*

14. In the previous fiscal year New York City had paid approximately 22 percent of the cost of WPA undertakings.

15. William F. McDonald, *Federal Relief Administration and the Arts* (Columbus, Ohio, 1969), pp. 309–10; Flanagan, *Arena,* p. 353; Mangione, *Dream and the Deal,* pp. 11–13; U.S. *Congressional Record,* 76th Cong., 1st sess., 1939, 84, pt. 7: 7291–94, 7363–74, 7385, 7957, 7958, 7962, 7978, 7966, and pt. 8: 8049, 8057, 8077, 8078, 8115–31, 8098–8102, 8084, 8086, 8089, 8131; New York *Herald Tribune,* 23 June 1939, p. 13; 21 June 1939, p. 1; *New York Times,* 1 July 1939, p. 2.

16. U.S. *Congressional Record,* 76th Cong., 1st sess., 1939, 84, pt. 8: 8450–52, 8453, 8456, 8457, 8459, 8407; Flanagan, *Arena,* p. 362; *New York Times,* 1 July 1939, pp. 1, 2; New York *Herald Tribune,* 2 July 1939, p. 4.

17. U.S. *Statutes at Large* (53), Emergency Relief Appropriations Act of 1939, section 16(b), p. 933; U.S. Congress, House Subcommittee of the

Committee on Appropriations, *Hearings on the Emergency Relief Appropriations Act of 1941*, 76th Cong., 3d sess. (Washington, D.C., 1940), pp. 438–39; Ellen Tarry, "How the History Was Assembled: One Writer's Memories," in *The Negro in New York: An Informal Social History*, ed. Roi Ottley and William J. Weatherby (New York, 1967), p. XII; Jacob Kainen, "The Graphic Arts Division of the WPA Federal Art Project," in *The New Deal Art Projects: An Anthology of Memoirs*, ed. Francis V. O'Connor (Washington, D.C., 1972), pp. 163–64; *New York Times*, 9 September 1939, p. 19; 31 January 1940, p. 13; 19 July 1939, p. 1.

18. Those signing included Robert Hutchins, president of the University of Chicago; Professor Franz Boas of Columbia; Frank Graham, president of the University of North Carolina; and acting president of New York City College, Nelson Mead.

19. U.S. Congress, House Subcommittee, *Hearings, 1941*, pp. 527–28; *New York Times*, 16 July 1939, p. 1; 29 July 1939, p. 13; 17 July 1939, p. 1; 7 August 1939, p. 1; New York City Department of Public Welfare, Report to Fiorello La Guardia from Com. William Hodson, 16 November 1939, Fiorello La Guardia Papers, New York City Municipal Archives.

20. New York WPA workers suffered actual pay cuts, as well, because another provision in the 1939 law required sectional readjustments of wage scales. The pay of rural, Southern WPA employees was to be raised, while that of urban, Northeastern workers was lowered.

21. U.S. *Statutes at Large* (53), ERA 1939, section 15 (a), p. 933; *New York Times*, 6 July 1939, p. 1; 7 July 1939, p. 1; 8 July 1939, pp. 1, 2; 1 September 1939, p. 13; 18 July 1939, p. 4; 20 July 1939, p. 1; 21 July 1939, p. 1; 6 August 1939, p. 20; 12 July 1939, p. 1; *New York Post*, 5 July 1939, p. 2; 6 July 1939, pp. 1, 12; 7 July 1939, pp. 1, 6; 14 July 1939, p. 1; Arthur Macmahon et al., *The Administration of Work Relief* (Chicago, 1941), pp. 156–57; U.S. Congress, House Subcommittee, *Hearings, 1941*, pp. 529–30, 434.

22. U.S. *Statutes at Large*, sections 12, 1 (d), 25 (a), 25 (b), pp. 932, 936; *New York Times*, 21 June 1939, p. 3; 24 July 1939, p. 1; 2 July 1939, p. 3; 3 July 1939, p. 23; 5 August 1939, p. 9; Elias Huzar, "The New WPA," *Survey Midmonthly* 75 (October 1939): 301; U.S. WPA for N.Y.C., *Final Report*, p. 114; *New York Herald Tribune*, 1 July 1939, p. 6; Mathews, *The Federal Theatre*, p. 295; U.S. Congress, House Subcommittee, *Hearings, 1941*, pp. 534–35.

10

The Last Years

The last years of the WPA, from 1 July 1939 to 1 February 1943, opened with the New York City agency attempting to recover from the disruptions caused by the Emergency Relief Act for 1939–40. During much of the summer of 1939, projects either halted entirely or operated at a fraction of their former size and efficiency. By late fall, however, Somervell's administration began to rally. The strike over the prevailing-wage issue came to an end in October. This eased the shortage of skilled laborers for the construction undertakings. Also, the colonel by then could rehire many of the experienced building trades workers dropped in July and August because of the eighteen-month-maximum rule. Furthermore, with all personnel required to put in thirty hours a week, the WPA started to make greater use of its engineers and other professionals.

As crews returned to their tasks, the community benefited once more from the fruits of relief labor. La Guardia Airport, the biggest job ever tackled by the WPA, opened for commercial flights in October, although it was not yet finished. For another year Somervell's workers continued to add runways and hangars. On a single day in April 1940, the mayor officially accepted from the colonel two newly completed firehouses, a school, and a wing of the registrar's headquarters in Queens. Meanwhile, another band of WPA laborers was transforming Bedloe's Island, home of the Statue of Liberty. They removed a hodgepodge of abandoned army barracks, replacing these with lawns, shrubbery, and living quarters for the members of the United States Park Service stationed there. On a reduced scale, the white-collar division also continued to supply New York with the extra personnel that permitted municipal departments to maintain and expand their services.[1]

The former units of Federal Project number 1 in New York, minus the theater group, faced the greatest adjustments under the Emergency Relief Act of 1939. Some of the arts survived the transfer from national control to local supervision better than others. The Writers' Project, which, along with the drama division, had been the prime target of the Dies Committee, suffered the most. First, the layoffs necessitated by the reduced appropriation and the eighteen-month rule removed many talented authors. Then many of the local and national administrators, including Alsberg, handed in their resignations. The congressional probe had also shattered the morale of the personnel who remained. As a result, the New York office initiated few imaginative new undertakings after July 1939. The momentum generated before that date, however, enabled the writers to complete a number of books that had been in preparation, such as *American Wild Life* (1940), *The Film Index* (1941) and *A Maritime History of New York* (1941). As the nation edged toward war, the work relief authors spent more and more of their time grinding out manuals for the armed forces and publicity releases for civil defense organizations.

The music and art endeavors fared better. The Music Project, now integrated into the service division of Somervell's agency, gave more performances in the season that began in November 1939 than ever before in its history. The pride of the WPA, the New York City Symphony Orchestra, made up of the top ninety-five relief musicians,

A poster designed by WPA artists to advertise the free classes offered by members of the Federal Music Project. *Photo by the Photographic Division, Federal Art Project, WPA.*

offered the public fifty concerts—double the number played the previous year. In addition, the WPA in the metropolis took over direction of eight dance orchestras, two bands, two choral groups, and three ensembles, as well as ninety-six centers where 188 music teachers instructed twenty-two thousand students free of charge.

During the 1940–41 season, the New York City Symphony Orchestra featured young American artists such as Susanne Fisher, soprano; Douglas Stanbury, baritone; and Edward Kilenyi, pianist. Sunday evening concerts at Carnegie Hall drew capacity crowds, demonstrating once again that there was an interested audience for classical music. The key to a big turnout seemed to be keeping the price of tickets low enough so that music lovers of limited means could afford to buy them. The WPA realized this and charged no more than $1.10 for the best seats and as little as $.28 for the balcony.

In January 1940 the artists also demonstrated that they were back at work. An exhibit of their creations opened at the American Museum of Natural History. Displays included models of sculpture destined to adorn the Community Center of the Queensbridge Housing Project and photographs of preliminary work by Ruth Gikow on a mural for the Children's Ward of Bronx Hospital.

At about the same time, another erstwhile section of Federal Project number 1, the Historical Records Survey, completed its first volume—"Inventory of County and Borough Archives of Richmond." The New York City WPA mimeographed 250 copies, which it distributed to the New York State Department of Archives, local newspapers, the Public Library, colleges and universities in the community, and various municipal officials.[2]

As spring approached, the yearly anxiety about the fate of these endeavors and the reliefers who worked on them mounted. Through the winter Francis Harrington had allowed the New York City job quota to expand slightly, until by March 1940 the rolls had grown to 115,000. By April, however, the inadequate appropriation for 1939–40 began to run out, necessitating austerity measures. National headquarters informed Somervell that he must reduce his personnel to 100,000 by 1 June. The colonel complied by not replacing the men he was forced to drop between March and June because they had reached their eighteen-month limit. This attrition, combined with the small but steady stream who left to take outside positions, accomplished the cutback without requiring another round of dismissals. What would happen on 1 July? Was the staff to remain at 100,000, increase, or decrease? The answers to these questions, of course, had to come from the president and Congress.

Roosevelt started the new year with optimism about the prospects for business revival. Expecting that the American economy, stimulated by war abroad and stepped-up defense spending, would soon absorb many of the jobless, he proposed that the lawmakers provide $985 million for the WPA to cover 1940–41. However, by April, when industrial recovery had not matched his anticipations, the president called the members of the Woodrum appropriations subcommittee to a conference at the White House. There he informed them that his January estimates of the WPA's needs had been too low. He now suggested that the committee draft a bill granting $975 million for the organization, with the proviso that all of the money could be spent in eight months rather than over a year's time if substantial unemployment persisted. Roosevelt's proposal aroused attacks from both the right and the left. Raymond Moley, earlier a presidential adviser but more recently a disillusioned critic of the New Deal, claimed that the state of the economy did not require such a large sum. Rather, he charged, the chief executive wanted the inflated fund to pad WPA rolls and buy Democratic votes in 1940.

The radical congressman who represented Harlem, Vito Marcantonio, on the other hand, called $975 million for the coming eight months "entirely insufficient." He pointed out that job openings remained scarce in New York, and any reductions in WPA employment would simply throw more people on home relief. Besides, providing for less than a year ahead made it next to impossible for cities to plan construction and other work relief projects sensibly. As an alternative, he introduced a bill that he named the American Standards Work and Assistance Act. Under its provisions the WPA would be allowed to hire three million men and women instead of the fewer than two million that Roosevelt's request would permit. His bill also attempted to undo most of the changes perpetrated by the conservatives the year before; it would eliminate the eighteen-month maximum and restore the prevailing-wage principle. Finally, Marcantonio desired to sever the connection between relief status and eligibility for public work entirely, making any unemployed person, on welfare or not, eligible for a WPA position. La Guardia, always an advocate of more federal help for depression victims, endorsed the Marcantonio bill.[3]

Needless to say, the House Appropriations Subcommittee paid little attention to Marcantonio's proposals. Woodrum and his economy-minded colleagues felt that federal work relief had operated badly. They differed among themselves only on how great the failure had been and what to do about it. On 15 May 1940 the subcommittee issued two reports concerning the WPA. J. O'Connor Roberts, committee counsel, wrote the majority statement, and the Democratic members signed it. The study focused on the situation in twelve states and in the city of New York. A dozen pages devoted to the latter condemned Somervell's agency. Most of the critical material was a rehash of the charges produced at the 1939 hearings, such as left-wing infiltration, poor administration, and inefficiency.

The Republican members of the subcommittee, headed by John Taber of upstate New York, presented an even harsher assessment of the metropolitan WPA in their minority report. They said that the Roberts inquiry had barely scratched the surface, neglecting to mention that the organization played politics and gave ruinous competition to private enterprise. They concluded that federal work relief had failed so miserably that it should be terminated at once. States and localities ought to administer their own welfare programs with the help of grants from Washington.

The Democratic majority, following Woodrum's leadership, rejected the advice of their Republican colleagues. Instead, they drafted a bill providing the WPA with $975,650,000 to be spent, if necessary, in the first eight months of the fiscal year ending 30 June 1941. In most other respects the subcommittee bill resembled the Emergency Relief Act of 1939. It retained the eighteen-month rule, despite Roosevelt's request for its modification, and the requirement of a 25 percent sponsor's contribution. A new feature placed specific ceilings on the number of people the WPA could hire during each season. The rolls were not to exceed 1.7 million in the summer, 1.8 million in the fall, or 2 million for the winter. By inserting these restrictions, the Southern Democrats and the Republicans on the subcommittee hoped to prevent the administration from greatly increasing work relief forces prior to the elections and thereby gaining additional votes for New Dealers.[4]

On the House floor the bill underwent some important changes. Liberals succeeded in softening the eighteen-month maximum somewhat by winning exemptions for widows and wives of veterans, as well as for the veterans themselves, and for WPA employees over forty-five years of age if they supported dependents. The ban on WPA construction costing more than fifty-two thousand dollars was also modified. The congressmen agreed to raise the ceiling to one hundred thousand dollars largely because many of them, beginning to worry about defense preparations, wanted the WPA to put idle men to work building armories, forts, air fields, and training camps. When Congressman Celler offered an amendment to revive the theater project, however, it quickly suffered defeat.

Congressman Francis Walter, Democrat of Pennsylvania, introduced an amendment that won House approval without any debate and on a standing vote. It barred Communists and Nazi Bund members from holding WPA jobs. All personnel on the rolls would be required to sign an oath swearing that they were not affiliated with either organization and did not advocate the overthrow of the government. Anyone who refused to comply would be dismissed. If a worker lied about his activities, he could be punished by a two-thousand-dollar fine and up to two years in prison.

Several things probably account for the ready assent of the House and later the Senate to this provision. Many lawmakers were worried about the radicals' infiltration of the WPA reported by the Dies and Woodrum Committees. The Nazi-Soviet Pact and the subsequent attacks by Germany and Russia on Poland and Finland heightened the fear and dislike of the two totalitarian states and of their sympathizers in this country. The war in Europe and defense preparations, moreover, kindled patriotic sentiments and brought forth demands for political cohesion and conformity. Governor Lehman of New York set aside one day a year for state residents to celebrate "I Am An American Day," and loyalty oaths became popular. In this atmosphere the House Un-American Activities Committee flourished.

The Senate made almost no changes in the House bill. With Hitler's blitzkrieg unleashed in the West, however, the lawmakers turned increasing attention to speeding American war readiness. WPA leaders, fully aware of this concern, did all they could to persuade Congress that their agency had a vital role to play. Testifying before the Senate Appropriations Subcommittee, Harrington pledged that the WPA would spend at least one-quarter of its funds for 1940–41 to employ five hundred thousand people on defense projects. He pointed out that in the previous fiscal year the organization had expended $125 million on national-preparedness endeavors. Without the WPA the nation's air power would have been in much worse shape since, in the past five years, the agency had been responsible for 85 percent of all airport construction. The senators apparently found such statements convincing because, for undertakings designated necessary to defense by either the secretary of war or navy, they waived the requirement that sponsors pay 25 percent of the costs. In conference committee the House agreed to this change. By mid-June the bill passed and went to the White House, where Roosevelt signed it into law.[5]

Of the various provisions in the Emergency Relief Act for 1940–41, the Walter Amendment produced the most immediate repercussions in New York City. Somervell announced that all of his employees would have to sign loyalty affidavits before July or face dismissal. He decided, moreover, to go farther than this in compliance with the law. Estimating that there must be at least one thousand Communists and fellow travelers on his rolls, he proposed to ferret them out. His staff checked the names of all persons working for the agency against Board of Elections records to find out if any were registered as Communists. The colonel asked both the FBI and the Dies Committee to help him investigate the politics of his personnel. In addition, he appealed to the public to report to him any relevant information they possessed about WPA laborers. Somervell, hoping that the citizenry would write him as many as fifty thousand letters with important leads, promised that he would screen out the obvious grudge and crank correspondence.

One might speculate as to why the New York administrator enforced the act with such zeal. After all, on assuming office he had renounced any interest in continuing his predecessor's red purge. Very likely, four years of dealing with the militant leaders of the left-wing unions, along with the frequent demonstrations, work-stoppages, and protests that they directed, had changed his mind. When Congress afforded this opportunity to get rid of some of his most troublesome adversaries, he seized the opportunity.

The new law and Somervell's efforts to implement it aroused heated debate. Much local opinion felt that the measures were long overdue. The New York *Sun* applauded the moves, saying: "For a government to take from loyal citizens their hard-earned money and bestow it as a subsidy on its enemies [is] ludicrous." The American Civil Liberties Union, with quite a different point of view, called such actions a "deprivation of civil rights wholly without justification." Many CIO unions wrote to WPA headquarters in Washington asking for Somervell's removal because of the way in which he was enforcing the provision, especially with regard to his cooperation with the Dies Committee and his encouragement of anonymous letters.[6]

Needless to say, the Workers Alliance and its allies, such as the WPA Teachers Union (AFL) and the United American Artists, Local 60 (CIO), resisted the new law with whatever force they still commanded. The Workers Alliance organized picket lines around Somervell's offices on Columbus Avenue. Maxwell Bodenheim, the Greenwich Village poet and novelist who had been fired by the colonel from the WPA's Bibliographies and Indices Project, led one of the demonstrations.[7] He admitted having once belonged to the party but claimed that he had not been a Communist since 1938. The Workers Alliance also offered to finance a test case in the courts for any WPA employee who refused to sign the oath. A fifty-seven-year-old stenographer named Charlotte Long, who handed in a blank affidavit, became the first to accept such aid. Arthur Garfield Hays, head of the ACLU, represented Long and a number of others who challenged the law, but they received little satisfaction. The U.S. District Court threw out their cases on the grounds that less than three thousand dollars was involved, which was not a large enough sum to bestow federal jurisdiction. The decisions were upheld on appeal.

Unmoved by the uproar, Somervell continued to look for and drop people he considered subversive. Even with his careful searching, he did not find as many Communists as he originally estimated were on the rolls. Scrutiny of 10,000 names of voters registered as Communists in New York revealed that 562 had worked for the WPA at one time or another. However, 551 of them no longer were employed either because they had left to take outside jobs or had been laid off in earlier cutbacks. The colonel immediately fired the 11 registered Communists who remained. He also discharged persons presumed to be fellow travelers, Trotskyists, members of other Socialist splinter groups, and one alleged Nazi. By the end of 1940, 365 persons had been dropped in the disloyalty purge.

Matters did not end there. The protests from suspended workers, the ACLU, and the unions against Somervell's methods led national headquarters to reopen many of the cases. Review officers sent from Washington conducted hearings at which the accused were permitted to defend themselves. As a result, by May 1941 all but forty-six of the discharged New Yorkers had been reinstated and given a chance to make up the pay they had lost while separated from the WPA.[8]

The projects that the WPA began to concentrate on in July 1940 contributed far more to national security than did the attempts to remove Communists. As Harrington had promised Congress, his organization moved increasingly into defense work. In fact, after the fall of France in late June, the WPA chief announced that soon one-third of all work relief employees would be engaged in such activities. The New York City agency built or rehabilitated barracks, installed gas and electric power lines, constructed sewers, laid water pipes, paved roads, and made other improvements at military bases throughout the metropolitan area, including Forts Tilden, Totten, Hamilton, Wadsworth, and Lafayette, the Marine Hospital, and the Brooklyn Navy Yard. WPA workmen renovated and outfitted the Tusitala, the oldest full-rigged ship in the U.S. Navy, as a training vessel for merchant marine sailors. At Miller's Field on Staten Island, Somervell's crews tripled the size of the landing field, put up a new administration building, enlarged hangars, and installed a modern lighting system.

White-collar employees in 1940–41 assisted the army by giving chest X-rays to inductees called for their physical exams. These WPA teams took the X-ray pictures at the Tuberculosis Clinic in the municipal Health Department on Worth Street and at the various induction centers. By the time that the army assumed full responsibility for the job in late 1941, the local WPA had X-rayed sixty-six hundred men.

During the summer of 1940, as American industry became increasingly involved in war production, a paradoxical situation developed. Although much unemployment persisted, there was a shortage of labor with the technical skills required by defense plants. To combat this problem, the New York City Board of Education and Somervell's organization cooperated in setting up an Emergency Training Program for National Defense. Some of the teachers came from the WPA's Adult Education Project. The board hired the rest. The instructors offered ten-week courses in gas and steam marine-engine repair, sheet-metal work, ship rigging, instrument and pattern making, welding, electrical installation, radio maintenance work, and airplane repairs. The first 1,250 people from the rolls of the New York City WPA entered training on 16 July 1940.[9]

In the midst of the WPA's efforts to assist rearmament and develop war industries training, the Army recalled Somervell to Washington to serve as chief of the Construction Division in the office of the quartermaster general.[10] The order to leave, which came in November 1940, was not the first one the army had issued to the colonel. The previous spring the War Department had summoned the New York administrator to the capital, but the mayor blocked the move at that time. La Guardia had begged Roosevelt to intercede in the matter, claiming that Somervell's leadership was the best thing that had happened to the work relief program. The president promised to help and wrote the secretary of war, gaining an extension for the colonel in his WPA assignment. Now, however, Somervell made it clear that he wished to resume his military career, and La Guardia agreed not to stand in the way.

Somervell's departure produced a mixed response in the city. The left-wing unions, which had been agitating for his removal because of the way he was handling the red purge, felt gratified. But most municipal officials regretted his leaving. After working with him for four years, they had come to respect and appreciate his executive abilities. James Lyons, borough president of The Bronx, expressed this view when he wrote: "Colonel Somervell has done a splendid job in supervising the WPA activities in the City of New York." The *World-Telegram,* certainly no friend of the work relief agency, admitted that the colonel had "transformed the WPA here from a sprawling, boondoggling enterprise that specialized in internal office intrigue . . . into a quietly efficient business organization able to spend a billion dollars with nary a scandal or criticism of greater than trifling proportions."

Once he had reconciled himself to the loss of Somervell, La Guardia began to discuss the choice of a successor with Roosevelt. The mayor was as certain as ever that he did not want a politician in charge of the WPA. The president shared this sentiment and on 26 November 1940 appointed Oliver Gottschalk, a forty-four-year-old former army officer, acting administrator. Gottschalk had retired from the Army Air Corps after World War I to become director of several aircraft companies. In the course of his work, he met Hugh Johnson, who, in 1935, brought Gottschalk into the New York City WPA as chief of the Finance Division. Gottschalk retained the post under Ridder and then Somervell, moving from it into the number one spot in November 1940. His term as head of the local agency proved brief, however, for in March 1941 Somervell invited Gottschalk to become an assistant in the quartermaster general's office. Raymond Branion, who ran the WPA's Northeastern Regional Headquarters, looked after the municipal unit until 9 April 1941, when the president finally named Irving Huie to the vacant position.

Huie, who would preside over the New York WPA for the last year and one-half of its life, came to the job on loan from the La Guardia Administration. In fact, his taking over the work relief organization brought Washington and the urban government into the closest possible cooperation, since Huie continued to act as the mayor's commissioner of public works as well. A man of stocky build with dark hair and brown eyes, Huie was born in Brooklyn on 8 March 1890. Like Somervell, he was an engineer with much experience in public construction, including participation in building the Seventh Avenue subway and the Henry Hudson, Marine, and Bronx-Whitestone Parkways. His induction into creating employment for welfare recipients came in 1931 when he was chosen to head the Works Division of the Emergency Relief Bureau. Later, Hugh Johnson appointed him to the staff of the WPA. In 1938 La Guardia launched a municipal Department of Public Works and named Huie its chief engineer and also liaison officer between it and the WPA. Less than a year afterward, the mayor put him in charge of the entire department, the position that he subsequently combined with that of WPA administrator.

While the New York WPA was undergoing this rapid turnover of leadership, the president and Congress attempted to assess what effect rearmament was having on unemployment and thus on the need for work relief. Undoubtedly, there had been a marked absorption of the idle into private industry. Between 1 July 1940 and 30 June 1941 the number of jobless Americans declined by almost four million. As of November 1940, people were resigning from the New York City WPA to take outside positions at the rate of two thousand a week. By February 1941 home relief offices did not have enough eligible, able-bodied clients to replace the WPA personnel who were departing. Consequently, in the spring national headquarters reduced the job quota of the local agency from one hundred thousand to eighty thousand.[11]

Did these encouraging statistics indicate that the WPA would not require a supplemental appropriation for 1940–41 and that the organization might soon be phased out entirely? Roosevelt believed that such expectations were premature. In his State of the Union Message, early in 1941, the president told Congress that, although the increase in defense spending was having a bearing on employment, preparedness would not employ all of the idle in the immediate future.

The situation in the country and especially in New York City justified the president's words of caution. Despite the stimulation of the economy by war abroad, as of July 1941 there were still over five million Americans unemployed. In the metropolitan area the inability of the relief offices to supply replacements for people leaving the WPA did not mean that all of those capable of working had obtained jobs. Rather, restrictions on WPA hiring imposed by Congress made some assignments impossible. For example, there were twenty-five thousand able-bodied aliens on welfare, but since 1939 work relief positions had been restricted to citizens. There were also twenty-two thousand women and nineteen thousand partially handicapped or older men on home relief who could have been employed if the WPA had been running more white-collar, white-apron, light manufacturing, and service projects.

As for the eighty thousand on the New York City WPA in April 1941, the prospects that most would soon be absorbed by industry appeared slim. Outside employers rejected some of them because of age—about half of the people on the local WPA were over forty. Blacks found all too true the old saying that they were the first fired in hard times and the last rehired when prosperity returned. Civil rights groups, Governor Lehman, and Mayor La Guardia all charged that management and unions were excluding blacks from defense jobs and industrial training programs. Because of this discrimination, blacks tended to remain on the WPA long after their more fortunate white colleagues left. In November 1937 a little over 13 percent of the WPA personnel in the metropolis was black; by April 1941 the figure had climbed to 22 percent; and as of 30 October 1942 nearly one-third of all those still on the WPA were black.[12]

Finally, the War Department did not spread defense contracts evenly throughout the nation. Some states and localities received more than their share, while other communities received few orders and thus became pockets of

The Last Years

unemployment. New York fell into the latter category. By the end of October 1942, war contracts in the urban area amounted to $198 per capita as compared to a national average of $480, or $2,750 for every man, woman, and child in Detroit.[13]

Because of the persistent unemployment in New York and other communities, Roosevelt permitted the WPA to spend the $975,650,000 granted in June 1940 during the first eight months of the fiscal period. Thus, in January 1941, the president had to ask Congress to supplement the original sum with $375,000,000. The lawmakers agreed to the request from the White House with a minimum of resistance. Perhaps they felt relieved that the total year's expenditure was well below what Colonel Harrington had earlier estimated the WPA would require for 1940–41.

In a message to Congress on 20 May 1941, Roosevelt spoke further about relief needs. He restated his belief that defense spending and lend-lease should continue to create new openings, reducing WPA rolls, but he also reemphasized his conviction that the federal program could not be terminated yet. For the fiscal year ending 30 June 1942, he suggested that the WPA would be able to get along on a budget of $875 million, or roughly two-thirds of what it had spent in the previous twelve months. The president also recommended that Capitol Hill eliminate the ban on positions for aliens and the eighteen-month maximum, and he called upon the WPA to step up its vocational training to help its personnel obtain jobs in defense industry.[14]

The modesty of the president's figure dismayed liberals, who pointed out that with such a limited appropriation the WPA would have to cut back its rolls from roughly 1.7 million to less than 1 million. A group of Southern Democratic and many Republican lawmakers, on the other hand, attempted to pare the sum to $500 million. The most conservative Republicans favored immediate elimination of federal work relief. The majority of both houses, however, accepted Roosevelt's recommendation on funding and also agreed to the virtual elimination of the eighteen-month rule.[15] Finally, in the Emergency Relief Act passed on 30 June 1941, Capitol Hill rejected the White House's suggestion that the WPA be allowed to hire resident aliens.

The new law had an immediate impact on the unemployed in New York City. The repeal of the year-and-one-half maximum saved some people on the WPA from mandatory discharges, but the small appropriation led to a new round of dismissals. Late in June national headquarters notified Huie that in light of the bill about to pass Congress he would have to cut his rolls from 73,000 to 59,200. The administrator complied reluctantly, stating his belief that few of those he fired could find jobs. He expected 50 to 75 percent of them to wind up on home relief.[16]

The reduced funds available for 1941–42 and Roosevelt's expressed desire to see the WPA give more vocational education to its personnel led the New York City organization to step up its training and placement efforts. In the summer of 1941, Huie initiated an in-plant training program. He and his staff members attempted to persuade factory managers to try out WPA men and women who had been taking courses in sheet-metal work, pattern making, welding, and so on. The federal agency offered to pay the wages of these individuals for a four-week breaking-in period. At the end of the month, if the novice proved satisfactory, the company was to hire him at the rates of compensation prevailing in the industry.

Huie's proposal met a cool reception from many businessmen. Some did not want to be bothered with training employees, preferring to look for experienced help. Quite a few were prejudiced against people who had been on relief, regarding them as bums and misfits. Big contractors cared little for the WPA's promise of a month's free labor since they operated on a cost-plus basis in the agreements they signed with the government. The WPA, however, managed to induce a number of firms to test the plan. The scheme appealed particularly to small subcontractors who worked on a competitive rather than on a cost-plus arrangement and who therefore appreciated the savings on labor that the

WPA's proposition entailed. The overall results were not as positive as Huie and his assistants had hoped. Slightly more than half of the trainees assigned to subcontractors pleased their foremen enough to be kept on after the initial month. The rejection of nearly 50 percent can probably be explained by the fact that the people still on the WPA in 1941 and 1942 tended to be the aging, the partially disabled, and the least skilled and educated.

The in-plant training program, nonetheless, scored some notable successes. The Carpenter Container Corporation and the Ledkote Products Company, both located in Long Island City, Queens between them, hired over three hundred WPA provisionals during a six-week period in 1941. The Ledkote Company up to that time had followed a restrictive employment policy, barring both women and blacks. The New York City WPA refused to go along with this discrimination and placed its people in the factory without regard to sex or race. After the month's trial, the establishment hired most of those the WPA had sent, including thirty women and thirty-nine blacks.

In addition to developing on-the-job training, the WPA endeavored to interest management in its personnel by other methods. Staff members repeatedly visited local businessmen to inquire if they had any openings. The agency ran a series of eight radio programs and printed brochures that described the vocational preparation the WPA gave its laborers and listed the occupations for which they were qualified. Mayor La Guardia and other city officials also praised WPA enrollees over the air and in the press. The efforts induced quite a few firms to send representatives to interview men and women on work relief. During 1941 and 1942 these contacts led to placements of five thousand individuals with such companies as Federal Shipbuilding, Sperry Gyroscope, and Wright Aeronautical.

Until its employees left to take outside positions, the New York City WPA found an increasing number of defense-related tasks for them to perform in the community. Throughout the summer and fall of 1941, these projects existed side by side with those serving the Board of Education, the Park Department, the libraries and museums, and other municipal authorities. After Pearl Harbor, however, the WPA closed out most undertakings filling primarily peacetime purposes and concentrated instead on programs contributing to the war effort or to basic civilian needs such as food, health, and clothing.[17]

Many of the new projects attempted to protect and prepare residents in case of enemy attack. The sewing shops manufactured armbands for air wardens, asbestos shields for fire fighters, emergency stockpiles of blankets, clothes, and sheets, and bandages and surgical dressings. Other crews constructed fifty portable first aid rooms complete with stretchers, cots, and the rest of the standard Red Cross equipment. White-collar personnel made a survey of bed space in volunteer and private hospitals and took microfilms of all essential local government records.

The WPA joined the police and the Red Cross in training New Yorkers to perform emergency services. Some of the men working for the WPA received instruction on how to repair sewers, the water supply system, and highways should they be damaged by bombing, fire, or natural disaster. Two hundred sixty WPA teachers ran eight hundred courses in first aid, home hygiene, home nursing, and nutrition, which were open to any resident of the city over seventeen years of age. Mayor La Guardia commented that the effort provided the community with a force of experienced people "essential to any program of civilian defense."

Huie's agency increased its help to hospitals, which were beginning to suffer from a shortage of nurses, doctors, and other trained personnel. In 1941 the WPA launched a drive to prepare people on its rolls to be medical aides. The individuals chosen reported to clinics and infirmaries throughout the city, where they acquired a variety of nonprofessional health skills. After their learning period, many became regular staff members of the institutions. Others went on assisting in various wards, but the WPA continued to pay them. The remainder returned to their original projects to form a reservoir of urban residents who could serve in case of emergency.

By 1942 the United States began to use steel and scrap iron faster than it could produce them. At the beginning of the year, industry officials predicted a six-million-ton shortage of scrap iron in the twelve months ahead. The New York City WPA did its bit to alleviate the problem. During the winter its laborers dug up thirteen thousand tons of streetcar tracks no longer in use in Brooklyn, Queens, and The Bronx. The reclaimed metal went to the War Department for fine quality scrap steel. A *New York Times* reporter estimated that the retrieved rails could be converted into 11,000 seventy-five-millimeter cannons or 220,000 machine guns. These varied projects led Gen. George Marshall, army chief of staff, to declare that "in the great task of preparing for national defense, the WPA has proved itself to be an invaluable aid."[18]

Conservatives in Congress did not share General Marshall's view about the usefulness of the WPA to the military effort. Immediately after Pearl Harbor, the enemies of the New Deal added participation in the war to their arsenal of arguments for curtailment of all federal welfare programs. The Joint Congressional Committee on Non-Essential Expenditures issued a majority report on 26 December 1941, written by its chairman, Sen. Harry Byrd of Virginia. This document urged reductions of more than $1 billion in nondefense spending in the coming fiscal year, to be accomplished by abolishing the Civilian Conservation Corps, the National Youth Administration, and the training activities of the Office of Education, and by cutting $400 million off the next appropriation for the WPA.

The president indicated considerable willingness to go along with the majority on the Byrd Committee. In his budget message, delivered to Congress on 7 January, he said that some work relief would be necessary in the year ahead, but estimated that the WPA could operate on a budget slashed by half. He promised Capitol Hill that he would make a more specific request in the spring. In fact, by May 1942 Roosevelt went further than the senators in supporting domestic economizing. Rather than asking the lawmakers for $400 million for the WPA for 1942-43, he proposed a sum of slightly more than $280 million. The drastic cutback meant that, instead of employing an average of one million Americans, as the WPA did in 1941-42, the organization could at best retain four hundred thousand.

In his May address the president admitted that there were still around three million jobless, but he predicted that most of them would surely be absorbed either by the armed forces or private industry before long. The $280 million appropriation for the WPA should be used to help those few who, because of age, lack of skill, or other handicap, were rejected by business and the military. The agency would assign them to day-labor projects that required a minimum of scarce materials.

The Democrats on the House Appropriations Subcommittee accepted the suggestion from the White House and submitted to the congressmen a bill allotting the WPA $280 million. On the floor, John Taber, speaking for the disgruntled Republican minority, led a drive of Southern rural Democrats and members of the GOP to end the life of federal work relief once and for all. When the congressmen voted on Taber's proposal, the conservatives nearly won, gaining 119 ayes to 123 noes.[19]

Among those who pleaded most eloquently against both the Taber move and the pitifully small allocation in the committee bill were members of the New York City delegation, particularly Congressmen Marcantonio and Celler. They pointed out that the WPA was disappearing at a time when their community still needed it desperately. Unemployment in New York, rather than dwindling as a result of participation in the war, had begun to climb again. The city had received only 2 percent of all prime contracts awarded in connection with the military effort, which meant that defense-plant jobs in the urban area were scarce. Furthermore, shortages of raw materials and rationing of civilian products were every day forcing garment factories, gas stations, retail stores, and other businesses to close down or reduce their operations and lay off personnel. Thus, in the spring of 1942, somewhere between three hundred thousand and four hundred thousand New Yorkers were out of work.

Although the efforts of the New York congressmen may have helped to defeat the Taber amendment, they did not succeed in enlarging the proposed WPA budget for 1942–43. By a vote of 279 to 52 the congressmen passed the $280 million measure and sent it to the Senate. The upper chamber added $3 million, and on 30 June a bill containing the slightly augmented sum won the approval of both houses.

From the attitude in Congress and the very limited appropriation granted by the Emergency Relief Act, Huie recognized that the life of the WPA was almost over. He instructed his staff to begin no new projects and to attempt to complete those in progress as quickly as possible. In compliance with orders from Washington, he also began to release his employees. In June 46,500 men and women worked for the local agency; by September 29,000 remained. Some of the shrinkage resulted from people leaving voluntarily to take other jobs, but most occurred through forced layoffs due to lack of funds.

The steady erosion of the WPA during the summer of 1942 did not satisfy its critics. They continued to harp on the idea that the organization had no place in a wartime economy. In October 1942 the *New York Times* wrote: "WPA should now be liquidated. In the present labor shortage there is no room for made-work." The Republicans, many of whom had been in the forefront of the fight to kill the WPA the previous spring, won substantial victories in the congressional races of November 1942, picking up forty-two seats in the House and nine in the Senate. Immediately after the elections, Sen. Arthur Vandenberg, Michigan Republican, proposed a bipartisan coalition with "politics and New Dealism" out for the duration of the war.[20]

These developments, together with an improving employment situation (workers in New York and other cities with few defense plants began migrating to more promising areas), must have influenced Roosevelt to hasten the end of the WPA. On 4 December 1942 the president ordered the "prompt liquidation" of the agency, asking that all projects be closed down by 1 February 1943. Roosevelt used most of the message terminating the federal emergency program to repeat for the last time his faith in the experiment he and Hopkins had launched in 1935:

> Seven years ago I was convinced that providing useful work is superior to any and every kind of dole. Experience has amply justified this policy.
>
> The WPA has reached a creative hand into every county in the nation . . . added to the national wealth, repaired the wastage of depression and strengthened the country to bear the burden of war.

Roosevelt concluded with the reminder that the lessons learned from the WPA should not be forgotten in the future.

The directive to shut down the WPA came at a time when more than twenty-five thousand New Yorkers still depended on it for their living, and many others were receiving services rendered by its 145 projects.[21] The latter included children enrolled in WPA nursery schools, adults in literacy and citizenship classes, patients in hospitals, and students eating free school lunches. Huie and his staff did what they could to ease the burden for both employees and the community. They urged the city to take over as many of the civilian projects as possible. The La Guardia Administration agreed to continue several, such as the free lunch program, the nursery schools, and the support of the hospital aides. Huie also attempted, with some success, to get the army and other government agencies that sponsored the defense activities of the WPA to hire the displaced employees. Finally, Huie made a plea over the municipal radio station for industry to engage the men and women about to be dismissed. Despite his efforts, Huie anticipated that about half of the former WPA personnel would wind up on home relief.

On 1 February 1943 the New York City WPA closed its Columbus Avenue headquarters. To its critics its passing represented no loss. The *New York Times* said: "It is to be hoped that the WPA in the form in which it has existed will never be revived." The *Sun* called it a "depression dinosaur" that should have become extinct long ago. On the other hand, many municipal officials regretted that the program was over. Spokesmen for the Board of Education stated that the ending of the special services that the WPA had performed for the schools since 1935 would be a distinct blow. La Guardia felt particularly sorry that the WPA orchestra would not play again over the municipal radio station.[22]

But neither foe nor friend commented upon the remarkable transition the WPA underwent in its last years. Nearly destroyed by the attacks of the Dies and Woodrum Committees and by parts of the Emergency Relief Act of 1939, the agency in New York, nonetheless, pulled itself together and resumed its work for the community. As it did so, World War II began in Europe, causing the president and Congress to place concern for national defense well ahead of the continuing unemployment problem. The leaders of the WPA recognized, under these circumstances, that the survival of the organization depended on its ability to convince the lawmakers that it had a vital role to play in preparedness. Increasingly, then, the WPA, including the New York office, closed out strictly peacetime endeavors. Instead, it concentrated on training workers for war industries; building forts, military roads, and airports; retrieving scrap metal; and aiding civil defense. While making this contribution to the preparedness and war efforts, it also eased the lot of thousands of unemployed persons whom private enterprise was slow to reabsorb, such as those past middle age, blacks, the under-educated and under-trained, and the physically handicapped.

The retooled WPA, however, did not win support from the majority on Capitol Hill. With heavy war spending, the conservatives became ever more insistent that all domestic programs be curtailed. And the New Dealers had not succeeded in convincing most legislators or the public that the government had an obligation to act as employer of last resort on a permanent basis. To the majority of Americans the WPA remained what it had always been, a depression aberration to be tolerated for a limited time only. It is therefore not surprising that Roosevelt eventually surrendered to the resurgent Republicans and conservative Democrats and terminated the WPA at a time when there were still several hundred thousand unemployed dependent on it.

NOTES

1. New York *Herald Tribune*, 5 April 1940, p. 19; *New York World-Telegram*, 4 April 1940, p. 3; New York *Post*, 1 March 1940, p. 6.

2. Jerre Mangione, *The Dream and the Deal: The Federal Writers' Project, 1935–1943* (Boston, 1972), pp. 330, 333, 336, 345; "Writers' Project: 1942," *New Republic*, 13 April 1942, p. 480; *Newsweek*, 31 March 1941, p. 63; New York *Herald Tribune*, 27 November 1939, p. 9; 9 January 1940, p. 15; 15 January 1940, p. 13.

3. New York *Herald Tribune*, 16 March 1940, p. 5; 18 April 1940, p. 12; *New York Times*, 29 May 1940, p. 24; New York *Post*, 5 April 1940, p. 14; Raymond Moley, "Perspective," *Newsweek*, 29 April 1940, p. 64; House Subcommittee of the Committee on Appropriations, "Statement of Vito Marcantonio," 18 April 1940, *Hearings on the Emergency Relief Appropriations Act of 1941*, 76th Cong., 3d sess. (Washington, D.C., 1940), pp. 1161–65.

4. New York *World-Telegram*, 15 May 1940, pp. 1, 3; New York *Herald Tribune*, 16 May 1940, p. 12; *New York Times*, 16 May 1940, p. 19; 24 May 1940, p. 1; Donald Howard, *The WPA and Federal Relief Policy* (New York, 1943), p. 523.

5. U.S. *Congressional Record*, 76th Cong., 3d sess., 1940, 86, pt. 6: 6746, 6753–55, 6746, 6762–63; New York *Herald Tribune*, 27 May 1940, p. 10; 6 June 1940, p. 14; Elias Huzar, "New WPA Rules Affecting Municipalities," *American City* 55 (July 1940): 5; *New York Times*, 24 May 1940, p. 1; New York *Post*, 6 June 1940, p. 18; New York *World-Telegram*, 5 June 1940, p. 3; Howard, *WPA and Federal Relief Policy*, p. 147.

6. New York *World-Telegram*, 22 June 1940, pp. 1, 2; *New York Times*, 23 June 1940, p. 1; New York *Herald Tribune*, 25 June 1940, p. 30; New York *Sun*, 25 June 1940, p. 18; Letters to Francis Harrington and Howard O. Hunter from United Retail and Wholesale Department Store Em-

The Last Years 279

ployees, Fur and Leather Workers Union, United Office and Professional Workers Union, Furniture Workers Union, and United Shoe Workers Union, fall 1940, Papers of the U.S. WPA for N.Y.C., National Archives, Washington, D.C.

7. Bodenheim was one of six employees whom Somervell fired because they had signed their names to a copy of Earl Browder's *People's Front*, which they gave as a present to a Writers' Project supervisor named Edwin Banta. Above their names they had written the following inscription: "Presented to Comrade Edwin Banta by the members of the Federal Writers' Unit No. 36s, Communist Party of the U.S.A. in recognition of his devotion to and untiring efforts on behalf of our party and communism—March 2, 1938." Banta subsequently turned the volume over to the Dies Committee.

8. *New York Times*, 1 July 1940, p. 8; 27 June 1940, p. 25; 17 July 1940, p. 23; 29 August 1940, p. 21; 14 September 1940, p. 1; 23 June 1940, p. 1; *Work* (National edition), 15 August 1940, p. 1; New York *Herald Tribune*, 2 August 1940, p. 1; 5 November 1940, p. 27; *Long v. Somervell*, 175 Misc. 119 affd. 261 App. Div. 946 (1940); *Carroll v. Somervell*, 116 F. 2d 918 (2d Cir., 1941); Howard, *WPA and Federal Relief Policy*, pp. 321-22.

9. New York *Herald Tribune*, 1 July 1940, p. 5; 21 October 1940, p. 29; 7 June 1940, p. 10; 4 May 1941, p. 29; 9 July 1940, p. 12; 19 July 1940, p. 15; *New York Times*, 15 June 1940, p. 8; 20 August 1940, p. 11; U.S. WPA for N.Y.C., *Final Report of the Work Projects Administration for the City of New York, 1935 to 1943* (New York, 1943), p. 207.

10. The national office also experienced a change of leadership at about the same time. In September 1940 Francis Harrington died suddenly of a heart attack and Howard O. Hunter replaced him as commissioner of the Work Projects Administration.

11. Roosevelt to H. A. Woodring, secretary of war, 22 May 1940, and James Lyons to Roosevelt, 2 October 1940, Papers of the U.S. WPA for N.Y.C., National Archives, Washington, D.C.; New York *Herald Tribune*, 8 November 1940, p. 4; 13 August 1941, p. 11; New York *Post*, 8 November 1940, p. 8; New York *World-Telegram*, 8 November 1940, p. 3; *New York Times*, 27 November 1940, p. 25; 3 November 1940, p. 45; 22 January 1941, p. 1; 21 February 1941, p. 20; 22 March 1941, p. 8.

12. Rilla Schroeder, "Here In Washington," *Survey Midmonthly* 77 (June 1941): 181; New York *Herald Tribune*, 13 August 1941, p. 11; 27 January 1941, p. 6; 7 May 1941, p. 15; *Survey Midmonthly* 77 (March 1941): 93; *New York Times*, 15 March 1940, p. 19; 1 February 1940, p. 15; U.S. WPA, "Interesting Facts" (Washington, D.C., 1941); Adelaide A. Matthews, special assistant to Irving Huie, to Layle Lane of the March on Washington Movement, 7 December 1942, Papers of the U.S. WPA for N.Y.C., New York City Public Library, Arthur Schomburg Collection.

13. New York received fewer war contracts than many other places because its leading industry, garment manufacturing, could not convert easily to war production. Typically, clothing manufacturers had small

shops with machines unsuitable to mass production of military equipment. Also, the armed forces hesitated to place contracts in the city because they feared the area was too vulnerable to enemy bombing.

14. New York *Herald Tribune*, 27 October 1942, p. 1; 11 February 1941, p. 10; New York *World-Telegram*, 20 April 1942, p. 3; 11 February 1941, p. 21; Schroeder, "Here In Washington," p. 181; *New York Times*, 21 May 1941, pp. 1, 17.

15. The law stated that an employee need be fired after eighteen months only if a person on welfare with the same qualifications could be found.

16. "Save the WPA," *New Republic*, 2 June 1941, p. 748; New York *World-Telegram*, 21 May 1941, pp. 1, 5; 22 May 1941, p. 18; New York *Herald Tribune*, 10 June 1941, p. 17; 1 July 1941, p. 1; U.S. *Statutes at Large* (1941), ERA of 1941, Section 1, p. 396, Sections 10 (b) and 10 (f), p. 402; *New York Times*, 27 June 1941, p. 12.

17. U.S. WPA for N.Y.C., *Final Report*, pp. 248–53, 258–59, 236, 141; *New York Times*, 19 August 1941, p. 19; U.S. WPA for N.Y.C., *Bulletin of the Training and Reemployment Division*, no. 1 (New York, 1942).

18. *New York Times*, 9 April 1942, p. 14; 24 May 1942, p. 31; New York *Herald Tribune*, 15 February 1942, p. 15; 18 June 1941, p. 12; 18 February 1942, p. 19; Special Report on WPA Assistance in Civilian Defense Activities in the City of New York, 10 February 1942, Papers of the U.S. WPA for N.Y.C., National Archives, Washington, D.C.; Lewis Bowen, "On the Home Front," *Hygeia* 19 (August 1941) : 628–30, 658–59; U.S. WPA for N.Y.C., *Final Report*, p. 239; Final Report of the Defense Health and Welfare Services of the New York City WPA, February 1943, Papers of the U.S. WPA for N.Y.C., National Archives, Washington, D.C.; *Nation*, 8 February 1941, p. 157.

19. New York *Herald Tribune*, 27 December 1941, p. 12; 26 May 1942. pp. 1, 10; New York *World-Telegram*, 7 January 1942, p. 26; 25 May 1942, pp. 1, 9; *New York Times*, 10 June 1942, p. 1; U.S. *Congressional Record*, 77th Cong., 2d sess., 1942, 88, pt. 4: 5149, 5159, 5163–64.

20. U.S. *Congressional Record*, 77th Cong., 2d sess., 88, pt. 4: 5150–51, 5175; New York *Herald Tribune*, 1 July 1942, p. 30; 6 November 1942, p. 1; U.S. WPA for N.Y.C., *Final Report*, p. 132; New York *World-Telegram*, 5 December 1942, p. 3; *New York Times*, 2 July 1942, p. 23; 31 October 1942, p. 14.

21. The national WPA rolls stood at 350,000.

22. *Time*, 14 December 1942, p. 29; New York *Sun*, 4 December 1942, pp. 1, 14; 5 December 1942, p. 6; New York *Herald Tribune*, 5 December 1942, pp. 1, 6; U.S. WPA for N.Y.C., *Final Report*, p. 132; Work Relief Committee of New York City (Joseph McGoldrick, comptroller; William Hodson, commissioner of the Department of Welfare; Irving Huie, commissioner of Public Works and administrator of New York City WPA) to Fiorello La Guardia, 20 December 1942, Fiorello La Guardia Papers, New York City Municipal Archives; *New York Times*, 11 January 1943, p. 17; 5 December 1942, pp. 14, 1.

11
Some Observations on the New Deal Record

The controversies over Franklin D. Roosevelt and the nature of his New Deal by no means ended with the 1930s. Two generations of historians have continued to disagree about the man and his programs as heatedly as did his contemporaries. To Sir Isaiah Berlin the four-term president was "the greatest champion of social progress in the twentieth century." On the other hand, Howard Zinn claims: "What the New Deal did was to refurbish middle-class America . . . to restore jobs to half the jobless, and to give just enough to the lowest classes . . . to create an aura of good will." What light does a study of the unemployment program in New York City shed on these widely divergent evaluations of the Roosevelt record?

First of all, whether the New Deal was essentially conservative or liberal, its job program appeared as a savior to millions of Americans. Roosevelt committed the resources of the federal government to relief at a time when large numbers of unemployed had run through any savings they once possessed. The administration stepped in as private charity was faltering and municipal and state funds proved inadequate to succor even a minority of depression victims.

One sees this demonstrated on an impressive scale in New York City. There, such philanthropic groups as the Prosser and Gibson Committees, which pioneered in work relief, had not been able to raise enough money to reach more than a fraction of the jobless. During Roosevelt's term as governor of New York, the state and city also struggled valiantly with emergency programs. It was the coming of the New Deal, however, that brought help to substantial numbers of urban residents, first with the Federal Emergency Relief Administration, then the Civil Works Administration, the FERA once more, and finally the WPA. At its peak in February 1936, this third and largest agency paid wages to 245,000 metropolitan inhabitants. Between 1935 and 1943 the WPA in New York City employed 700,000 people. If we count their dependents, we find that roughly two million New Yorkers, or more than one-quarter of the community, received some support from the federal organization.

On the most elementary level, these government jobs allowed their holders to survive until private enterprise could again absorb their labor. As one former WPA worker explained, a position on the program "gave you bread and butter, cigarettes, rent money, an occasional movie. . . . It saved your life."[1] But creating work that attempted to utilize the individual's skills and training did much more for him than fill his stomach and provide shelter. A government job often gave the man or woman who had been idle for several years renewed faith in himself and in the future. Anzia Yezierska, who was on the Writers' Project in New York, recalled the reaction she and her friends had when they first heard about the emergency work program: "People who no longer hoped or believed in anything but the end of the world began to hope and believe again." As she queued up with others to be interviewed for WPA placement, she noticed the changed manner of her companions. "I had seen these people at the relief station, waiting for the investigating machine to legalize them as paupers. Now they had work cards in their hands. Their waiting was no longer the hopeless stupor of applicants for mass relief; they were employees of the government. They had risen from the scrap heap of the unemployed, from the loneliness of the unwanted. . . . The new job look lighted the most ravaged faces."

If a government job could rekindle the spark of life in a person, it also carried important implications for stability and order within the society. Frances Piven and Richard Cloward, in *Regulating the Poor,* point out the relationship between work and social control in these words:

> So long as people are fixed in their work roles, their activities and outlooks are also fixed. . . . But mass unemployment breaks that bond, loosening people from the main institution by which they are regulated and controlled. Without work people cannot conform to familial and communal roles; and if the dislocation is widespread, the legitimacy of the social order itself may come to be questioned.

This breakdown, according to the authors, manifests itself in mass protests, demonstrations, and riots, which may even escalate into revolution. Putting the unemployed on home relief does not curtail disorder, for it is not privation that triggers unrest but, rather, the "deterioration of social control" that work establishes.

By 1934 the Roosevelt Administration must have discerned signs of the malaise that Piven and Cloward discuss. Hopkins, while head of the FERA, asked local welfare officials and assistants he sent into the field to report on the mood of the reliefers. From New York City he received communications that told of a growing mood of radicalism among the jobless. The Unemployed Councils and other groups close to the Communists were recruiting members in almost all neighborhoods. Any leader who promised jobs was likely to gather a following, New York caseworkers warned. Meanwhile, penniless young writers and artists marched in the streets, joined the John Reed Clubs, and denounced the capitalist system.

Whether there would have been an uprising had Roosevelt not intervened with his WPA we cannot ascertain. Many sociologists and historians believe that the unemployed make poor material for a revolution because they respond to their enforced idleness with apathy as often as rebellion. In any case, emergency jobs did tend to mute the bitterness and discontent of those hired. The secretary of the New York Emergency Relief Bureau noted this when he said: "Even if these relief workers never did anything more than dig holes and fill them up again, the WPA avoided major class riots during the depression."[2]

A young man of Marxist persuasion, who was on the payroll of the Writers' Project in New York, suspected the same thing, although with much less approval than the welfare official. As he and his colleagues celebrated with their first week's wages, he remonstrated:

> Mass bribery, that's what WPA is. Government blackmail. We'd fight, we'd stage riots and revolutions if they didn't hush us up. We're all taking hush money. The Mellons and the Morgans and the holy crusaders of the Liberty League must laugh when they think how cheaply they silenced the voice of an entire class and averted a revolution with a few billions of the people's money.

His comrades' reactions to his speech may well have substantiated his charge. As they ordered round after round of drinks and a good meal with their WPA remuneration, they shouted at him to sit down and cut the gloomy ideology.

The belief that work relief might be the best way to save the self-respect and courage of the unemployed as well as to maintain their faith in the system did not come to the New Dealers out of thin air. The welfare undertakings of the Roosevelt Administration owed a heavy debt to the professional social worker, the settlement house movement, and private philanthropy. Robert Bremner, in *From the Depths: The Discovery of Poverty in the United States,* goes so far as to claim that "without minimizing the importance of the social reforms inaugurated during the 1930s, it may be said that the measures then adopted were largely implementations, amplifications and partial fulfillments of the programs of preventive social work."

In New York City the social worker certainly played an important role in bringing about the WPA. The trained personnel of the Welfare Council issued reports on the psychological damage that home relief inflicted on community residents. William Hodson and other social workers campaigned ceaselessly for a job program. The Prosser and Gibson Committees demonstrated by their activities the desire of the unemployed for useful labor. Many of the projects that those two charitable groups initiated, especially in the white-collar field, were later continued and expanded by the FERA, the CWA, and ultimately the WPA. Hopkins, of course, was a social worker who began his career at a settlement house in New York City. Roosevelt, in his message to Congress of 4 January 1935, adopted the insights and even the language of the social workers. The president called for ending the federal dole and replacing it with government jobs that would protect both the bodies and the morale of the American people.

Although it is certainly true, then, that the New Deal's work relief policies drew inspiration from humanitarian reformers and aided an impressive number of New York City residents, one can also see (as Howard Zinn and other Roosevelt critics claim) that the government's efforts fell far short of providing fully for depression victims. The president never asked for, nor did Congress appropriate, enough money to hire all of the jobless. When FDR requested $4.8 billion for work relief and other public works programs in 1935, it must have seemed like a huge sum. In fact, it was the largest single peacetime fund Capitol Hill had ever made available, and represented more than half of the total federal budget that year. However, it would have taken nearly double the amount to give employment to every able-bodied person who was involuntarily idle. Therefore, the president made the decision at the start to limit WPA assignments almost exclusively to people who were receiving public assistance. This requirement for getting on a project had some unfortunate consequences.

First, undergoing an investigation in which the applicant had to prove he was destitute robbed the future WPA employee of some of the very self-respect that the New Dealers wanted to protect. Many of the jobless resented this. When Anzia Yezierska expressed her repugnance to going on welfare in order to qualify for the Writers' Project, her acquaintances told her bitterly: "We all had to go through it. You've got to be a goddamn charity case. The relief mill has to put the stamp of a legalized pauper on your forehead."

Secondly, limiting participation to those on welfare vitiated the point that Roosevelt and Hopkins hoped to make —that WPA enrollees were legitimate wage earners. The fact that they had been declared destitute and lived on home relief, however briefly, left a taint on them as far as public opinion was concerned. A substantial portion of more fortunate Americans always viewed the WPA laborers as parasites burdening the taxpayers. David Lasser, head of the Workers Alliance, testified before a congressional committee on this matter, saying that the relief certification was "degrading to the worker," gave the WPA a "bad name," and made "employers less willing to provide private employment for those . . . on the program."

Further, inadequate and short-term funding of the WPA brought continual fluctuations in the size of the rolls, with frequent cutbacks and layoffs. In the latter part of the 1930s, Congress added to the confusion by introducing new rules and sudden procedural changes. All of this operated to make life on the WPA terribly insecure. Orrick Johns, first head of the Writers' Project in New York, noted the pervasive "group fear" that arose from "the hazard of quota reductions and the unknown quantity of legislative action." Another ex-WPA worker recalled: "Fears [got] into you and sapp[ed] the blood and weaken[ed] the tissue of independence." She and her colleagues engaged in a seemingly endless dialogue that went more or less as follows:

Will the government appropriation run out, with the result that the project will be closed down? Shall I be fired tomorrow for some red-tape reason? Did you see in the paper yesterday that Congress is going to cut WPA in half? I notice the Federal Theatre was discontinued; maybe our project is next on the list.[3]

While the limited appropriations caused the WPA personnel ceaseless worry, the failure of the president to ask for and of Congress to vote adequate sums of money denied many destitute jobless any employment at all. At the beginning of 1936, an estimated one hundred thousand able-bodied New Yorkers, eager to work, subsisted on home relief because the local WPA's quota was not large enough to permit hiring them. The Writers' Project in New York consisted of three hundred people during the summer of 1938, but it had a waiting list of eighteen hundred applicants. Congress, in 1939, chose to handle the problem of too few jobs not by making more funds available but by forcing out all the men and women who had been with the organization for a year and one-half or longer to make room for new individuals.

The cutbacks, layoffs, and denial of work to destitute employables accounted for much of the disorder and radicalism that persisted after the WPA got underway. Each reduction of the rolls brought a round of frantic marches, sit-ins, picket lines, and fights with police. Many non-Communists joined the Workers Alliance and other left-wing unions in hopes that these groups could somehow induce the president and Congress to preserve and expand the program. Earl Conrad, once a member of the writers' unit in New York City, explained that he and his colleagues had the feeling that their "organization and protest and demand alone held the Project together." "It was all very precarious," he recalled, and they believed that if they relaxed their militancy for a moment the project "would fold up."

Before one can join Roosevelt's critics and denounce his failure to provide adequate work relief for the unemployed, however, one must ask whether it was within his power to do more. This is a difficult question to answer. Perhaps in 1935 and 1936, had FDR requested bigger appropriations from Congress, he might have gotten them. But the president decided against such action because of his own fears about mounting budget deficits—Roosevelt never wholly embraced the idea of deficit spending—and his hope that recovery would occur soon. By the late 1930s and the early 1940s, however, it is most doubtful that the White House could have wrung anything extra from Capitol Hill. After 1938 the coalition of conservative Southern Democrats and resurgent Republicans held the reins in Congress. These legislators became increasingly balky about voting money for work relief, killed the Federal Theatre in 1939, and came within four votes of scuttling the whole WPA in the spring of 1942. Furthermore, the chief executive, concerned primarily with foreign affairs after 1939, was reluctant to endanger congressional support for measures like lend-lease by engaging in fruitless battles for increased WPA funds.

Those who blame Roosevelt for accomplishing too little do not take into account sufficiently the conservative forces that impeded him. Consider for a moment the opposition to the WPA. Prominent Republicans like Herbert Hoover and Arthur Vandenberg, powerful congressional Democrats, including James Byrnes and Clifton Woodrum, businessmen such as J. P. Morgan, budget-conscious members of the administration like Secretary of the Treasury Henry Morgenthau, the majority of the press—including practically every New York City newspaper but the *Post*—all called for curtailment of government spending on work relief. These critics charged that continued outlays would drive taxes sky-high and eventually bankrupt the country. They pictured the WPA enrollees as chiselers and misfits whose moral fiber was being weakened further by government coddling. On top of this, by 1937, as it became clear that the chief beneficiaries of the WPA were the urban poor, congressmen from rural districts expressed growing hostility toward it.

To understand this opposition one must recognize that

the economic notions of the Hoover era and belief in rugged individualism and self-help did not completely disappear during the 1930s. In 1935 the enemies of the WPA were in a weak position because the majority of the American people were willing, at least temporarily, to put aside their orthodox ideas to combat an emergency situation. But as the worst days of the depression passed, the views of the conservatives carried increased weight. In 1939 a Roper poll found that the great majority of those interviewed favored a balanced federal budget even if that meant welfare cuts. Perhaps Piven and Cloward are correct when they state: "WPA ran against the grain, it violated the American Way. Once Main Street began to feel that things were better, it wanted to return to that Way."[4]

Anoher criticism of Roosevelt's approach to unemployment relief involves the distinction he repeatedly made between the dole and emergency work. Briefly, this argument runs as follows: The president missed a golden opportunity to educate the public on the subject of welfare. He should have stressed that poverty frequently arose not from defects in an individual's character but from the inequitable operation of the economic system. Since the society caused much of the problem, it was the responsibility of the state to provide for the distressed both through direct relief and jobs. Had Roosevelt been truly progressive in the matter of relief, he would have called for a decent guaranteed income for all Americans. Instead, by denigrating the dole as harmful to morale and self-reliance, Roosevelt reenforced long-standing prejudices against the poor. As a result, to this day the thinking of the average American on the topic of welfare is woefully unenlightened.

There are several explanations for Roosevelt's denunciation of the dole and his preference for work relief. First, the president, as thoroughly imbued with the work ethic as most citizens, probably did have a natural dislike for supporting the unemployed in idleness. Besides, he was a shrewd enough politician to see that the conservatives, who basically wanted to spend as little as possible on relief, found it harder philosophically to oppose aiding a man who worked for his welfare check than one who received a "handout" without giving anything in return. Furthermore, since Congress hesitates in the 1970s to endorse the principle of a guaranteed income for everyone and since many Americans still reject the idea, those who suggest that Roosevelt could have convinced the lawmakers to approve such a proposal in the thirties are unrealistic. Much more important than Roosevelt's personal preferences, politics, or public opinion in determining the New Deal's espousal of work relief was the administration's advanced thinking, not its conservatism. It was progressive social workers and settlement house reformers who reported to the president and Hopkins that home relief did nothing to alleviate the psychological distress of their clients. In a society that judged individuals largely on the basis of their occupational roles, people had to have jobs to receive the respect of others and to face themselves. Understanding this, Roosevelt and Hopkins tried to explain to the public that the WPA was not just another welfare program. It was a public works effort that created important jobs that needed to be performed.

It may also be said in defense of the New Deal that if it did not embrace the notion of a guaranteed income, it was groping in the direction of an equally liberal idea and perhaps a sounder one—that is, the right of every American to a job. If the private sector of the economy could not offer work, then it was the obligation of the government to act as employer of last resort. Admittedly, the WPA, for reasons already discussed, fell far short of achieving this goal, but the concept that motivated its creation was progressive.

Recently, scholarly writings on the New Deal have not only been critical of Roosevelt for the inadequacies of his relief and recovery efforts but have also taken his administration to task for its treatment of black Americans: the president refused to fight for a federal antilynching law, the CCC ran segregated camps, and the WPA paid Southern black laborers less than it gave its Northern white employees.[5] These discriminatory actions, as well as others, cannot be denied. But, again, in order to arrive at a balanced assessment of the New Deal, historians should study every agency and program of the depression era and try to evaluate exactly what impact each had on the black.

In the case of the New York City WPA, the question of equal benefits for blacks arose almost immediately. Black leaders claimed that the first director, Hugh Johnson, was insensitive or prejudiced and, as a result, their people got too few jobs in the organization. Johnson's successor, Victor Ridder, attempted to right past injustices with a deliberate policy of hiring blacks, especially for clerical and professional positions. During his tenure the proportion of blacks on the projects climbed from 8 to 12 percent of total WPA personnel and continued to rise thereafter. His efforts did not completely solve the problem, however, since blacks remained concentrated at the lowest levels within the agency. In 1937 three-quarters of the blacks on the New York City WPA worked as unskilled laborers. Only 5 percent held professional and technical assignments, and .5 percent served as supervisors. Conscious discrimination may explain these figures in part, but they also reflect the low educational attainments of black welfare recipients at that time and the tendency of WPA placement officers to assign people to jobs that resembled their former occupations.

Despite this shortcoming of the New York City WPA, the organization aided blacks tremendously. Since private industry reemployed blacks far less readily than whites, the proportion of blacks on the government payroll rose steadily until, by the early 1940s, black people constituted nearly one-third of the New York City WPA personnel. Consequently, the agency became one of the leading sources of income in Harlem. The importance of the WPA as a provider was reflected in a song the novelist Richard Wright heard blacks singing on the streets:

> Roosevelt! You're my man!
> When the time come
> I ain't got a cent

> You buy my groceries
> and pay my rent.
> Mr. Roosevelt, you're my man!

Between 1939 and 1943 the WPA began to concentrate more on retraining its employees to enable them to find work in defense plants. Among those who benefited were the black New Yorkers on the rolls. The industrial education courses, the on-the-job training, and the placement efforts of the WPA helped blacks get positions in war-production factories that had previously excluded them. In fact, when the WPA began in 1935, almost all private businesses in New York refused to hire blacks for skilled, white-collar, or professional work. The policy of the Consolidated Gas Company, as stated by its vice-president, was typical: "Negroes employed by us render common labor, maid service and the like. We do not assign Negroes as stenographers, clerks, or inspectors." The WPA, on the other hand, used qualified blacks as secretaries, typists, research workers, and payroll clerks, and approximately 10 percent of the relief teaching assignments went to black instructors.

The organization also gave substantial support to black artists. During the 1920s black talent in writing, painting, music, sculpture, and theater had begun to gain recognition in the Harlem Renaissance, but private patronage for black creativity dried up after the crash. The WPA came to the rescue of black artists who had started to make a name for themselves and of those waiting to be discovered. At one time or another, the Writers' Project in New York City employed such talented black literary figures as Claude McKay, Ralph Ellison, Richard Wright, and Roi Ottley. The Art Project included, among other black painters, Ronald Joseph, Jacob Lawrence, Robert Blackburn, and Charles Alston. The Lafayette Theater, which shut down after 1929, reopened under the auspices of the Negro Theater Unit. Ralph Ellison summed it up when he said that black "writers and would-be writers, newspaper people, dancers, actors— they all got their chance" on the WPA.[6]

Besides those blacks who actually worked for the New York City WPA, many black residents benefited from the projects. The hospitals and schools of Harlem were among the shabbiest and most overcrowded in the community. WPA laborers repaired and made additions to these facilities. Relief personnel opened nursery schools, aided the staff at Harlem Hospital, and operated free clinics in the ghetto neighborhood. Harlem received a large share of the WPA adult education, art, music, and recreation centers, and the Writers' Project promoted scholarly studies of black life.

Many city dwellers, in addition to blacks, gained from WPA projects. Historians who minimize the significance of New Deal measures should consider the impact of work relief on the urban scene. Through the FERA, CWA, and especially the WPA, the federal government for the first time in American history dispensed large-scale aid to cities. As the cost of relief threatened to bankrupt many communities, programs of the Roosevelt Administration assumed much of the burden. The WPA, moreover, carried on what amounted to a gigantic urban renewal effort. In New York City this took the form of creating an outstanding system of parks and playgrounds, beaches, swimming pools, and other recreational facilities. New hospitals, clinics, housing developments, and schools went up, while older structures were renovated and expanded. The WPA built for New York City what was then the most modern airport in the nation, resurfaced streets and bridges, and constructed highways.

Along with the physical rebuilding of cities that the New Deal underwrote, the federal government began to finance social services on an unprecedented scale. The WPA spent large sums employing people in the fields of education, health care, research, recreation, and culture. Because of these expenditures many poor New York City residents received benefits not available to them in the prosperous 1920s. Quite a few of the programs, such as the operation of day-care centers and the dispensing of free school lunches, became so popular that when the WPA ended they were continued, even if frequently on a smaller scale.

If the urban aid supplied by the New Deal was almost without precedent, the WPA sponsorship of the arts broke still more sharply with the past. The poet W. H. Auden observed:

> [N]o other state has ever cared whether its artists as a group lived or died; other governments have hired certain individual artists to glorify their operations and have even granted a small pension from time to time to some artist with fame or influence, but to consider, in a time of general distress, starving artists as artists and not simply as paupers is unique to the Roosevelt Administration.

Hopkins, with the backing of the president, based the WPA arts projects on two beliefs that were very new in the 1930s: (1) unemployed creative individuals, who get just as hungry as manual laborers, have the same right to a government job in their specialty as the bricklayer has in his, and (2) an enlightened state ought to concern itself with the welfare of the arts as well as with that of agriculture and industry. The extent of Republicans' and conservative Democrats' criticism of Federal Project number 1 indicates just how radical these two propositions seemed at the time and may help explain why no administration followed in Roosevelt's path after 1943. Washington did not openly commit itself to encouraging and subsidizing the arts again until John F. Kennedy entered the White House.[7]

Since New York had long been the creative capital of the nation and the mecca to which would-be writers, actors, composers, and painters journeyed, the WPA there ran the biggest and generally most successful efforts in the arts. Many young people with talent received their first recognition while on the payroll of the New York City unit. At the same time, theater, music, and art reached a much wider urban audience than ever before.

The work of the arts projects, moreover, very likely encouraged the growth of the cultural nationalism that marked the 1930s. The guidebooks turned out by the writers, the Index of American Design produced by the artists, the Music Project's emphasis on introducing new American composers—all contributed to heightened awareness and deeper appreciation of the country's cultural heritage and accomplishments. This was not a narrow, chauvinistic patriotism. Rather, the WPA endeavors stressed as never before the rich diversity within the United States and the nation's debt to manifold ethnic groups.

Although one might conclude from this examination of the WPA in New York that the New Deal, or at least its work relief policy, was progressive and humanitarian even if it did not come close to caring for all of the jobless, it is reasonable to ask how representative of the national program was the WPA in the country's largest city. Was it typical of the WPA in the nation as a whole? Essentially, yes; there were many local variations upon the main theme, however, because the WPA functioned in cooperation with the states and not as a single centralized body run solely from Washington.

Diversity across the country was evident with respect to politics in the WPA. Hopkins and his assistants declared that the jobless should be hired on the basis of their needs and abilities without reference to their party affiliations. Nonetheless, local politics did creep into the program in many areas.[8] In Kentucky in 1938 Gov. Albert (Happy) Chandler and Sen. Alben Barkley were locked in a primary contest for the senatorial nomination. The governor filled state offices with his supporters, while Barkley sought to strengthen his political organization through WPA assignments. In that same year in Cook County, Illinois, the WPA, under pressure from the Democratic district leaders, hired 450 men, 70 of whom did no work on projects but canvassed their precincts on behalf of the Horner-Courtney-Lucas ticket. The WPA assignment cards of these employees were signed by the Northern Illinois Democratic campaign manager.

E. Wight Bakke, in his study of the unemployed in New

Haven, found that although politics had little impact on securing ordinary WPA jobs, a man's affiliations did help him obtain supervisory positions or what were called "the gravy jobs." One local Democratic activist told Bakke: "We got somebody in there now [the head of the WPA in Connecticut] who'll look out for us." Rank-and-file WPA workers, aware of favoritism, respected their foremen less and felt diminished job satisfaction.

Where local political interference became especially blatant, Hopkins stepped in, but even so he was not always successful in altering the situation. To counter the attempts of James Curley's Democratic machine to control the Massachusetts WPA, Hopkins appointed an outsider, Paul Edwards, to direct the work relief agency.[9] Governor Curley, Congressman John McCormack, and State Democratic Chairman Joseph McGrath protested bitterly when Edwards instituted a nonpartisan hiring policy. Curley and company enlisted the support of James A. Farley and in the closing days of the 1936 campaign forced Edwards to knuckle under to their wishes, enabling the governor to boast to Farley that there were twenty-two hundred project supervisors under the control of the Massachusetts Democratic party. Curley's defeat in his races for senator in 1936, for mayor of Boston in 1937, and for governor in 1938 removed much of the pressure, and thereafter the WPA in Boston and elsewhere in the state exhibited less bias in hiring.

The New York City WPA, while not totally free of patronage considerations in its job assignments, largely escaped this type of political interference. It was not enmeshed in Empire State partisan battles because the urban WPA existed as an independent unit reporting to Washington, one of the earliest instances of direct city-federal cooperation. Its separation from metropolitan factional struggles owed much to the particular political situation in New York City. Fiorello La Guardia, at least nominally a Republican, had spent his early political career fighting Tammany Hall. In fact, his credentials as one of the longest standing and most outspoken critics of the New York City regular Democratic organization helped win him the city Fusion party's nomination for mayor in 1933. That party came into being in reaction to the scandals that took place during the administration of James Walker, the Democratic mayor driven from office by the Seabury investigations. The Fusionists included old-time municipal reformers, anti-Tammany Democrats, and a number of prominent Republicans. With the endorsements of both the Fusion and the Republican parties, La Guardia went on to defeat the Tammany candidate, John O'Brien, and the Recovery party nominee, Joseph McKee, who had been urged to run by Franklin Roosevelt. The new coalition, however, did not make a clean sweep. The Democrats still held a majority on the Board of Aldermen, along with the borough presidencies of Manhattan and The Bronx.[10] Smarting over the loss of city hall, the local Democrats looked for opportunities to embarrass the mayor. That was a chief motive behind the aldermanic investigation of the city work relief program in 1935.

Naturally, La Guardia did not want members of this opposition running the New York City WPA. His fear that Tammany Hall might get a foothold in the agency expressed itself in his repeated warnings to Hopkins not to let the "politicians" in. At the same time, La Guardia depended on a Democratic president and a Democratic governor to funnel home and work relief funds to the city. It behooved him to stay on good terms with them. In addition, appointees to WPA supervisory jobs had to be acceptable to New York's Democratic senators. This situation would have prevented La Guardia, if he had been so inclined, from recommending administrators primarily on the basis of their political loyalty to him. His best course under these circumstances lay in backing a relatively nonpartisan work relief hierarchy.

La Guardia must have realized, moreover, that he did not have to control the WPA for it to enhance his reputation. He benefited simply from its being active and efficient. The federally financed programs of the WPA made it possible for his administration to offer broader services to New

Yorkers than they had ever enjoyed before, while the construction projects built much needed facilities. A lot of the credit for these accomplishments went to La Guardia. When he dedicated a new firehouse, accepted a new clinic, or officiated at the opening of the North Beach Airport, soon named after him, his fame as a mayor who got things done for the city grew. It is interesting to speculate on whether La Guardia would have been nearly as popular a mayor without this federal largess. In fact, one wonders if anyone could have governed New York during the depression had the city been forced to carry the relief burden and the cost of services and construction out of its own resources.

Unfortunately, not all local officeholders found that it accorded with their principles and was to their political advantage to cooperate with the WPA. The first three administrators of the New York City WPA became involved in widely publicized clashes with Robert Moses, the city park commissioner, who resented any federal supervision of his use of relief funds and labor. The fight between Republican borough president George Harvey, who hoped to further his career through public attacks on the WPA, and Victor Ridder reached such proportions that it nearly halted WPA activities in Queens. Such instances of conflict between municipal leaders and the New Deal agency, however, were more the exception than the rule.

Besides the question of politics, other variations in the operation of the WPA from city to city or from state to state prevent one from citing the New York unit as typical of the larger program in all respects. In some areas public officials either would not or could not raise the required sponsors' contributions for work relief projects, with the result that WPA quotas in their communities went unfilled. The WPA allotted New Orleans two thousand WPA positions in 1940 for its approximately ten thousand eligible unemployed workers, but even this meager number were never hired because the state of Louisiana and the city of New Orleans did not come forward with the necessary funds. On the other hand, New York City, perhaps because of its stronger tradition of giving both private and public assistance to the poor, consistently managed to meet its obligations under the program. It also appears that New York City's administrators, particularly Ridder and Somervell, compiled a better record in their treatment of minority groups than did WPA directors in certain other localities. One study of Boston during the depression revealed that the hiring practices of the work relief agency there tended to favor the Irish and discriminated against blacks.

In addition, the large size of the New York City WPA made it possible for it to run projects varied enough to employ approximately two-thirds of its personnel in jobs similar to those they had held prior to the depression. Thus it could be claimed that the WPA fulfilled the purpose of preserving the skills of those individuals. In cities with smaller enrollments, however, the organization was less successful in this regard. A survey conducted by a Harvard Public Administration research team found that the WPA in Massachusetts cities frequently used skilled and semiskilled workers in jobs that did not take into account their past training and experience. In one community only 35 percent of the skilled workers and as few as 25 percent of the semiskilled were employed in their customary trades.

Despite these differences, the most important observations about the New York unemployed and what the WPA meant to them hold true for other communities also. Evidence from all over the nation indicated that home relief, while it kept people from starving, did nothing to solve the psychological crisis of unemployment. Martha Gellhorn, after visiting Boston in 1934, wrote to Hopkins that in the households of the jobless she saw "fear, fear driving them into a state of semi-collapse; cracking nerves," and causing "an overpowering terror of the future."

Just as the coming of the WPA brought new hope to the unemployed in New York, it apparently did the same for the destitute elsewhere. Bakke noted the "real satisfaction" among WPA personnel in New Haven, where the jobless "could hold their heads up as normal citizens aware that the community looked upon them as such." That was in 1935. But Bakke observed an increasingly critical attitude toward the WPA employee on the part of Connecticut residents from 1937 on. This is strikingly similar to developments in New York. Bakke explained this change in public opinion as follows: "With the increasing belief that industry was once more offering opportunities for able workers, citizens began to renew their opinion that any competent man could find a job if he really wanted it. In short, the curve of community attitude toward the unemployed had begun a descent toward pre-depression points of view."

Just as the New York WPA left the city more livable, so the organization built, repaired, and renewed in community after community. And alongside the construction went the white-collar projects, which extended services to the urban poor on a scale never before available. In Boston the WPA laid twenty-five miles of sewers, constructed the Huntington Avenue subway, built the Commonwealth Avenue underpass across from the Harvard Club, completed a new runway at the East Boston Airport, recatalogued the public library, ran a medical treatment program for alcoholics, and by 1938 sewed and distributed over one million articles of clothing for families on welfare. The arts projects provided that community with low-priced and free concerts and plays, exhibiting the same appreciation for the culture of ethnic minorities as their New York counterparts. WPA theater in Boston included Yiddish and black troupes, and when the black thespians presented William E. B. DuBois's *Haiti* they sold out every seat. In New Haven, also, the work undertaken by the WPA needed to be done and, according to Bakke, was "a useful addition to the assets of the community."

Despite these impressive achievements, the WPA in New Haven and Boston, as well as in New York, was unable to hire many of the eligible unemployed. During the summer of 1938, out of thirteen thousand able-bodied jobless in New Haven, the WPA employed twenty-eight hundred, or roughly 21 percent. At the start of 1940 the federal agency was supporting only about one-third of Boston's jobless, and there were thirty-eight hundred employables on home relief.[11]

Another development that one notes in the New York City WPA illustrated a trend throughout the work relief organization—that is, the growing use of military personnel as administrators. Col. Francis Harrington replaced Hopkins as national director when the latter became secretary of commerce. Army men ran the Los Angeles and New York offices and predominated in the engineering and construction divisions all over the country. Several things explain this dependence on career officers. First, since the WPA carried on more building than any other activity, it desperately needed engineers with experience in public works construction. Finding competent people with these qualifications on the limited wages that the WPA paid its administrators proved nearly impossible. Unable to attract sufficient civilian staff, the WPA turned to the Army Corps of Engineers, which had a long tradition of supervising public works. Second, in the 1930s the nation did not possess a group of trained public servants capable of running large enterprises. The era of big government was in its infancy. The few people who did possess such experience had mostly gotten it during World War I, and many were members of the armed forces. Hugh Johnson, a retired army man who launched the New York City WPA, offers a prime example. Third, the use of military officers served still another purpose. It placed the running of district, city, and state branches in the hands of men not associated with or indebted to local politicians. By interspersing these careerists throughout the organization, Hopkins and his assistants hoped to ease the partisan pressures that impinged on the operation of the program.

Hopkins did not call on this help without trepidation. He worried that the army men might turn out to be martinets who treated the jobless like draftees in basic training. This fear partially materialized, as one can see in Somervell's conduct. Unlike Hopkins, Aubrey Williams, and Jacob

Baker of the national office, who were idealistic social reformers (despite their attempts to deny it), the colonel functioned like a hardheaded engineer. A stickler for discipline, he made his subordinates feel that they had to pass military inspection each day. Artists, writers, and actors charged that he lacked sympathy for creative people, and the left-wing unions accused him of conducting a witch-hunt in 1939–40. In short, his autocratic tendencies at times impaired relations between the WPA and its employees.

On the other hand, Somervell's insistence on efficiency, planning, and accountability turned the New York City WPA into an agency capable of serving the community well. His reforms gave the taxpayers more parks, firehouses, and clinics for their dollars and made the WPA a little less vulnerable to the attacks of its enemies. Ultimately, Somervell's emphasis on productivity, sound engineering practices, and tighter management earned the grudging respect of even the otherwise hostile New York press. The New York WPA also benefited from his independence of all local political factions. Finally, as a military careerist from Arkansas, he offered a counterweight to the vociferous group of radicalized intellectuals on the metropolitan WPA. The allegations of the Dies and Woodrum Committees that the Communists had taken over the agency seemed less plausible with Somervell at the helm.

The WPA had still another connection with the military. Ironically, before the agency became a wartime casualty, along with many other New Deal social welfare efforts, it made important contributions to preparing the nation for World War II. If there had been no job program and millions of Americans had been left for a decade to suffer the physical and psychological damages of unemployment, it is hard to believe that they would have fought to defend democracy with very high morale. Besides, WPA projects in the thirties and early forties built military roads and airports, refurbished army bases, and trained workers for defense industry, all of which were vitally needed when war came. With justification, then, Roosevelt, on terminating the WPA, reiterated his belief that "providing useful work is superior to any and every kind of dole."

Has postwar America learned from the WPA experiment, as FDR predicted it would? The answer to that question is far from certain. In 1946 liberal Democrats backed the Murray-Wagner Full Employment Bill, which recognized the public obligation to make work available for all, if necessary through government spending and planning. Because of the objections of conservative Republicans and Southern Democrats, however, the measure finally signed by President Truman was considerably watered down. The law adopted as its goal not full but "maximum" employment and contained no specific commitment of federal funding for achieving this objective.

Between 1945 and 1960 the nation experienced four recessions, with sharp increases in the number of jobless Americans. The downturn in February 1958 threw more than five million persons out of work, establishing an unemployment rate of 7.7 percent of the labor force. A handful of liberal Democrats proposed to remedy the situation by reviving New Deal programs. Sen. Albert Gore of Tennessee introduced a public works bill in 1958, but a Democratic-controlled Congress rejected it. President Eisenhower denounced the Gore proposal, saying: "I am concerned over the sudden upsurge of pump-priming schemes, such as setting up of huge federal bureaucracies of the PWA and WPA types."

The issue arose again in 1961, with Pennsylvania Democratic Sen. Joseph Clark calling for a $1 billion public works effort in preference to more home relief spending: "I urge that we put our emphasis on buying things of lasting value . . . rather than pay it out in the form of a dole which brings no tangible public benefits of any kind." Just as in the 1930s, the mayors of the nation's big cities, ever short of funds to carry on services and construction, backed Clark's bill enthusiastically. However, President Kennedy, worried about enlarging the budget deficit in the spring of 1961, refused to endorse the measure. Eventually, a much modified proposal, known as the Accelerated Public Works Act, passed Congress, and the president signed it in September 1961. Rather than authorizing a national program, the law was used to combat structural unemployment in specific depressed areas.

In the early 1970s the United States slid into the worst economic downturn it had suffered since the Great Depression. By the summer of 1975 national unemployment hovered around 8 percent, and New York City, suffering its bleakest economic disaster since the thirties, experienced a local jobless rate above 11 percent of the labor force. Spurred by these frightening developments, Democratically controlled Congresses passed, and two Republican presidents reluctantly approved, new work relief laws. The Comprehensive Employment and Training Act, signed into law by Richard Nixon on 28 December 1973, allotted grants of federal money to the states and gave local authorities wide powers to create and run public service job programs. The measure, underfinanced and undersupervised by the national government, got off to a slow and uncertain start. In New York City hiring did not begin until September 1974, and months later, despite high unemployment in the city, the quota of emergency positions had not been filled. As the economy slumped still further, Congress amended the C.E.T.A. with the Emergency Jobs and Unemployment Assistance Act. This law, signed by President Ford in December 1974, appropriated $1 billion to create roughly one hundred thousand jobs, of which New York City hoped to obtain sixty-five hundred, financed by its expected share of $61 million.[12]

Since New York City, on the verge of bankruptcy by 1975, was laying off thousands of teachers, firemen, policemen, and other civil servants, a federal job program of such limited size could hardly make a dent in the urban unemployment situation. The Ford Administration, nonetheless, indicated its opposition to spending much more on public works projects, instead relying largely on tax reductions to revive the economy.[13] In fact, President Ford repeatedly warned against new appropriations for public employment or other social welfare programs on the grounds that they would lead to rampant inflation. These post-1945 developments reinforce the conclusion that the Roosevelt Administration's response to the needs of the unemployed was not only progressive for its day, but is still too liberal for many contemporary conservatives to accept.

NOTES

1. William E. Leuchtenburg, "Franklin D. Roosevelt: A Profile," and Howard Zinn, "Roosevelt: The Liberal Myth," in *Myth and the American Experience*, ed. Nicholas Cords and Patrick Gerster, 2 vols. (New York, 1973), 2:266 and 277; U.S. WPA for N.Y.C., *Final Report of the Work Projects Administration for the City of New York, 1935 to 1943* (New York, 1943), p. 4; Jo Sinclair, "I Was on Relief," *Harper's* 184 (January 1942): 162.

2. Anzia Yezierska, *Red Ribbon on a White Horse* (New York, 1950), pp. 150, 156; Frances Fox Piven and Richard Cloward, *Regulating the Poor* (New York, 1971), pp. 6–7; Narrative Reports on New York City from Wayne Parrish to Hopkins, 11 November 1934 and 17 November 1934, Harry Hopkins Papers, Franklin D. Roosevelt Library, Hyde Park, N.Y.; *New York Times*, 16 December 1934, p. 17; William F. McDonald, *Federal Relief Administration and the Arts* (Columbus, Ohio, 1969), p. 405; Edmund B. Butler, as quoted in Donald Howard, *The WPA and Federal Relief Policy* (New York, 1943), p. 789.

3. Yezierska, *Red Ribbon on a White Horse*, pp. 162–63, 152–53; Robert Bremner, *From the Depths: The Discovery of Poverty in the United States* (New York, 1956), p. 261; House Subcommittee of the Committee on Appropriations, *Hearings on the Emergency Relief Appropriations Act of 1941*, 76th Cong., 3d sess. (Washington, D.C., 1940), p. 922; Johns, *Time of Our Lives: The Story of My Father and Myself* (New York, 1937), p. 346; Sinclair, "I Was on Relief," p. 162.

4. *New York Times*, 9 October 1935, p. 1; Jerre Mangione, *The Dream and the Deal: The Federal Writers' Project, 1935–1943* (Boston, 1972), pp. 169, 153; Piven and Cloward, *Regulating the Poor*, p. 112.

5. See, for example, Raymond Wolters, *Negroes and the Great Depression: The Problem of Economic Recovery* (Westport, Conn., 1970); Bernard Sternsher, ed., *The Negro in Depression and War* (New York, 1969); and August Meier and Elliott Rudwick, *From Plantation to Ghetto* (New York, 1966).

6. U.S. WPA for N.Y.C., *The Administration of Work Relief in New York City, August 1936–December 1937,* Report of Brehon B. Somervell to Harry Hopkins (New York, 1938), p. 147; Adelaide Matthews to Layle Lane, 7 December 1942, Papers of the U.S. WPA for N.Y.C., New York City Public Library, Arthur Schomburg Collection; Yezierska, *Red Ribbon on White Horse,* pp. 161–62; Bernard Sternsher, ed., *Hitting Home* (Chicago, 1970), p. 108; Mangione, *Dream and the Deal,* pp. 155, 159, 260–63, 255; Alain Locke, *The Negro in Art: A Pictorial Record of the Negro Artist and the Negro Theme in Art* (New York, 1940), pp. 130–36.

7. W. H. Auden, Introduction to *Red Ribbon on a White Horse,* by Yezierska, p. 17; McDonald, *Federal Relief Administration,* pp. ix, 830.

8. The repeated refusal of Congress to place WPA supervisors under civil service and the insistence of that body that it approve appointments of state WPA directors contributed to the politicizing of work relief administration.

9. Edwards later served as business manager for the New York City arts projects.

10. James Patterson, *The New Deal and the States* (Princeton, N.J., 1969), pp. 80–84; Arthur Macmahon et al., *The Administration of Work Relief* (Chicago, 1941), p. 285; E. Wight Bakke, *The Unemployed Worker* (New Haven, Conn., 1940), pp. 405–7; Charles H. Trout, "Boston during the Great Depression: 1929–1940" (Ph.D. diss., Columbia University, 1972), pp. 334–37, 338–339; Arthur Mann, *La Guardia Comes to Power, 1933* (Chicago, 1965), pp. 19–20, 68, 95–96, 123.

11. Howard, *The WPA and Federal Relief Policy,* pp. 149, 234; Trout, "Boston during Great Depression," pp. 391, 348, 340–41, 369–70, 376, 372, 357; Bakke, *The Unemployed Worker,* pp. 323–24, 399, 391, 341.

12. Oscar T. Barck, Jr., and Nelson M. Blake, *Since 1900: A History of the United States in Our Times* (New York, 1974), p. 533; James L. Sundquist, *Politics and Policy: The Eisenhower, Kennedy, and Johnson Years* (Washington, D.C., 1968), pp. 17, 21, 25, 24, 92–93, 97; *New York Times,* 12 December 1974, p. 1; 19 December 1974, p. 23; 20 December 1974, pp. 1, 4; 6 January 1975, pp. 1, 14; 17 June 1975, p. 29; 26 September 1975, pp. 1, 21.

13. The Roosevelt Administration in 1935 was spending $4.8 billion on public works out of a total budget of slightly more than $8.5 billion. In 1975 spending on public works programs averaged about $10 billion out of a budget of some $200 billion. *New York Times,* 8 January 1935; 27 August 1975.

Selected Biblography

Manuscripts

Hyde Park, N.Y. Franklin D. Roosevelt Library. Harry Hopkins Papers.
Hyde Park, N.Y. Franklin D. Roosevelt Library. Aubrey Williams Papers.
New York. Columbia University Oral History Research Office. Reminiscences of Holger Cahill, 1957.
New York. Columbia University Oral History Research Office. Reminiscences of Luther Evans, 1966.
New York. New York City Municipal Archives. Fiorello La Guardia Papers.
New York. New York City Public Library. Arthur Schomberg Collection. Papers of the U.S. Works Progress Administration for New York City.
Washington, D.C. National Archives. Papers of the U.S. Works Progress Administration for New York City.

Interviews Conducted by the Author

Angoff, Allan. 20 November 1976. Teaneck, N.J.
Buxton, Alan. 22 November 1976. Paramus, N.J.

Publications of the Works Progress Administration

U.S. Works Progress Administration. *Index of American Design Manual.* WPA Technical Series, Art Circular no. 3. Washington, D.C., 1938.

———. *Intercity Differences in Cost of Living in March, 1935, in Fifty-nine Cities,* by Margaret Loomis Stecker. Washington, D.C., 1937.

———. "Interesting Facts." Washington, D.C., 1941.

———. *Urban Workers on Relief, May 1934,* by Gladys Palmer and Katherine Wood. 2 vols. Washington, D.C., 1936.

U.S. Works Progress Administration for the City of New York. *The Administration of Work Relief in New York City, August 1936–December 1937.* Report of Brehon B. Somervell to Harry Hopkins. New York, 1938.

———. *Brief Review of Developments in New York City during the Past Two Years.* Report of Brehon B. Somervell to Harry Hopkins. New York, 1937.

———. *Bulletin of the Training and Reemployment Division,* no. 1. New York, 1942.

———. *Education and Recreation Programs of the U.S. Works Progress Administration in Cooperation with the Board of Education of the City of New York.* New York, 1938.

———. *The Employment Program.* New York, 1939.

———. *General Statistical Bulletins, 1938–39.* New York, 1938–39.

———. *Reports on Public Assistance to the Administrator of the Works Progress Administration for the City of New York,* by Donald D. Lescohier. New York, 1939.

———. *Study and Development of Home Care of Recipients of Old-Age Assistance.* New York, 1937.

———. *The WPA in New York City: The Record for 1938.* New York, 1939.

U.S. Work Projects Administration for the City of New York. *Final Report of the Work Projects Administration for the City of New York, 1935 to 1943.* New York, 1943.

———. *The WPA Federal Art Project: A Summary of Activities and Accomplishments.* New York, 1940.

Selected Bibliography

———. *The WPA in New York City: The Record for 1939.* New York, 1940.

———. *WPA: Research and Records Programs in New York City.* New York, 1941.

Other Government Documents

New York City Aldermanic Committee to Investigate the Administration of Relief. *In the Matter of the Investigation of the Administration of Unemployment Relief in the City of New York.* New York, 8 July 1935.

New York City Board of Education. *All of the Children.* Thirty-ninth Annual Report of the Superintendent of Schools for New York City, 1936–37.

———. *All of the Children.* Fortieth Annual Report of the Superintendent of Schools for New York City, 1937–38.

New York City Mayor's Committee on Unemployment Relief. *Report of Mayor La Guardia's Committee on Unemployment Relief.* New York, 1935.

New York Governor's Commission on Unemployment Relief. *State and Local Welfare Organization in the State of New York.* Albany, N.Y., December 1935.

———. *Work Relief in the State of New York, A Report Submitted to Governor Herbert H. Lehman, August 10, 1936.* Albany, N.Y., 1936.

U.S. Advisory Committee on Education. *Educational Activities of the Works Progress Administration,* by Doak S. Campbell. Washington, D.C., 1939.

U.S. Community Improvement Appraisal. *A Report on the Work Program of the Works Progress Administration by the National Appraisal Committee.* Washington, D.C., April 1939.

U.S. Congress. House Subcommittee of the Committee on Appropriations. *Hearings on the First Deficiency Appropriations Bill.* 74th Cong., 2d sess. Washington, D.C., 1936.

———. *Hearings on the Emergency Relief Appropriations Act of 1937.* 75th Cong., 1st sess. Washington, D.C., 1936.

———. *Investigation and Study of tht WPA.* 76th Cong., 1st sess. Washington, D.C., 1939.

310 THE NEW DEAL AND THE UNEMPLOYED

———. *Hearings on Work Relief and Relief for Fiscal Year 1940.* 76th Cong., 1st sess. Washington, D.C., 1939.

———. *Hearings on the Emergency Relief Appropriations Act of 1941.* 76th Cong., 3d sess. Washington, D.C., 1940.

U.S. Congress. Senate Subcommittee of the Committee on Appropriations. *Hearings on the First Deficiency Appropriations Bill for 1936.* 74th Cong., 2d sess. Washington, D.C., 1936.

———. *Hearings on the Emergency Relief Act of 1937.* 75th Cong., 1st sess. Washington, D.C., 1936.

———. *Hearings on the Supplemental Appropriation: Relief and Work Relief, Fiscal Year 1938.* 75th Cong., 3d sess. Washington, D.C., 1938.

U.S. Congress. Special House Committee for the Investigation of Un-American Activities. *Investigation of Un-American Propaganda Activities in the United States.* 75th Cong., 3d sess. Washington, D.C., 1938.

———. Report—Pursuant to H.R. 282. *Investigation of Un-American Activities and Propaganda.* 75th Cong., 4th sess. Washington, D.C., 1939.

U.S. *Congressional Record.* 74th Cong., 1st sess., 1935, 79; 76th Cong., 1st sess., 1939, 84; 76th Cong., 3d sess., 1940, 76; 77th Cong., 2d sess., 1942, 88.

U.S. Department of Health, Education, and Welfare. Social Security Administration. Office of Research and Statistics. *Public Attitudes Toward Social Security, 1935–1965,* by Michael E. Schiltz. Washington, D.C., 1970.

U.S. Department of Labor. *Family Income and Expenditure in New York City, 1935–1936.* 2 vols. Washington, D.C., 1941.

U.S. Government. Executive Order no. 7034, 6 May 1935; no. 7046. 20 May 1935; no. 7060, 5 June 1935.

U.S. *Statutes at Large* (49), Emergency Relief App. Act, 1935; (53), Emergency Relief App. Act, 1939; (55), Emergency Relief App. Act, 1941.

Newspapers

Amsterdam News, April, June, July 1936.
Bronx *Home News,* August 1935, July 1936, August 1937.

Brooklyn *Citizen,* May 1937.
Brooklyn *Eagle,* August, October 1935, February 1936, October 1938.
Carpenter, July 1938.
Long Island *Daily Press,* July 1936, August 1937.
New York *Daily News,* 1935–43.
New York *Evening Journal,* March 1936.
New York *Herald Tribune,* 1931–43.
New York *Post,* 1935–43.
New York *Sun,* 1935–43.
New York Times, 1930–43.
New York *World-Telegram,* 1935–43.
North Shore Journal, August–September 1937.
Staten Island *Advance,* April 1937.
Staten Island *Transcript,* June–July 1937.
Variety, May 1937.
Work (national edition), September 1938, February 1939, August 1940.
Work (New York edition), April 1938.

Periodicals

"A $20,000,000 Investment in Emergency Work Jobs." *American City* 48 (February 1933): 70–71.
Adams, Grace. "The White-Collar Chokes: Three Years of WPA Professional Work." *Harper's* 177 (October 1938): 474–84.
American City 52 (November 1937): 89; 57 (June 1942): 9.
Amidon, Beulah. "WPA—Wages and Workers." *Survey Graphic* 24 (October 1935): 493–97.
Archibald, Raymond Clare. "The New York Mathematics Tables Project." *Science,* 25 September 1942, pp. 294–96.
Baker, Ella, and Cooke, Marvel. "The Bronx Slave Market." *Crisis* 42 (November 1935): 330–31.
Botkin, Benjamin. "WPA and Folklore Research: Bread and Song." *Southern Folklore Quarterly* 3 (March 1939): 7–14.
Bowen, Lewis. "On the Home Front." *Hygeia* 19 (August 1941): 628–30, 658–59.

Calverton, V. F. "The Cultural Barometer." *Current History* 46 (July 1937) : 94–95.
———. "The Cultural Barometer." *Current History* 49 (October 1938) : 45–47.
Cameron, Donald. "Research Projects Aid Schools and Scholars." *American Scholar* 8, no. 2 (April 1939) : 248–50.
"Can the Librarians Help the WPA?" *Library Journal*, 1 November 1936, pp. 854–56.
"Citizenship Education for Aliens." *American City* 57 (September 1942) : 79.
Colby, Merle. "The Work of the Federal Writers' Project." *Publishers Weekly*, 18 March 1939, pp. 1130–35.
Current History 48 (May 1938) : 58–59.
"CWA Nursery Schools for Children." *Literary Digest*, 24 February 1934, p. 21.
"Dig Up Rich Data; Can They Use It?" *Business Week*, 8 May 1937, pp. 38–41.
Dryden, Maude. "What Games for the Day Camp?" *Recreation* 31, no. 2 (May 1937) : 81–84.
Editorial. *New Republic*, 4 September 1935, p. 88.
Editorial. *Opportunity* 17, no. 2 (February 1939) : 34.
"Farewell to the Gibson Alms." *Literary Digest*, 24 June 1933, pp. 17–18.
Feinstein, Isidor. "New York's Relief Crisis." *Nation*, 22 August 1934, pp. 213–14.
Fortune 19 (March 1939) : 132–35.
Frazier, Corinne Reid. "WPA Serves the Blind." *Commonweal*, 11 August 1939, pp. 371–72.
Geist, Sidney. "Prelude: The 1930's." *Arts* 30 (September 1956) : 52.
Grumpelt, H. J. "Little Theaters in Libraries." *Library Journal*, 15 May 1935, pp. 426–28.
Huzar, Elias. "The New WPA." *Survey Midmonthly* 75 (October 1939) : 300–301.
———. "New WPA Rules Affecting Municipalities." *American City* 55 (July 1940) : 5.
Isaacs, Edith. "The Negro in the American Theatre." *Theatre Arts* 26 (August 1942) : 519–21.

Selected Bibliography

———. *Theatre Arts* 21 (March 1937) : 184–85.

Kolodin, Irving. "Footlights, Federal Style." *Harper's* 173 (November 1936) : 621–31.

Lescohier, Donald. "Hybrid WPA." *Survey Midmonthly* 75 (June 1939) : 166–69.

Lindeman, Edward C. "Recreation Rehabilitates the Shut-In." *Recreation* 31, no. 7 (October 1937) : 417–20.

Literary Digest, 5 October 1935, p. 8; 11 September 1937, pp. 18–20.

Moley, Raymond. "Perspective." *Newsweek*, 29 April 1940, p. 64.

Moore, Earl V. "Men, Music, and Morale." *Musical America*, 25 April 1942, pp. 5, 41.

Motherwell, Hiram. "Uncle Takes the Stage." *Survey Graphic* 26 (April 1937) : 212–13.

Nation, 8 April 1936, p. 438; 31 October 1936, p. 510; 8 February 1941, p. 157.

"Negroes Under the WPA, 1939." *Monthly Labor Review* 50 (March 1940) : 636–38.

Newsweek, 31 March 1941, p. 63.

New Yorker, 10 February 1940, pp. 22–27; 17 February 1940, pp. 28–30.

"New York Relief." *Commonweal*, 12 April 1935, p. 681.

"Power Is WPA Public Ownership Propaganda." *Life*, 22 March 1937, pp. 22–23.

Recreation 31, no. 5 (August 1937) : 287–88; 31, no. 7 (October 1937) : 418–19; 31, no. 7 (October 1937) : 452.

"Save the WPA." *New Republic*, 2 June 1941, p. 748.

School and Society, 2 July 1938, pp. 18–19; 5 November 1938, pp. 594–96.

Schroeder, Rilla. "Here In Washington." *Survey Midmonthly* 77 (June 1941) : 181.

Sinclair, Jo. "I Was on Relief." *Harper's* 184 (January 1942) : 161–63.

Springer, Gertrude. "The Job Line." *Survey* 65 (February 1931) : 497–99.

Stark, Louis. "All I Want Is Work." *New Republic*, 4 February 1931, pp. 317–18.

Survey 74 (September 1938) : 288, 291, 295; 74 (October 1938) : 324.

Survey Midmonthly 75 (July 1939) : 224; 75 (December 1939) : 379; 76 (September 1940) : 270; 76 (December 1940) : 362–63; 77 (March 1941) : 93.

"Thanks to the CWA." *Survey* 70 (March 1934) : 87.

Time, 14 December 1942, p. 29.

Toubey, Eleanor. "The American Baedekers." *Library Journal,* 15 April 1941, pp. 339–41.

"Unemployed Arts: The WPA's Four Art Projects: Their Origin, Their Operation." *Fortune* 15 (May 1937) : 108–17.

"Unemployed Help Catalogue Department." *Library Journal,* 1 October 1932, p. 815.

Vernon, Granville. "Injunction Granted," *Commonweal,* 21 August 1936, p. 407.

Wellman, Ruth. "Open-Air Reading Rooms." *Library Journal,* 15 September 1936, pp. 668–70.

Wilder, Grace. "Puppetry in a New Age." *Recreation* 30 (July 1936) : 207–8.

"Writers' Project: 1942." *New Republic,* 13 April 1942, p. 480.

Wyatt, E. V. "The Federal Theatre Project." *Catholic World* 149 (August 1939) : 598–601.

Books

Adams, Grace. *Workers on Relief.* New Haven, Conn., 1939.

Alexander, Charles. *Nationalism in American Thought, 1930–1945.* Chicago, 1969.

Bakke, E. Wight. *The Unemployed Worker.* New Haven, Conn., 1940.

Barck, Oscar T., Jr., and Blake, Nelson M. *Since 1900: A History of the United States in Our Times.* New York, 1974.

Bernstein, Barton, ed. *Towards a New Past.* Westminister, Md., 1968.

Bremner, Robert. *From the Depths: The Discovery of Poverty in the United States.* New York, 1956.

Brown, Milton W. *Jacob Lawrence.* New York, 1974.

Selected Bibliography

Colcord, Joanna C. *Emergency Relief as Carried Out in Twenty-six American Communities.* New York, 1932.

Conkin, Paul. *The New Deal.* New York, 1967.

Cords, Nicholas, and Gerster, Patrick, eds. *Myth and the American Experience.* 2 vols. New York, 1973.

Degler, Carl N. *Out of Our Past.* New York, 1959.

Derber, Milton, and Young, E., eds. *Labor and the New Deal.* Madison, Wis., 1957.

Flanagan, Hallie. *Arena.* New York, 1940.

Gassner, John, ed. *A Treasury of the Theatre from Henrik Ibsen to Arthur Miller.* New York, 1956.

Graham, Otis L., Jr., ed. *The New Deal: The Critical Issues.* Boston, 1971.

Howard, Donald. *The WPA and Federal Relief Policy.* New York, 1943.

Johns, Orrick. *Time of Our Lives: The Story of My Father and Myself.* New York, 1937.

Johnson, Hugh. *The Blue Eagle from Egg to Earth.* New York, 1935.

Kazin, Alfred. *On Native Ground.* New York, 1942.

Leuchtenburg, William E. *Franklin D. Roosevelt and the New Deal.* New York, 1963.

Locke, Alain. *The Negro in Art: A Pictorial Record of the Negro Artist and the Negro Theme in Art.* New York, 1940.

McDonald, William F. *Federal Relief Administration and the Arts.* Columbus, Ohio, 1969.

Macmahon, Arthur, et al. *The Administration of Work Relief.* Chicago, 1941.

Mangione, Jerre. *The Dream and the Deal: The Federal Writers' Project, 1935-1943.* Boston, 1972.

Mann, Arthur. *La Guardia: A Fighter Against His Times, 1882-1933.* Chicago, 1959.

―――. *La Guardia Comes to Power, 1933.* Chicago, 1965.

Mathews, Jane D. *The Federal Theatre, 1935-1939.* Princeton, N.J., 1967.

Meier, August, and Rudwick, Elliott. *From Plantation to Ghetto.* New York, 1966.

Millett, John D. *The Works Progress Administration in New York City.* Chicago, 1938.

O'Connor, Francis V., ed. *The New Deal Art Projects: An Anthology of Memoirs.* Washington, D.C., 1972.

Ottley, Roi, and Weatherby, William J., eds. *The Negro in New York: An Informal Social History.* New York, 1967.

Patterson, James. *Congressional Conservatism and the New Deal.* Lexington, Ky., 1967.

———. *The New Deal and the States.* Princeton, N.J., 1969.

Perkins, Frances. *The Roosevelt I Knew.* New York, 1946.

Piven, Frances Fox, and Cloward, Richard. *Regulating the Poor.* New York, 1971.

Porter, James A. *Modern Negro Art.* New York, 1969.

Rauch, Basil. *History of the New Deal, 1933–1938.* New York, 1944.

Rice, Elmer. *The Living Theatre.* Westport, Conn., 1972.

Robinson, Edgar E. *The Roosevelt Leadership 1933–1945.* New York, 1955.

Rose, Barbara. *American Art Since 1900: A Critical History.* New York, 1967.

Roskolenko, Harry. *When I Was Last on Cherry Street.* New York, 1965.

Schiltz, Michael E. *Public Attitudes toward Social Security, 1935–1965.* Washington, D.C., 1970.

Schlesinger, Arthur M., Jr. *The Age of Roosevelt.* 3 vols. Boston, 1957–60.

Sherwood, Robert. *Roosevelt and Hopkins.* 2 vols. New York, 1948.

Sternsher, Bernard, ed. *Hitting Home.* Chicago, 1970.

———. *The Negro in Depression and War.* New York, 1969.

Sundquist, James L. *Politics and Policy: The Eisenhower, Kennedy, and Johnson Years.* Washington, D.C., 1968.

Williams, William Appleman. *The Contours of American History.* New York, 1961.

Wolthers, Raymond. *Negroes and the Great Depression: The Problem of Economic Recovery.* Westport, Conn., 1970.

Yezierska, Anzia. *Red Ribbon on a White Horse.* New York, 1950.

Zinn, Howard, ed. *New Deal Thought.* Indianapolis, Ind., 1966.

Ziskind, David. *One Thousand Strikes of Government Employees.* New York, 1940.

Miscellaneous Materials

American Federation of Labor. *Report of Proceedings of the Fifty-sixth Annual Convention.* Washington, D.C., 1936.

Brandt, Lillian. *An Impressionistic View of the Winter of 1930–1931 in New York City Based on Statements from Some Nine Hundred Social Workers and Public Health Nurses.* Report to the Welfare Council of New York City. New York, 1 February 1932.

―――. *Relief of the Unemployed in New York City, 1929–1937.* Report to the Welfare Council of New York City. New York, 1938.

Carroll v. Somervell. 116 F. 2d 918 (2d Cir., 1941).

Long v. Somervell. 175 Misc. 119, affd. 261 App. Div. 946 (1940).

Morris, Richard B. "Pioneering Days of Regional Archives." Transcripts from the symposium The Historian and Archives, 23 October 1969, Columbia University. Mimeographed.

Trout, Charles H. "Boston during the Great Depression: 1929–1940." Ph.D. dissertation, Columbia University, 1972.

Index

Abel, Lionel, 195
Accelerated Public Works Act, 304
Adams, Grace, 159
Alexander, Charles, 184, 198, 200, 213
Alsberg, Henry G., 195, 196, 200, 230, 255
Alston, Charles, 80, 212, 292
American Art Since 1900: A Critical History, 214
American City, 130
American Civil Liberties Union, 262–63, 264
American Federation of Labor (AFL), 94; strikes the New York City WPA for prevailing wage, 52, 54, 56; wins the prevailing wage, 57, 138; makes no attempt to organize work relief employees, 92; denounces WPA vocational training, 115; strikes the New York City WPA over loss of prevailing wage, 246, 247

American Legion, 93
American Writers Association, 90
Angoff, Allan, 59, 92, 196, 197, 200, 230
Arent, Arthur, 189
Association for Improving the Condition of the Poor, 19, 26, 37
Auden, W. H., 294

Baker, Jacob, 301–2
Bakke, E. Wight, 295–96, 299, 300
Ball, William, Major, 90
Bankhead, John H., Senator, 240
Bankhead, Tallulah, 189, 240
Bannarn, Henry, 80
Banta, Edwin P., 229, 231
Barber, Philip, 187
Barkley, Alben, Senator, 295
Bay, Howard, 189
Belmont, Mrs. August, 20
Benjamin, Herbert, 91, 233
Blackburn, Robert, 292
Blacks. *See* Works Progress Ad-

ministration for the City of New York and blacks
Blitzstein, Marc, 191, 205
Bodenheim, Maxwell, 195, 200, 263
Boileau, Gerald, Representative, 104, 105
Bookkeepers, Stenographers, and Accountants Union, 56
Brandt, Lillian, 22, 23, 32
Branion, Raymond, 266
Bremner, Robert, 284
Bronx, The, 27, 28, 64, 129, 153, 156, 166, 196, 209, 257, 266, 273, 297
Brooklyn, 77, 78, 161, 234, 238, 267; abandonment of babies in, 22; work relief musicians give lessons in, 27; apartment rents in, 28; WPA workers and projects in, 63, 65, 129, 131, 160, 171, 264, 273; description of WPA headquarters in, 170
Brown, Alvin, 51
Buchanan, James, Representative, 87
Building Trades Employers Association, 136, 139
Business Week, 158
Buxton, Alan, 92, 170–71, 179, 180
Byrd, Harry, Senator, 273
Byrnes, James, Senator, 106, 247, 288

Cahill, Holger, 207, 209, 214
Calverton, V. F., 203
Catholic Charities Organization, 19
Celler, Emanuel, Representative, 231, 238, 239, 242, 260, 274
Chandler, Albert (Happy), Governor, 295
Cheever, John, 198
City Projects Council, 56, 91, 94, 102, 105, 107. *See also* Unemployed, unions of
Civilian Conservation Corps (CCC), 45, 273, 290
Civil Works Administration (CWA), 23, 27, 28, 37, 40, 207, 285; Hopkins outlines plan for, 31; La Guardia assists in planning program for, 32; hires workers and runs projects in New York City, 32–34; opposition to, 34; Roosevelt orders ending of, 34; protests in New York against ending of, 34–35; decline of work relief in New York City after end of, 35–36; Civil Works Service and; different hiring practices of WPA and, 46; employment of creative artists by, 183; aid to urban residents by, 282, 293
Clark, Joseph, Senator, 303
Clifton, Chalmer, 201
Cloward, Richard, 283, 289
Columbia University, 39, 113, 201, 215
Communists, 23, 38, 39, 90–95, 101, 233. *See also* Works Progress Administration for New York City and Communists; Unemployed, protests, demonstrations, and radicalism of; Unemployed, unions of; Federal Project number 1, charges of Communist influence on
Comprehensive Employment and Training Act, 304
Congressional Conservatism and

Index

the New Deal, 228
Conrad, Earl, 38, 61, 287
Costigan, Edward P., Senator, 29
Cotton, Joseph, 189
Coughlin, Father Charles E., 53
Crisis, 153
Curley, James, Governor, 296
Current History, 172, 203

Dahlberg, Edward, 200
Democrats, 70, 100, 105, 239, 259–60, 278; receive preference over Republicans in early New York City work relief program, 24; 1934 congressional election gains of, 40; role in New York City WPA of, 50, 71, 297; conservative and Southern, 34, 189, 226–27, 228, 231, 269, 274, 288, 294, 303; use WPA in some states for their political advantage, 295–96
De Sola, Ralph, 229, 234
Dickstein, Samuel, Representative, 73, 237, 238
Dies Committee. *See* House Committee on Un-American Activities
Dies, Martin, Representative, 173, 228
Diller, Burgoyne, 211
Douglas, Lewis, 34, 40
Downes, Olin, 204
Duty, Frankie, 233

Eccles, Marriner, 108
Edwards, Paul, 296
Eisenhower, Dwight D., President, 303
Emergency Jobs and Unemployment Assistance Act, 304
Emergency Relief Act (1933), 29–30
Emergency Relief Appropriations Act (1935), 41, 45, 49, 52
Emergency Relief Appropriations Act (1937), 106
Emergency Relief Appropriations Act (1939): provisions and passage of, 137, 237–43; impact on New York City of, 243–50, 254–57, 277
Emergency Relief Appropriations Act (1940): provisions and passage of, 260–62; impact on New York City of, 262–64
Emergency Relief Appropriations Act (1941), 269–70
Emergency Relief and Construction Act (1932), 29
Emergency Work and Relief Bureau (Emergency Work Bureau), 19, 20, 21, 23
Evans, Luther, 215

Family Welfare Association, 28
Farley, James A., 296
Fay, James, Representative, 227, 228, 239
Fearing, Kenneth, 195
Federal Art Project, 59, 80, 185, 207–14, 243, 257. *See also* Federal Project number 1
Federal Emergency Relief Administration (FERA), 23, 33, 34, 39, 40, 125, 207, 283, 285; creation of, 29–30; pays laborers in hospitals and clinics, 149; and relief labor in schools, 166–67; begins employment of creative artists, 183; and aid to cities, 282, 293

Federal Music Project, 185, 201–6, 255–57, 295. *See also* Federal Project number 1
Federal Project number 1, 47, 102, 103, 104, 201, 223, 249, 294–95; effects on the arts and artists of, 184–85, 186, 215, 216–17, 223; charges of Communist influence on, 229–31, 234; ended by Congress, 237–40, 241–42; operation of the arts projects in New York City after end of, 255, 257
Federal Theatre Project, 90, 185, 186–95, 228, 231, 234, 237, 239, 240, 241, 242–43, 249–50, 288. *See also* Federal Project number 1
Federal Writers' Project, 61, 62, 82, 92, 185, 195–201, 228, 234, 239, 243, 255, 282, 284, 286, 287, 292, 293. *See also* Federal Project number 1
Federation of Architects, Engineers, Chemists, and Technicians, 56, 91, 104. *See also* Unemployed, unions of
Flanagan, Hallie, 186, 187, 194, 195, 229, 230, 239, 241
Ford, Gerald, President, 304
Francis, Arlene, 189
Free Employment Bureau, 18
From the Depths: The Discovery of Poverty in the United States, 284
Fusion party, 31, 100, 297

Gall, Oscar, 234
Gellhorn, Martha, 299
Gibson Committee, 20, 21, 23, 166, 207, 282, 285
Gibson, Harvey, 20, 21

Gilbert, Joseph, 91
Gill, Corrington, 58, 70
Goldwater, Dr. S. S., 152
Gompers, Samuel, 31
Gore, Albert, Senator, 303
Gottschalk, Oliver, 266
Green, William, 53
Grofe, Ferde, 205
Gullino, Frank, 205
Guston, Philip, 211

Hale, Ralph, 111
Hamer, Philip, 215
Harlem Community Art Center, 33, 80, 212
Harrington, Francis, Colonel, 100, 234, 239, 247, 248, 257, 261, 264, 269, 301
Harris, Roy, 204, 205
Harvey, George U., 84–86, 298
Hein, Peter, 136, 137
Hill, T. Arnold, 78
Hillman, Sidney, 53
Historical Records Survey, 186, 215, 257. *See also* Federal Project number 1
Hodson, William, 24, 25, 28, 29, 32, 37, 38, 39, 41, 113, 245, 285
Hoffman, Clare, Representative, 231
Hoover, Herbert, President, 25, 29, 87, 288, 289
Hopkins, Harry, 41, 47, 48, 53, 58, 66, 70, 78, 108, 117, 133, 139, 147, 186, 188, 207, 234, 276, 285, 286; becomes director of TERA, 25; biography of, 26; as director of TERA, 26–28; outlines plan for a federal relief program to Frances Perkins, 29; as administrator of FERA,

30, 37, 38, 39, 283, 299; outlines plans for CWA to Roosevelt, 31; as head of CWA, 32, 34, 35; presents plans for work relief program to Roosevelt, 40; becomes head of WPA, 45; creates separate WPA administrative unit for New York City, 49; names Hugh Johnson administrator of New York City WPA, 50; defends security wage of WPA, 54, 55; denounces strike against WPA, 56; gives into demands of AFL unions, 57; appoints Victor Ridder head of New York City WPA, 71; creates Division of Investigation to fight corruption on WPA, 72; and politics on WPA, 74, 295, 296, 297; asks La Guardia to help handle Robert Moses, 84; underestimates funds needed for WPA, 87; orders employment cutbacks on New York City WPA, 86, 102, 103, 104; disapproves of Ridder's anti-Communist drive, 93–94; defends hiring of creative artists, 183, 294; sets up Federal Project number 1, 185; uses military personnel on WPA, 100, 301; appoints Brehon Somervell head of New York City WPA, 100–101; responds to House Committee on Un-American Activities probe of WPA, 229; sees WPA workers as employees, not welfare recipients, 222, 290

House Committee on Appropriations, Subcommittee of. *See* Woodrum Subcommittee

House Committee on Un-American Activities, 173, 228–31, 234, 255, 261, 262, 263, 277, 302

Houseman, John, 189, 191

Huffman, Hazel, 229, 230

Huie, Irving, 266–67, 270, 271, 272, 275, 276

Ickes, Harold, 31, 32, 40, 45

Irvine, Harry, 192

Irwin, Robert, 143

Isaacs, Edith, 194

Jewish Social Services Association, 19

John Reed Clubs, 38, 59, 283

Johns, Orrick, 62, 195, 286

Johnson, Hugh S., General, 52, 54, 62, 63, 70, 71, 72, 77, 101, 186, 266, 267, 301; becomes head of New York City WPA, 50–51; biography of, 50–51; dislikes WPA security wage, 53; appeals to AFL unions not to strike New York City WPA, 56; reaches a settlement with the unions, 57; simplifies WPA recruitment of labor, 58; resigns WPA post, 65; criticizes idea of work relief, 66; contributions to New York City WPA of, 66–67; replies to Democratic congressmen asking for jobs for constituents, 73; accused of discrimination against blacks, 78, 291; disputes with Robert Moses, 83; rejects idea of WPA turning work over to private contractors, 139; comments on difficulty of creating projects for white-collar jobless, 148

Johnson, John H., Reverend, 79

Joint Legislative (Hofstadter) Committee, 24
Joseph, Ronald, 212, 292

Kainen, Jacob, 59, 243–44
Kazin, Alfred, 184, 198
Kellogg, Paul, 28
Kennedy, John F., President, 294, 303
Kerr, Florence, 111
Kirstein, Lincoln, 195
Knauth, Oswald, 37, 135, 139

Lafayette Theater, 80, 192, 194, 292
La Follette, Robert M., Jr., Senator, 29
La Guardia (North Beach) Airport, 126, 132–34, 135, 136, 137, 246, 250, 254, 298
La Guardia, Fiorello, Mayor, 78, 126, 127, 130, 137, 168, 172, 177, 178, 255, 266, 267, 271, 276; becomes mayor of New York City, 31; biography of, 31; cooperates with the Roosevelt Administration on relief matters, 32; urges continuation of CWA, 35; asks Albany for new taxing power, 36; battles with Democratic aldermen over work relief program, 36–37; leads delegation of mayors to Hyde Park to urge federal takeover of relief for employables, 38; proposes projects for WPA, 48; obtains a separate WPA administrative unit for New York City, 49; urges appointment of Hugh Johnson, 50; protests against WPA security wage, 53– 54; helps settle AFL strike against New York City WPA, 57; participates in ceremonies starting work on Franklin D. Roosevelt Drive, 65; uses influence to obtain appointment of Victor Ridder, 70–71; and political influence on New York City WPA, 73, 296–98; intervenes in disputes between local officials and WPA, 84–86; protests against cutbacks on WPA, 88, 103; and Brehon Somervell, 100–101, 118, 265; calls for bigger appropriations for WPA, 104, 105, 106, 108, 259; pledges larger New York City contribution to WPA, 105, 117; commends efficiency of New York City WPA, 112; urges WPA to build airport for New York City, 133; presides at opening of La Guardia Airport, 134; acknowledges debt of cities to WPA and other New Deal agencies, 144; protests against Emergency Relief Appropriations Act (1939), 238, 240, 249; charges blacks being kept out of defense plants, 268; commends WPA civil defense work, 272; regrets end of WPA orchestra, 277
Lamont, Thomas, 20
Laning, Edward, 208, 211, 213
Lasser, David, 91, 233, 235, 286
Lawrence, Jacob, 80, 292
Lehman, Herbert, Governor, 35, 57, 261, 268
Lescohier, Donald, 115, 127, 139, 140, 149, 162
Levy, Edmund, Major, 100

Index

Lewis, John L., 53
Library Journal, 160
Life, 188
Locke, Alain, 212
London Times, 202
Long, Huey, 53
Long Island *Press,* 124, 130, 144
Lord, Clifford, 215
Losey, Joseph, 189
Lyons, James, 266

McClendon, Rose, 194
McCormack, John, Representative, 296
McGrath, Joseph, 296
McKay, Claude, 82, 199, 200, 292
McKee, Joseph, 297
McMahon, Audrey, 21, 38, 207, 213
Mangione, Jerre, 239
Manhattan, 27, 38, 51, 65, 94, 129, 130, 179, 297
Marcantonio, Vito, Representative, 231, 238, 258-59
Marshall, George, General, 273
Maverick, Maury, Representative, 105
Mead, James, Senator, 240, 241
Meany, George, 53, 55, 57
Mehaffy, Joseph, 52
Modern Negro Art, 212
Moley, Raymond, 258
Monthly Labor Review, 172
Morgan, J. P., 87, 288
Morgan, Willis, 91, 94
Morganthau, Henry, Jr., 105, 288
Morris, Richard, 161, 215-16
Murray, Thomas, 246
Murray-Wagner Full Employment Act, 303

Namm, Benjamin, Major, 161
Nation, 93, 195
National Education Association, 172
National Urban League, 78, 83
Nationalism in American Thought, 184, 198
New Deal, 53, 54, 162, 221, 228, 258, 273, 298, 302, 303; victory in 1934 congressional elections, 40; aid to cities, 125, 144, 293; aid to education, 166, 172; and the arts, 184, 185, 188, 189, 294; newspapers hostile to, 225; and use of work relief to gain votes, 227; conflicting historical interpretations of, 281, 285, 291, 295; espousal of work relief over the dole, 290
New York City: numbers of unemployed in, 17, 28, 36, 108, 275, 304; private charity unable to care for unemployed in, 20-22, 282; starts its municipal relief and work programs, 24; establishes Home and Work Relief Bureaus, 27; receives money from Reconstruction Finance Corporation loan, 29; uses FERA money to expand work relief, 30; La Guardia becomes mayor of, 31-32; protests against end of CWA in, 34-35; finances, 36, 126, 127, 248-49, 304; mood of the unemployed in, 39-40, 283-84; role in helping to bring about WPA, 41, 285; welfare certification rules in, 46-47, 112-13; start of WPA in, 48, 52; gets its own WPA administrative unit, 49; welfare

spending of, 49; WPA wages in, 53–54, 226; cost of living in, 54; number on welfare in, 86, 108, 268, 287; protests against WPA cutbacks in, 88–89, 102–3, 104–5, 107, 232; average relief payment in, 226; unions of the unemployed in, 90–91; financial contributions to the WPA of, 105, 117–18, 249, 298–99; physical deterioration in early thirties of, 124–25; improved physical condition due to WPA of, 135, 293; deterioration of schools in early thirties in, 165; high proportion of white-collar unemployed in, 147; unemployed artists in, 183, 195; predominance in WPA arts projects of, 185, 294; writing of the guidebooks for, 196–97; receives largest WPA expenditures, 228; WPA employees testifying before Dies Committee, 228–29; low rate of labor turnover on WPA in, 235–36; ablebodied unemployed without WPA jobs in, 238, 249, 268, 287; efforts on behalf of WPA by the congressional delegation of, 238–39, 242, 258–59, 260, 274–75; repercussions of the Emergency Relief Appropriations Act (1939) on, 243–50, 254–55; repercussions of the ERA (1940) on, 262–64; repercussions of the ERA (1941) on, 270; receives few contracts from War Department, 268–69, 274; workers migrate from to cities with more defense plants, 276

New York City Aldermanic Committee to Investigate the Administration of Relief, 37
New York City Board of Education, 165, 166, 167, 168, 171, 173, 175, 176, 178, 180, 265, 272, 277
New York City Central Trades and Labor Council, 53, 56, 57
New York City Department of Health, 149, 150, 162, 232, 264
New York City Department of Hospitals, 77, 149, 162
New York City Department of Housing and Buildings, 156
New York City Emergency Relief Bureau, 37, 38, 51, 52, 54, 55, 77, 267 284
New York City Emergency Work Bureau, 27, 28, 32, 33, 35
New York City Home Relief Bureau, 27
New York City Park Department, 20, 75, 84, 127, 272
New York City Public Welfare Department, 36–37, 112–13, 154
New York *Daily News*, 188, 224
New York *Herald Tribune*, 224
New York League for the Hard of Hearing, 33
New York *Post*, 61, 106, 188, 195, 288
New York *Sun*, 136, 225, 262, 277
New York Times, 28–29, 71, 87, 115, 188, 204, 226, 227, 273, 275, 277
New York Tuberculosis and Health Association, 26, 152
New York University, 20, 157
New York *World-Telegram*, 189, 266

New Yorker, 135
Newell, James Michael, 209
Niles, David, 93
Nixon, Richard M., President, 304
Norton, Mary, Representative, 239

O'Brien, John, 297
O'Connor, John J., Representative, 227
Ottley, Roi, 199, 292

Patterson, James, 228
Perkins, Frances, 29
Piven, Frances, 283, 289
Pollock, Jackson, 211
Porter, James, 212
President Roosevelt's Advisory Committee on Education, 167, 180
Project Workers Union, 91. *See also* Unemployed, unions of
Prosser Committee (Emergency Employment Committee), 19, 20, 282, 285
Prosser, Seward, 19, 23
Public Works Administration (PWA), 31, 45, 111, 125, 126, 131, 136, 139, 166, 236, 303

Queens: mood of the unemployed in, 39; WPA projects in, 64–65, 76, 117, 125, 128, 129, 130, 131, 133, 144, 156, 225, 255, 273; dispute between Victor Ridder and George U. Harvey, borough president of, 84–86, 298; WPA in-plant training program in, 271

Reconstruction Finance Corporation (RFC), 29

Regulating the Poor, 283
Republicans, 70, 221, 278, 298; discriminated against in early New York City work relief program, 24; accuse CWA of waste and corruption, 34; defeated in 1934 congressional elections, 40; fear liberal bias of some plays produced by Federal Theatre, 189; fear WPA building a vote-getting machine for Roosevelt, 226–27; form anti-New Deal coalition with conservative Democrats, 228; attempt to reduce appropriations for WPA, 105, 231, 269, 288; attempt to kill WPA, 237, 259–60, 274, 275, 288; criticize Federal Project number 1, 294; back La Guardia for mayor in 1933, 297; weaken Murray-Wagner Full Employment bill, 303
Reynolds, Robert, Senator, 231
Rice, Elmer, 186, 187
Rice, Dr. John, 152
Richmond (Staten Island), 27, 65, 128, 152, 156, 257, 264
Ridder, Victor F., 100, 101, 108, 112, 148, 266; asked to become head of New York City WPA, 70; biography of, 71; fights graft on WPA, 72–73; and politics on WPA, 73–74; attempts to employ more women, 77–78; fights discrimination against blacks on New York City WPA, 78–83, 299; fights with Robert Moses and George U. Harvey, 83–86, 298; lays off WPA employees, 86, 89; institutes anti-Communist campaign, 90, 92–

95; resigns, 94–95
Robinson, Joseph, Senator, 105
Rollins, William, Jr., 198
Roosevelt, Franklin D., Governor, 24, 25, 26, 28, 29, 282
Roosevelt, Franklin D., President, 30, 32, 37, 38, 39, 49, 50, 73, 101, 117, 133, 135, 147, 154, 221, 241, 246, 249, 262, 283, 297; begins federal aid to relief, 29; appoints Harry Hopkins head of FERA, 30; agrees to creation of CWA, 31; orders Hopkins to end CWA, 34–35; breaks with some conservative advisers, 40; calls for a national job program, 40–41; creates WPA and appoints Hopkins head, 45–48; and security payments for WPA workers, 52–53, 54, 55, 56; gives into AFL on prevailing wage for WPA workers, 57; asks Victor Ridder to head New York City WPA, 70–71; and short-term and inadequate funding of WPA, 47–48, 86–87, 88, 89, 103–4, 105–6, 108–9, 226, 231, 232, 233, 237, 250, 258–59, 267, 269–70, 273–74, 286, 287–88; and aid to cities, 125, 293; and aid to education, 165–67; and aid to the arts, 183, 185, 188, 191, 203, 294; and politics on WPA, 227; faces growing opposition in Congress, 228; reorganizes work and public works agencies, 236; denounces the eighteen-month rule for WPA workers, 238; puts up little fight to save Federal Theatre, 239; criticizes Emergency Relief Act, 1939, 242–43; favors end of prevailing wage on WPA, 247; asks Congress to modify the eighteen-month rule, 260, 269; asks Army to extend Brehon Somervell's WPA assignment, 265; names Irving Huey head of New York City WPA, 266; asks WPA to increase vocational training efforts, 269–70; ends WPA and praises its accomplishments, 276, 278, 302–3; historical controversy about, 281, 285, 287, 289–90, 291, 292, 305; influence of social workers on relief programs of, 284–85; and blacks, 290–93
Rose, Barbara, 214
Rose, Herman, 208
Roskolenko, Harry, 200, 201
Rourke, Henry, 234–35
Ryan, Joseph, 53

Saunders, Sallie, 229, 231
Savage, Augusta, 33
Scherer, Marcel, 91
Science, 158
Seabury, Samuel, 24, 297
Shahn, Ben, 209
Sirovich, William, Representative, 73, 238, 239
Smith, Alfred E., 20, 50
Smith, Gus, 194
Snell, Bertrand, Representative, 105
Social workers, 22, 23, 25, 26, 28, 30, 37–38, 39, 41, 46–47, 77, 113, 284–85, 290
Sokoloff, Nikolai, 201, 204
Solman, Joseph, 208
Somervell, Brehon B., Colonel,

105, 107, 129, 130, 131, 132, 152, 156, 157, 162, 232, 243, 245, 254, 255, 259, 267, 299; becomes director of New York City WPA, 99; biography of, 99–100; and La Guardia, 101, 265; halts anti-Communist drive, 101; and unions of the unemployed, 101; cuts back employment and handles protests, 103, 106–7; announces end of WPA layoffs, 108; administrative and supervisory reforms of, 109–112, 225; imposes strict discipline and angers employees, 110–11, 112–16, 301–2; and planning of WPA programs, 116–19; La Guardia proposes building airport to, 133; sets up committee to review New York City WPA projects, 135; replies to charges of excessive WPA building costs, 136–40; hires physically handicapped, 142; on difficulty of placing white-collar unemployed, 148; attempts to enlarge white-collar employment, 149; doubts value of some white-collar projects, 159; exercises little control over arts projects prior to 1939, 186; and Audrey McMahon, 207; sends questionnaire to local businessmen, 222; prohibits certain political activity on New York City WPA, 227; not invited to appear before Woodrum Committee, 233; replies to charges made before the Woodrum Committee, 235; handles 1939 strike for prevailing wage, 246–48; takes over arts projects, 249; reduces WPA rolls by attrition, 258; conducts drive against Communists on New York City WPA, 262–64; recalled by the Army, 265; praised for work as head of New York City WPA, 266

Staten Island *Advance*, 116
Stephens, Allen, 136, 137
Straus, Jesse, 25
Survey, 28
Survey of Federal Archives, 186, 215–16. See also Federal Project number 1

Taber, John, Representative, 231, 237, 259, 274, 275
Tarry, Ellen, 82, 89, 195, 243
Temporary Emergency Relief Administration (TERA), 71, 207; created by Governor Roosevelt, 25; Hopkins becomes director of, 25; rules governing projects of, 26; projects of, 27; inadequacy of, 28; receives RFC loan, 29; receives FERA funds, 30; continues CWA projects after demise of that agency, 33; funds used to employ workers in hospitals and clinics, 149
Theatre Arts, 194
Thomas, J. Parnell, Representative, 228
Thomson, Virgil, 189, 205
Tinney, Mary, 77–78, 79, 82
Truman, Harry S., President, 303

Unemployed: living conditions of, 17, 18, 19, 28, 54, 55, 59, 61; attempts to find work, 18, 19, 20, 23, 32, 58–62, 232; family life of, 22, 23; emotional and physical state of, 22, 23, 28, 39, 62, 299; protests, demonstrations, and radicalism of, 34–35, 38, 39, 56–57, 88–89, 102, 104–5, 107, 232, 283, 287; unions of, 35, 38, 39, 56–57, 61, 88–89, 90–93, 101, 102, 104, 105, 106, 283

United Neighborhood Houses, 37, 88

United States Corps of Engineers, 51, 99, 100

United States Conference of Mayors, 38, 49, 105, 108

United States Employment Service (National Employment Service), 32, 46, 58, 66–67, 112

Vandenberg, Arthur, Senator, 275, 288

Veterans' Theater League, 90

Voorhis, Jerry, Representative, 105

Wagner, Robert, Senator, 29, 35, 53, 224, 231, 240–41

Walker, James, 24, 297

Walter, Francis, Representative, 260

Walton, Charles, 234

Watkins, Perry, 194

Welfare Council, 22, 23, 88, 285

Welles, Orson, 80, 189, 191, 194

Wicks Act, 24, 25

Wilder, Charlotte, 198

Williams, Aubrey, 40, 94, 101, 222, 227, 301

Woodrum, Clifton, Representative, 235, 237, 239, 242, 260; attempts to cut appropriations for WPA, 106, 231, 288; calls for investigation of WPA, 233; defends the eighteen-month rule for WPA workers, 238; announces intention of killing Federal Theatre, 249; criticizes New York City WPA, 259

Woodrum Subcommittee (House Committee on Appropriations, Subcommittee of), 233–36, 237, 247, 258, 259, 261, 274

Work relief: programs run by private charitable organizations, 19, 20, 21, 22, 23; politics in, 24, 36–37; programs run by New York City and state, 24, 25, 26, 27–28. See also Temporary Emergency Relief Administration, Federal Emergency Relief Administration, Civil Works Administration, Works Progress Administration, Works Progress Administration for New York City

Workers Alliance, 94, 232, 233, 246, 286; leads work stoppages, marches and demonstrations, 56–57, 104, 107, 263; formation of, 91; reasons why workers joined, 92, 287; demands larger appropriations for WPA, 104; criticizes Somervell, 116; collects campaign funds to help elect friends of WPA, 227; called front group for Communists, 229, 233, 234; charged with controlling WPA hiring and firing, 230–31, 234; break up of, 234–35

Works Progress Administration (later Work Projects Administration) (WPA), 23, 26, 33, 35, 53, 54, 66, 108, 183, 207, 236, 237, 238, 239, 303; creation of,

45–46; eligibility for, 46–47; rules and regulations of, 47, 72, 74, 95, 111, 148, 158, 243, 268; short-term and inadequate financing of, 48, 86–88, 101–2, 103–7, 109, 179–80, 226, 231–33, 236–37, 250, 257–60, 269, 274–75, 285–88, 300–301; Army officers as administrators of, 51–52, 100, 111, 116, 301–2; wage scales, 52–53; attitudes of the public toward employees of, 72, 115–16, 223–24, 225, 247, 270, 286, 288, 300; opposition to, 87, 105, 106, 135, 221–42, 259–60, 269, 273, 274, 275, 277–78, 288–89; impact on cities of, 124–25, 126, 130, 135, 144, 161–62, 228, 240, 293–94, 300; construction contractors' complaints against, 126, 226, 235; politics on, 227, 295–96, 301; defense and war projects of, 261–62, 264–65, 272–73, 277, 302; role in avoiding riots and unrest of, 283–84

Works Progress Administration for the City of New York (New York City WPA), 65, 67, 100, 226; creation of, 48–49, 51, 52; appointment of Hugh Johnson, first director of, 50; disputes over security payments versus prevailing wage on, 52, 53, 54, 55, 56–57, 66, 92, 138–39, 237, 246–48; strikes against, 52, 55–57, 66, 89, 102, 104–5, 223, 246–48; wages and hours of employees of, 53, 57, 226; placement of workers on, 58–63, 67, 72, 112–13, 149; number of persons employed by, 63, 67, 74, 95, 108, 109, 148, 244, 257, 267, 268, 270, 275, 276, 282; attitudes of its employees toward their jobs on, 63–64, 75, 82, 107, 282–83, 286, 287, 299–300; appointment of Victor Ridder, second director of, 70–71; supervision on projects of, 72, 110–12; control of graft and corruption on, 72–73; politics on, 73–74, 227–28, 296–98; young people employed by, 75, 184, 195, 205; women employed by, 77–78, 271; and blacks, 78–83, 153–54, 168, 172, 178, 184, 192–94, 198–99, 204, 205, 212–13, 268, 271, 290–93; relations between local government officials and, 83–86, 298; employment cutbacks and layoffs of employees by, 86–88, 102–3, 104–5, 106–7, 108, 232, 243–44, 250, 270, 275; and Communists, 90–94, 185, 200–201, 213–14, 216, 228–31, 233–35, 302; drives against Communists by administrators of, 90–95, 262–64; appointment of Brehon Somervell, third director of, 99–100; job training on, 114–15, 154, 167, 178, 265, 270–71; planning of its projects by, 116–19; construction projects of, 64–65, 76–77, 125–26, 127–37, 143–44, 166, 238, 250, 255; reasons for the high cost of construction done by, 137–40; manufacturing and sewing projects of, 114, 140–44, 245; white-collar and white-apron projects of, 65, 76–77, 147–49, 161–62, 245, 250; health projects of, 149–53;

housekeeping projects of, 83, 153–56; prison projects of, 156; clerical projects of, 156–57; research projects of, 157–59; library and museum projects of, 159–60; education projects of, 166–77, 179–80, 245; recreation projects of, 177–79; characteristics of employees of, 137, 147–48, 224, 268, 271; efficiency and diligence of employees of, 160–61; and recall of Somervell and appointment of his successors, 265–67; end of, 276–77

Wright, Richard, 197, 198, 200, 291, 292

Yezierska, Anzia, 63, 195, 200, 282, 286

Zinn, Howard, 281, 285